T0277103

AFTERNESS

AFTERNESS
Home and Away

ASHOK S. GANGULY

EBURY
PRESS

An imprint of Penguin Random House

EBURY PRESS

USA | Canada | UK | Ireland | Australia
New Zealand | India | South Africa | China

Ebury Press is part of the Penguin Random House group of companies
whose addresses can be found at global.penguinrandomhouse.com

Published by Penguin Random House India Pvt. Ltd
4th Floor, Capital Tower 1, MG Road,
Gurugram 122 002, Haryana, India

Penguin
Random House
India

First published in Ebury Press by Penguin Random House India 2022

ISBN 9780670096770

Typeset in Adobe Garamond Pro by MAP Systems, Bengaluru, India
Printed at Replika Press Pvt. Ltd, India

Afterness: The misty musings of a lifetime, near the end of the innings, the joys and sadness, people and events, looking back, just that, only once!

Contents

Part I

Prologue: A Speck in Timelessness

I frequently think of certain events during my long lifetime. I have happy memories of my carefree and happy childhood, followed by an unpromising and indifferent decade of school, in stark contrast to the subsequent heady and exciting years of higher education. I fondly remember some of my older relatives, who were dedicated leftists, and one of them even went on to become the mayor of Patna, for two terms. I used to be fascinated listening to the stories of Prahlad, who owned the barbershop across our street, a staunch communist and the election agent for my relative, the mayor. Amongst my prized possessions were several free, hardbound copies of books on Marxism, distributed by the Soviet Embassy. I spent a brief, delusional spell, formally, as a leftist president of my college union.

In 1947, newly independent India was in thrall of Pandit Nehru and the Indian National Congress. In my very young days, politics seemed to happen in distant Delhi, while the rest of the world was recovering from the ravages of the war. Socialism, self-reliance and non-alignment were the clarion call of our leaders, as well as the newly independent, former colonies. The trauma of the communal riots due to the partition of India remains an indelible scar, marking the end of British colonial rule.

Comparatively, Bombay (now Mumbai) was insulated, and preoccupied with trade and commerce. The liberation of Hyderabad from the Nizamshahi was the extension of India's Independence movement, and Goa was liberated not long after.

By the time I left for my graduate studies in America, I was imbued with a deep sense of national pride and with a somewhat amorphous sense of the future. Looming, on the horizon, were the new 'temples' of modern India, the large dams, the steel plants and the emergence of a gigantic and overarching public sector, occupying the 'commanding heights' of a nation, of the future.

As students in America, we hardly received any news of what was happening in India, other than the monthly bulletins from the Indian embassy. The infrequent and informal gatherings of our small group of Indian friends on the campus were mostly speculations of the forward march of our country.

India's border skirmish with and humiliation by Mao's China, the country's perennial food scarcity and dependence on the American PL 480 wheat imports, the demise of Pandit Jawaharlal Nehru and, not very long after him, of his successor Lal Bahadur Shastri, cast a dark shadow over our country. I returned to an India of shortages and social stresses. Soon, I embarked on my professional life with a strong sense of energy and purpose.

Middle-class Indians, especially of my generation, were very hopeful of the future; however, the reasons for our optimism, I am no longer able to recall. I was amongst the very tiny fraction of my peer group of Indians to return home from America, while the majority stayed back after completing studies and staked their future in that prosperous country which valued talent. Though I did not hear any of them say so, their view of India had become somewhat distorted during our student days. The emergence of Indira Gandhi as the prime minister, and the success of the Green Revolution, revived a renewed sense of optimism, in spite of India's severe and persistent economic problems, burgeoning poverty and widespread unemployment. India's role in the birth of Bangladesh, renewed hopes for the future, which soon and sadly came crashing down with the imposition of the Emergency, the subversion of the Constitution as well as compromising the independence of the judiciary.

My generation continued working hard, with nose to the grindstone; but these were dark times and seemed hopeless.

Droves of Indians left the country in search of livelihood, especially in the oil-rich countries of the Middle East, and even the trickle of those who went to study in the West, and were planning to return home, stayed back. Those employed in the private sector in India had to bear the brunt of the rising political interference and scrutiny, which were without any value or substance. While interactions with politicians and bureaucrats were unavoidable, those experiences may have been the reason behind my personal aversion towards politics.

As I cast my mind back, my expectations of life in India became moderated. Still, the hopes of our generation regarding India's future survived as the driving force which propelled the post-Independence and succeeding generations forward. Personal as well as the collective hopes of the people, their aspirations and hard work are critical for a nation to progress. Not necessarily, all the time, and in all matters. I harbour a growing sense of disquiet, of late, regarding certain emerging trends, which I wish to briefly share.

Historically, India has been and remains a multicultural, multi-ethnic, multilingual and multi-religious land of people. There were Hindu kingdoms, Muslim rulers, followed by British and European traders; the country was eventually colonized by the British, alongside hundreds of rajas and sultans, of all shapes and sizes, most of whom survived, as also their extravagant personal lifestyles. With the accumulated history of the ruled, independent India emerged as a republic as did the Constitution of India, protecting the rights of every citizen, the independence of the judiciary and an unfettered media, without caveats and preconditions.

Recent attempts to change India into a majoritarian Hindu nation can only be at the cost of dismembering the Indian Constitution and disowning the nation's solemn promise to 'We the People', by the founding fathers of our republic.

I was born a Hindu and will die a Hindu. I recall my thread ceremony at the age of twelve, with tonsured head and holes pricked in my ear lobes. I had to remain in isolation and incommunicado for three days as a brahmachari, learning to chant the Gayatri Mantra. To this day, I continue to recite the Gayatri Mantra every morning, not as a Hindu Brahmin, but as a lifelong habit, since my thread ceremony. I pray for peace and harmony. Therefore, the not-so-subtle attempts to redefine India as a 'Hindu' nation are not only a gross distortion of the Indian Constitution, but also the ground realities, and given India's history, are unlikely to succeed. The hopes and aspirations of the majority of Indians and succeeding generations continue in search for progress. So while I remain hopeful of the future, I do not underestimate the potential damage which attempts to distort India's unity in diversity pose— an unlikely and unsustainable proposition.

Historically, there is no nation which is spared periodic, domestic threats and upheavals, mostly by the unachievable ambitions of a few. However, my optimism is now tempered by my own experience of a lifetime, of a notional mix of progress and setbacks. History is replete with examples that better sense always prevails, to fend off unachievable dreams, and so it will, for India's present and future generations. Hopes, energy and optimism of succeeding generations provide the energy to sustain humankind and civilizations.

Part II

Early Days

The story of my early days revolves primarily around three cities. Bombay, where I grew up; Patna, home of my mother, Binapani, and where I was born; and Benares (now Varanasi), home of my father, Sekharnath. Our family of four and our relatives, some of whom I got to know or hear about, belonged to the growing Indian middle class, professionals from the late nineteenth to the early twentieth century, some in the service of the British India government. My mother's maternal uncle lived in Dhaka, now in Bangladesh, her father, Jogendra, belonged to what is now West Bengal. It so happened that my paternal grandfather, Anathbandhu, was born and grew up in the village of Barti, in Barisal district, now in Bangladesh, while his wife—my paternal grandmother, Surangini Devi—hailed from Burdwan in West Bengal. So the genes from both the eastern and western parts of Bengal were fairly mixed amongst the expanding clan, some moving in pursuit of livelihood, across different parts of India.

Part of the gene pool has been sustained. My late wife, Rooma (Connie), was born in Dhaka ten days before the British departed from India. Her mother, Neelima, belonged to the family in Dhaka and was distantly related to my mother. Rooma's father, Sasankha, belonged to the Bhattacharya family of Brahmanbaria in Comilla district, now in Bangladesh. The family moved to Burma, which was at the time a part of British India. Upon completing his medical education, Sasankha trekked back to India along with hundreds of thousands of Indian refugees fleeing the advancing Japanese forces during the Second World War. My father, Sekharnath, was one of eleven brothers and sisters. Although he was the second son, he became the principal bread earner of the family, moving to Bombay from Benares, in the early years of the twentieth century, in search of employment. It is thus that Bombay, Patna and Benares became the triangle for my and my sister Protima's childhood of happy memories and carefree days.

My earliest childhood memory was of an event, when the family gathered around Surangini Devi's dying moments in Benares. I was not yet three, standing next to my solemn parents, uncles and other relatives, while my grandmother was propped up against pillows, with her backside resting on an inflated tyre tube. I, later on, came to know that she had developed bed sores and resting on an inflated rubber tube gave some relief. The house in Benares had to be approached from a main square, named Godhaulia, which had a large parking space for horse-drawn 'phitons' and 'ekkas'. The heavy smell of hay, horse dung and urine hung in the surrounding area. We usually travelled by train from Bombay to Benares via Mughalsarai. From the station, we travelled in a taxi to my grandfather's house in an area called Agasthkunda, next to Godhaulia. We reached home, usually in the very early hours of the morning. Didi, my sister, and I would be drowsy and tired after the long journey from Bombay. But as we neared home, the odour of the Godhaulia signalled that we were close to our destination, and we would be suddenly wide awake. We would alight at the bottom of a flight of broad steps, like the ones in Rome or Venice, and trudge up the few broad steps to a cobbled street, which led us to a narrow passage a few feet wide, at the end of which, was our front door. The main door would already be open in anticipation of our arrival. The front door led to an open courtyard surrounded by the rooms of the house. The prayer room, the kitchen, bed rooms and a sitting room. All the rooms faced the open courtyard across a passage running at right angles. At the corner of the house, a set of stone steps led to the terrace, at one end of which rose an enormous Banyan tree, home to a regiment of monkeys, for which Benares is famous.

My grandmother, Surangini Devi, lay dying on a bed, which was spread out in the living room. She was surrounded by all of us, as life slowly ebbed away and she eventually breathed her last. Apparently, Surangini Devi had taken to bed a few months earlier, shocked by the death of her fourth son, Laloo, at the age of thirty. As she neared her end, I remembered my grandmother crying aloud 'Laloo, Laloo', before lapsing into eternal silence. It was said that Surangini died in peace and joined her son, who had 'come' to fetch her eternal spirit. As I still vaguely recall, Surangini's rather dramatic last moments were seen as an auspicious omen and tempered the collective grief which engulfs families. It reminded me of my mother, Binapani, who told us of another event, when she had accompanied her sister-in-law, Nandarani, for a condolence visit to a friend's house in Bombay. My mother was then newly married and had come recently to Bombay. Upon entering the home of the bereaved, Nandarani embraced her just-widowed friend, or rather accurately, an acquaintance and burst into copious tears of grief. Young and newly-wed, Binapani was quite taken aback by the turn of events and remained demurely silent, until Nandarani nudged her as a signal to join in the grieving. This Binapani found extremely difficult to fall in line with, to the mild annoyance of the gentle Nandarani. On their way back home, Nandarani said, 'It would have been right and proper for you to have shed a few tears as the new bride in our family.' Binapani said, 'But I have never met them before and know nothing about the departed gentleman.' 'It does not matter,' Nandarani said, 'a few tears would have been the right and proper thing to do.' Binapani complained that it was difficult to produce tears instantaneously. Nandarani, by now only slightly mollified, advised, 'If you stare long enough at the wall without blinking, tears will well up without effort. You may wish to remember that for the future.'

Surangini Devi's four surviving sons and one daughter could have made a parent proud, the way they arranged a grand funeral on the banks of the Ganges, at the Dashaswamedh ghat, near our house, and during the days following, were devoted to endless religious ceremonies, presided over by scores of priests, praying for the safe passage of Surangini Devi's soul towards the gods, and final resting place, alongside Laloo. I imagine, being the only grandson in the family at the time, I got to accompany my father and his brothers on their collective religious errands, including once, a boat ride on the Ganga, to immerse Surangini Devi's ashes and, on another occasion, to immerse the remains of the religious ceremonies. I still remember, in addition to a large number of family members, for eleven days, a number of Brahmins were also fed, as a daily ritual, culminating in a grand finale of prayers and giving 'daan' (gifts) to Brahmins, including a live cow, amongst several other paraphernalia, which were handed over to the head priest. This was grander even than the usual gestures of expressing public piety, signifying both devotion and the means to put the soul of one's parent to rest in grand style. Nowadays, the priests are more practical and have monetized such prerequisites, for the convenience as well as to the relief of grieving siblings.

Ever since watching the dying of Surangini Devi, I have been curious about my memories of childhood, as I was growing up. I can still recall some smells and tastes of my childhood, and for a time, I was convinced that I was possessed of some unique memory. The other day, I asked my daughters, Nivedita and Amrita, what they could recall from their earliest memories. I was hoping at least one of them would recall how I balanced them in the air on my palm, while they shrieked in fear and joy. Neither of them could recall those exciting moments, or events at an age when they were as old as I was when Surangini Devi lay dying. Nivedita could vaguely recall her first pram ride, and Amrita, her sighting a chameleon in infant school.

The bulk of my sister's (Didi) and my growing-up years were spent in Bombay, where our father (Baba) had his job and our mother (Ma) managed a neat and orderly household, well within the budget of my father's modest monthly salary. Baba was a well-built, handsome man, given to smoking Cavender cigarettes. He was not a heavy smoker. He lived within his means but was also caring and generous. We had a full-time domestic help, named Maruti. Didi and I had a happy childhood, grew up with the usual ups and downs of primary and secondary school education. We lived in the front portion on the top floor of a four-storey building. The building was midway between a tenement and an apartment house. It was the second building on the right as you entered our lane off a main street called Tardeo, in the central part of Bombay. It was a longish lane with similar neighbourhood buildings, with a fairly large gated portion at its far end, a typical Bombay Parsi colony.

The Parsis are a close-knit community, who are followers of the Zoroastrian faith. They are the descendants of immigrants from Persia, who came in the fifteenth century to escape religious persecution. The first wave landed on the coast of Gujarat. Their leaders had been summoned to the court of the local monarch, having sought permission to live in India. The story goes that the reigning sultan had told them that India was already overcrowded, to which the Zoroastrian leaders are supposed to have responded that their small numbers would be like a few crystals of sugar, which would mix and melt in the bowl of the Indian ocean of milk of kindness. This response impressed the local sultan, who granted them permission to make India their new home, provided they desisted from any religious conversion. Over the centuries, the Parsi community has made, disproportionate to their numbers, contributions to the social, political and economic progress of India. They had settled along the coast of Gujarat, established many fire temples or 'agiaries'—their religious temples—and over a period of time, adopted the Gujarati language as their mother tongue, along with the dress and social customs of the local people. The Parsis, however, have maintained their religious practices inviolate, until the present day. Entry into their fire temples and witnessing their religious rituals are strictly forbidden to non-Parsis. For example, after they die, their body is left on a hillock, a landmark in Bombay called the Tower of Silence, to be devoured by vultures. Intermarriage with other communities is forbidden. As a consequence of inbreeding, over the centuries, the

Parsi population in India has slowly dwindled, exacerbated by large numbers emigrating, mainly to Canada, USA and Australia.

In the course of time, many Parsis became rich and famous, starting with their success in cotton trading and exporting opium to China. Many prospered in trade and commerce, especially when the British ruled India. A Parsi established India's first steel mill, in the nineteenth century. The community excelled in trade, commerce, education and philanthropy. The Parsis remain a close-knit community, and continue to be at the forefront, both for their piety and charity. Building housing colonies to provide for their less well-endowed compatriots was a major act of charity of rich and prosperous Parsis. The community wanted to provide a roof over every Parsi family, at very cheap and affordable prices. The Parsi Colony in our lane was one such subsidized housing colony.

In the rest of the lane, all the other houses were also occupied mostly by Parsis, other than the one in which we lived. There was also one fire temple and a good-sized playground. The end of the lane had some shops and an Irani restaurant, typical of the nineteenth- and early-twentieth-century Bombay. Iranis were later immigrants from Persia, a few were Zoroastrians and some others followers of Islam. The Iranis specialized in ubiquitous tea shops and bakeries, both of which were spread across Bombay, and because of their inexpensive and very tasty offerings, were patronized by Bombayites from all walks of life.

The lane in which our house was situated provided the perfect setting for bare-feet cricket matches, very popular on Sunday mornings and in the evenings; we hung around in the lane as young boys, in clusters, chatting away for carefree hours. At home, we spoke Bengali, which is our mother tongue. On the street with friends, we spoke 'Hindian'—this is a mix of Gujarati, Marathi, Bombay Hindi and a few other, minor languages. The way one spoke Gujarati clearly distinguished a Parsi from a native of Gujarat. In reality, the accent in any Indian spoken tongue identifies the geographical region of one's origin. We were, of course, not conscious of such fine distinctions until much later, as we grew up. The Marathi spoken in Bombay is a mix of the dialects of the regions from where people had migrated to Bombay, in search of employment. The Hindi spoken in Bombay is unusual in its utilitarian adaptation for local use, of what may be called classical Hindustani. Bombay Hindi is much scorned by the votaries of the language, not that it mattered.

The Ganguly House

My mother's home in Patna was bought, developed and built by Deena's husband (the wife of my grandmother's cousin), Baroda Kanta Ganguly, who worked in the colonial civil service. The main Ganguly house, facing the road, had served as the 'kacheri' or front office, when Deena's late husband used to be the district judge in Patna. This narrative belongs to a time well before I was born. The judge presided over his domestic affairs from his sitting hall, the interior, but met visitors in the 'Baithak-Khana' or the reception hall, situated in the main building, which was separated from the domestic quarters, by a large stretch of garden. The judge had two attendants whom I have seen not met and who continued to live in their old quarters, long after they had retired. They told us stories of their working life when they would be resplendent in their long khaki coats with epaulettes and broad red sash across the shoulders. Ramnareshji and Tiwariji used to wear their red-and-gold pugri caps at a jaunty angle. A white dhoti and a pair of polished black pump shoes would complete their accouterment. Once the judge had been ushered into his two-horse-drawn, closed carriage, Ramnareshji would climb next to the 'Garwan', the driver, carrying all the files and official papers, while Tiwariji would travel standing on a platform attached to the rear end of the carriage. Must have been very impressive! The two of them would provide all that the judge needed, near at hand, while he attended to his court duties. Although I had not seen the judge, there were many stories of his fame, during his working life and of how he provided for the comfort and security of the rest of the large joint family, none of whom seemed to have quite distinguished themselves in the public domain. There was a particular story which riveted my attention no matter how many times it had been repeated.

Whenever the judge sentenced someone found guilty to be hanged, following the hanging, the bodies would be brought later on covered in a shroud and laid out on the outer balcony of the Ganguly House, facing the main road, with mourning relatives in train. It was a rule which required the judge to identify the deceased before clearing them, to be handed over to their family. It all sounded gruesome but was a part of the colonial judicial system.

By the time I, as a child, met Ramnareshji and Tiwariji, they were well into their eighties. They lived in the same outhouse which used to be their 'quarters'.

As strict Brahmins, they still cooked their own meals and tended the milch cows, belonging to the Ganguly House. Once a month the Pandeyjis, as we respectfully addressed them, would dress in their former official tunics of long coats with a red sash, to go and collect their pension. On many evenings, we children sat around the old Pandeyjis, listening to the stories of the heyday of the judge, and let our imagination drift.

Summer Holidays

Most of our summer holidays were spent in Patna, at the home of our maternal grandparents, with scores of our cousins, who lived in Ganguly House. Patna, one of the oldest urban settlements in India, emerged during the last couple of millennia, from the ancient capital of Pataliputra of the Gupta dynasty. Our neighbours, of the Gupta House, were not related to the historic Guptas but were fellow Bengalis. Ma used to get a once-a-year yearning to visit Patna; I imagine she was drawn by her memories of childhood, before she got married at the age of sixteen, moved to Benares, my father's home, and soon thereafter to Bombay, to join him. Didi and I were born in Patna.

Ma felt the urge to visit Patna usually during summertime, but sometimes these urges did not coincide with our school holidays. My father would make one of his rare visits to our school, to seek the headmaster's permission for us to leave before the annual summer holidays. Didi and I knew that we would be going to Patna along with Ma, happy to miss school; we would, the same evening, board the train for the thirty-six-hour journey to Patna, full of anticipation of the happy days which lay ahead. My childhood memories of Patna are of a slow-moving gentle city, of cycle rickshaws and horse-drawn 'phitons'. The broad tarred boulevards would start wilting in the intense heat and haze during the afternoon of the central Indian summer. Deep grooves were formed along the melting tar roads by the cycle rickshaws and the phitons. I was left with a childhood impression that all roads in north India were corrugated!

All along, the road was flanked by broad open drains ('nullahs'), covered with large stone slabs. The open drains carried the city's effluent and were also the breeding ground for Anopheles mosquitoes. Mosquitoes bred and rested during the day and emerged in hordes to feast on the blood of humans and animals after dark. This was the only unattractive feature of our holiday, mitigated somewhat by the joy of being with our grandmother Hironbala, listening to her telling us stories from the Ramayana and Mahabharata, and falling asleep under the mosquito net, in the coolness of the night.

Ganguly House used to be a large red-brick, four-storey building on one of the main arterial roads of Patna, and across the street from the Anglo High School, where my grandfather, Yogendra Nath Mukherjee, used to be a teacher. A passageway alongside the middle patch of the garden led into the main courtyard. Along the passageway, the drain was covered with large stone slabs as well. This main outlet collected effluent from a number of narrow and open tributaries, fed by the effluent from the domestic bathing enclosures, the cattle pen, two wells, which supplied the bulk of the potable water, toilets and the kitchens. The night soil was separately collected, as head loads, every morning, by women whom the Hindu caste system called untouchables and assigned this hereditary role.

There were two bungalows, side by side in the interior of the larger rear potion. One was occupied by Deena, our grandmother Hironbala, her son Nalini and his family. The other bungalow housed Hironbala's brother, his wife and their seven daughters and three sons. The roofs were flat and the main terrace provided space for several cots in the summer and rare privacy to young people during the hours of dusk. They were supposedly seeking peace and quiet to 'study'. I was too young to understand the need for 'peace and quiet' then!

The large courtyard had a cattle shed on one side where there were generally three or four milch cows. There was also an outhouse for the domestic help. The houses were shadowed by an enormous jamboon tree and a graceful wood apple (bale) tree. Bale panna (juice) is an extract from the round 'bale' fruit. The juice is a very soothing, aromatic and sweet drink, especially comforting in summer. The jamboon tree in season used to carry a full load of a huge number of fruits, in the summer. The black juicy jamboon fruit used to hang temptingly within easy reach from the ground, and one of our pastimes was to shake the branches, to collect and consume the fruits.

The flagstone-covered passage next to the house in which Hironbala lived with her son Nalini and his family, led to the inner courtyard, whose other three sides were taken up by another cottage where Hironbala's brother, Gangaprasad Ganguly, and his family lived. A third standalone unit was the main kitchen and storeroom.

My grandfather, Yogendra Nath Mukherjee, lived in a book-lined room of his own, situated in the main building, up front, where he enjoyed a degree of privacy, to read, smoke the 'hookah', and play 'daba' or bridge, with his friends, in the evening.

Grandmother Hironbala was a towering personality who dominated the household, although the property was built and belonged to the widow Deena's husband and Hironbala's uncle, the judge. Deena was widowed at a relatively young age and inherited the handsome property, the Ganguly House. Deena had two sons and a daughter, besides her own grandchildren, all belonging to the large joint family.

My playmates were my Mama's sons, Bubul and Tutul, and my mother's maternal uncle Gangaprasad's sons, Gopal and Munua. Didi's companions were a number of Gopal's and Munua's younger sisters, while their two elder sisters were closer in age to my mother and were her close friends.

Soon after we reached Patna, from Bombay, for our once-a-year visit, and just about finished unpacking, we children would get together and drift in small groups, exchanging stories and playing games. The fun of our summer holiday always started spontaneously, and we behaved as if we had not been away for a year and grown older since the previous summer. Shooting marbles was a principal pastime for us boys, and we played most mornings, after breakfast.

During our marble games, some of the marbles would roll into one of the shallow open tributaries of the drains. If any one of us was caught retrieving a marble from a drain, clothes had to be given for washing, and one also had to take a bath. The trick was to recover any drain-lodged marble out of sight of the elders. Afternoons were for plucking jamboons and bale, and a short, forced siesta. In the evening, we joined a soccer game at the Gupta House, which had a large open ground in front of their big house.

In a corner of that forecourt and a wooded recess lived an old widow named Bhati. As I grew older, I became more curious to know who she was and why she lived in such a secluded and deprived condition, alongside the splendour and old wealth of the Guptas. It turned out that she was one of the Gupta sisters who had been widowed in childhood and had withdrawn into a shell since that time. The rest of the family had tried to make her as comfortable as they would have liked to, but this was the way she wished to live, by herself. Bhati's only pastime was to watch us playing soccer and at times raising hell, without reason, all around her.

As we grew older, I did realize that the fun holidays of our childhood were a maze of relationships and issues, which were anything but simple.

Over the years the large Ganguly House gradually started dispersing. Our visits from Bombay became less frequent. Our maternal uncle bought a house in Mahendru Mohalla, and moved there with his mother, our grandmother, and the rest of his family. The last time I went to Patna and Ganguly House was in 1967, along with my wife, Connie. We spent a day at Mahendru with Grandmother. My childhood playmates, cousins Bubul and Tutul were soon to move to Calcutta and start their jobs. Gopal had got married, found a job and settled in Bombay. His younger brother Monua died in a motorcycle accident in Patna on his way to work to the State Bank of India, leaving behind his widow and their newly born son. Ganguly House in Nayatola was virtually deserted.

Part III

Growing Up: 1935–47

My grandfather, Anathbandhu, shifted from his ancestral home and family, in Barishal (now in Bangladesh), in the last quarter of the nineteenth century, to Benares.

He acquired a house, to spend his years close to the banks of the Ganga. Stories of his years in Benares are fuzzy; for example, what he did for a living, or who arranged his marriage to Surangini Devi, from the village of Chanok, in Burdwan, etc. My grandparents had eleven children—five sons and six daughters. Five of the daughters died in infancy.

Anathbandhu died at the relatively young age of sixty years or as per average longevity of the period. After his death, widowed, Surangini Devi had to struggle to bring up her children without a steady source of income to make ends meet. Surangini had to frequently sell her ornaments, exhausting all the other valuables to feed, educate and raise her six children and arranging her daughter's marriage. My father, Sekhar Nath, had to sacrifice his studies after matriculation and travelled to Bombay in 1924, where his close relatives had settled. His maternal uncle worked in the GIP (Great Indian Peninsular) Railways, and his two sons, Bonomali and Tarakeshwar, worked in a private company known as Bombay Electric Supply and Tramways (BEST). My father was recruited by BEST, as a junior officer; his fluency in English must have helped. Bonomali had converted to the Christian faith and held a senior position in BEST. The British preferred to recruit Anglo–Indians and Indian Christian converts.

In Bombay, my father started life at first staying with the joint family of his maternal uncle. Although as children, I don't recall hearing many stories of his early days in Bombay. As my sister and I were growing up, we frequently took out the old boxes and enjoyed looking at old photographs of our father and his British colleagues playing tennis. He was a reasonably good tennis player; in those old sepia-tinted photos, he looks young and handsome in his tennis whites. His other passion, as a bachelor, was going to the cinema with his cousin Tarakeshwar and a couple of other friends.

Baba's marriage with Bina Pani Mukherjee was arranged by their parents and solemnized at Bina Pani's home, in Patna, in 1931. Bina Pani was born and grew up in a joint family. Her father, Yogendranath, was a school teacher in Patna, although his ancestral home was in Belgharia, in the outskirts of Calcutta. My grandmother Hiron Bala's family roots were in Dhaka.

After their marriage, my parents returned, as newly-weds, to Bombay, after a break in Benares. They briefly stayed with the joint family of Baba's uncle and, shortly thereafter, moved to a neighbouring flat, of their own, on Lamington Road. Bina Pani was sixteen years of age when she got married. She and Nandarani, Tarakeshwar's wife, soon became close friends. My mother used to be a very good raconteur and told us that both she and Nandarani were given one anna each every month by Tarakeshwar's father, the head of the joint family, as pocket money. Both of them would soon walk to Chowpatty, which was nearby, for their monthly treat of bhel-puri. During their stay in the joint family, my father and his cousins handed over their salaries to Bonomali and Tarakeshwar's father, the head of the joint family, who oversaw and managed the monthly household expenditure. Thus commenced our parents' happy and carefree life in Bombay. Baba sent money orders every month, to his mother in Benares, to manage the household expenses, as well as to a few widowed aunts and cousins.

My sister Protima (Ruby—all Bengalis have a 'pet' name) was born in December 1933 in Patna, during a massive earthquake which struck north India. I was born in July 1935 at the Patna Medical College Hospital. Sometime after my birth, my mother returned, along with Ruby and me, to Bombay, where we lived and grew up.

After a few years, Baba's cousin, Tarakeshwar, his father and his wife, Nandarani, moved from Lamington Road to another apartment in Body Guard Lane, and our family moved into a neighbouring lane, on Ratan Tata Road, in Tardeo. That was where we lived for many years, and where Didi and I grew up, through our childhood, infant and secondary schools, as well as college, carrying memories of happiness and contentment. Over time, Baba arranged for his brothers, Kalo, Lalu and Probhat, to also come to Bombay and found Kalo and Lalu jobs. Our home became a slightly crowded Ganguly joint family. Baba's elder brother Bholanath and his family, and our grandmother Surangini Devi, continued to live in the house in Benares. Our summer holidays, for several years, were spent between Patna and Benares. As we grew older, our short trips to Poona (Pune) or Matheran, especially in winter, led to happy memories. I remember, one year, while we were in high school, Didi, Ma and I spent several months in Patna, long enough to have to be admitted to a local school there. I cannot recall the reason for our long sojourn to Patna, but it may have been due to some tension in our joint family, of which I am happily ignorant.

After the initial excitement of that one, rather long stay in Patna, and the fun of the company of our cousins slowly wore off, we were very happy to return to Bombay and to our old school routine, and friends whom we had missed. One of my earliest memories is being cared for as a baby by our domestic help and majordomo, Maruti. He helped me bathe in the mornings, laid out my clothes, delivered Ruby (Didi) and me to our nursery school, waited around for school to get over and then walked us back home. In the evening, Maruti perched me on one of his shoulders, while Didi held on to Maruti's hand, for our evening outing via Body Guard Lane, to Mahalaxmi Maidan, a vast expanse of a leafy commons and some days to play in the beautiful garden in the grounds of the Bombay Central Station.

I think we were fortunate to grow up in the Bombay of that time, probably the prettiest and cleanest city in india. Evenings passed quickly at home. Bina Pani was a voracious reader of Bengali novels and periodicals. Some evenings, she would bring out her harmonium from its wooden box and her notebook of songs, to render a few songs in her mellifluous voice. Teaching Didi and me to read and write Bengali was her passion and our fright. Our home-tutored Bengali started with primary-level Bengali, with the help of a beginner's textbook procured from Calcutta, followed by progressively advanced texts. For a while, we had almost a parallel education, learning to read and write Bengali at home, while attending up to class four at an English convent school in Bombay. I am ever grateful for Ma's perseverance in teaching Didi and me Bengali. As we grew older, the ritual of Sunday morning Bengali dictation, which we had to write without making spelling mistakes, used to be a torture as it delayed my joining the tennis-ball cricket game with friends, on the road where we lived. I am very grateful that Ma determinedly taught us to read and write Bengali. During my years in the USA, a weekly Bengali letter was the only means of communicating with my mother, and reading hers. Baba, Didi and I wrote letters in English.

Didi and I studied up to the third standard at Sunny Dale Convent, and then moved to Masters Tutorial High School for higher classes. Both schools were within walking distance from our home, in Tardeo. While Maruti took us every day to Sunny Dale, Didi and I walked to Master Tutorial by ourselves, to Gowalia Tank.

We were growing up and moving on from our idyllic childhood, of evening outings with Maruti and our happy home, sometimes witnessing the occasional tiffs between the grown-ups, without really comprehending what the hullaballoo was all about.

My childhood image of Sekhar Nath (Baba) was that of a tall, handsome Baba, who carried a silver cigarette case lined with Capstan or Cavender cigarettes. His job with BEST was mostly outdoors. He wore long brown socks, brown shoes, khaki shorts, white shirts and cotton jackets. These were his work clothes, and that was, at the time, the working man's attire. He went around in an Austin van, with a junior Parsi colleague, Poly Mehta, driving him, attending to his outdoor work around Bombay.

On Saturdays, when our school got over at lunchtime, my father would usually be waiting in his Austin van outside, to pick my sister and me up, and take us home for lunch. I cannot recall why Didi and I felt a bit shy to get into his van, while being watched by our classmates.

Didi was a diligent and disciplined student; I was almost totally uninterested in studies. Our teachers may have been OK, as far as I can recall, none, however, was inspiring. My lack of interest in studies, short attention span and a wandering mind were a mix fated for failure, or underperformance. A succession of private tutors at home, arranged by Baba, neither improved my performance nor kindled my interest. Two other related developments at the time are worth recalling. A close family friend, Sudhir, was almost a daily evening visitor to our home. Sudhir had played a critical role on one issue, for my sister and me to choose Sanskrit, which was the reason for my failing the SSC examination. Opting for Sanskrit happened to be the first 'fork on the road', and being forced to choose Sanskrit, a wrong decision. From then onwards, my subconscious decisions at various forks on the road, during my lifetime, may have been influenced; I became what I am and remain there.

To be fair, the outcome may not have been different if Didi and I had chosen French instead of Sanskrit. But there is no way of knowing, since I remained mediocre and indifferent, throughout my school years anyway. My mother welcomed him, my father enjoyed his company. Sudhir and my father seemed to have endless conversations, played carom, worked on crossword puzzles in the *Illustrated Weekly of India*, and Sudhir, who was a confirmed bachelor, usually ended up having dinner with us. From class six in school, we had to opt for French, German or Sanskrit as an additional subject. Didi and I were keen to choose French. Sudhir persuaded Baba instead, for us to choose Sanskrit. On one of his annual trips to Calcutta, Sudhir brought for us a thick Bengali–Sanskrit dictionary. Didi and I never found any use for the dictionary. Not surprisingly, learning Sanskrit became even a greater disaster. An additional tutor, solely for Sanskrit, was engaged by Baba. No one succeeded in sparking my academic interest. Didi, however, used to be diligent and hard-working—just my opposite. In school I remained a consistent underperformer. It was an ordeal for me to show my weekly report card to Baba, for his signature. Even though he never reprimanded me, Ma was quite vocal about her disappointment regarding my poor performance.

As we grew slightly older, Didi and I got one anna (one sixteenth of a rupee or approximately six paise in decimal currency) as pocket money, daily. The pocket money was meant to buy small tucks in school. I was a spendthrift, and Didi was a saver. I invariably ended up borrowing small change from her, quite frequently. Over the years, this must have amounted to a significant sum, which, of course, I never repaid.

I twice played truant, in my lifetime, around the age of 10–12. Once from home, being very upset after receiving a good thrashing from Ma for some lapse, I vaguely recall crying my eyes out and deciding to 'leave' home. I walked from our home in Tardeo to Haji Ali, and then along the sea face, called the Hornby Vellard, at the end of which there used to be a giant model of a Dunlop tyre, as an advertisement. The Dunlop advertisement is no longer there and the beautiful sea front is now dotted with slums and a potted sidewalk, in harmony with the present disrepair of the city.

After walking out from home without telling anyone, I sat on the parapet, facing the sea, next to the Dunlop advertisement. In my state of feeling sorry for myself, I passed time watching the fisher folk unloading fish from a boat which had just returned from sea. After they sat down to rest nearby, they got to chatting with me, as if that was a perfectly normal thing to do. The boatmen also seemed to be in a carefree mood and did not seem curious about my presence. By now, it was midday, and it being summer, it was getting quite hot.

Ma became very worried about my whereabouts, because I was not responding to her calls at home. Baba came home at noon every day for his lunch break, and was informed by my nervous Ma, in tears, that I had gone missing. In the meantime, I was persuaded by the boatmen to take a dip in the sea along with them, which I did. Baba, on hearing the news that I had gone AWOL, got back into his van and went out looking for me. I never discovered how he reached the spot where, on the seafront, I had taken a dip in the sea and was basking in the sun, while my underclothes were drying on the rocks. I was chatting away, with the fisher folk, about what I cannot recall. He came down to the spot where we were chatting. I got up sheepishly, relieved that I had been found! I followed him to his van, and we drove back home, in silence. I was now really worried about another spanking awaiting me, from my mother. To my pleasant relief, she received me with a warm embrace and not a single word was spoken about the episode, either at that moment or ever after. Baba, not surprisingly, like always, remained silent. We sat down to a quiet lunch, while Ma took a little time to recover. In retrospect, I am ashamed that I was not repentant of my behaviour, and secretly hoped Ma would be more careful in the future, scolding me or disciplining my wayward ways. However, very soon, life returned to its usual pattern under Ma's watchful discipline, and not much changed.

It must have been a couple of years later that my particularly poor and worse-than-usual monthly school report triggered my second escapade. The monthly reports of performance in school were handed over to each student, on the last Saturday of the month. The report card of the month's performance had to be shown to parents, signed by Baba, and returned by each student to Principal Banaji on the following Monday morning.

My sister regularly received average to better-than-average school reports, which Baba would see at a glance and then sign. In contrast, my reports remained consistently poor. That particular month's report, and the principal's comments, were even more caustic than usual. Baba never reprimanded me on my consistently poor performance, while Ma freely expressed her disappointment. This particular monthly report was even worse than my usual poor performance and made me feel very scared. In panic, but in a foolishly contrived plot, I decided not to show my report to Baba. In his preoccupation, he also did not ask to see my report, although he had just signed Didi's report card. Instead, at an opportune moment, on Sunday, when Ma was busy cooking lunch and Baba was visiting a friend, I got hold of the rubber block of his signature facsimile from his desk drawer, along with the ink pad, and pressed the copy of his signature on my report card. It was a wily but a very stupid act on my part. As usual, the report cards were collected on Monday morning by our class teacher and sent to the principal's office. That was the moment I panicked. Before the next class started, I walked out of my classroom and out of the school gate, and thus began the second episode of my being AWOL. I had no specific plan, other than wandering aimlessly and avoiding school, until the end of the day, and return to the school gate, catch up with Didi as she came out, and for both of us to walk back home. She was in the 'girls' section, and was unaware of my escapade.

I continued to stay away from school for the rest of the week. I had not thought out how my escapade would end. After seeing the 'rubber stamp signature' on my report card, Principal Banaji had sent for me to appear in his room. He was informed that I was not in the class. Every day, I walked around aimlessly, from the Nana Chowk fire brigade station, along the sidewalk, up to Gowalia Tank. One day, during my escapade, I bought a packet of 'bidis', and for the first time, smoked them all, till I felt really ill. I was then ten or twelve years old. Another day, I espied one of my parent's acquaintances approaching from the opposite end of the footpath. I quickly hid behind a lamp post, to escape being asked what I was doing on my own, at that time of day. It turned out to be an unnecessary manoeuvre on my part. On the fourth day of my escapade, as usual, I joined my sister at the school gate, at the end of school, to walk back home. She was carrying a letter addressed to Baba, from the principal. I guessed the letter was regarding my misdeed and my absence from school. I felt horrified and panic-stricken. My sister was oblivious of the contents in the sealed envelope. When we reached home, Didi kept the principal's letter on Baba's table. By now I was in deep panic, thinking of the likely outcome. Ma instantly guessed that something was amiss and tried vainly to get the truth out of me, before Baba returned home from work. As usual, after returning, he changed his work clothes and sat down on the easy chair, with a cup of tea and the day's newspaper, lit a cigarette and relaxed. I awaited my fate. Instead of going out to play with friends, I quietly sat down with one of my school textbooks, chosen at random. The words appeared blurred, my mind kept wandering to one of the several possible punishments which was about to befall me. My tension at that point was such that I am unable to describe in words. Didi, as usual, settled down to do her homework. Time seemed to have stopped for me, although at that time I did not know what that feeling actually meant! My mother seemed to have lost interest and was engrossed in reading a Bengali novel, her usual habit, and at the usual time, got busy to get the dinner ready. At the usual time, we sat down to dinner. Baba, Didi and I each sat on separate *ashones* (floor mats) and we were then served, by my mother, on thalis. Usually, there was mostly small chat between Ma and Baba while we ate our chapattis, with vegetable curry and dal. After we finished, Ma would have her dinner, then after a while, all of us were off to bed.

That night, I went to bed with a certain sense of relief, as well as fear, as no conversation had taken place all evening about my escapade, even though I had noticed that in the meantime, Baba had opened the envelope. Baba had apparently read the principal's letter and also seen my report card.

Baba usually left for work very early in the morning, Didi and I ate 'lunch' around 10 a.m. and then walked together to school. Baba had apparently asked Didi to hand over my report card and his reply, addressed to our principal. In retrospect, Baba provided a strong aura of quiet confidence and reassurance all through my school and college years. It was not in his nature to appear either upset or annoyed or overly cheerful. It was later in my life, and especially in my lonely moments in America, that I realized how difficult his own growing-up years may have been, while he rolled out the rotis and his mother cooked endlessly to feed her children, under difficult economic circumstances. His move to Bombay soon after matriculation, starting to work to help his mother and after some time arranged marriage with Ma, the birth of Didi and me must have been sources of satisfaction, happiness and confidence and had set the course for the future. My own growing up with perpetual lack of interest in studies must have bothered my parents deeply. While Ma was frequently visibly upset, Baba remained stoic, other than engaging private tutors and an aura of helpful resolve. When I think of those times, I recall his self-confidence and silent resolve to light a spark in me. Baba's personality and resolve failed him once when Didi married against his wishes, which he took to heart and which lasted his lifetime. Sadly, I was away in America during this episode and only came to know about the intensity after my return to India. I realized that he had not mentioned anything to Ma. I had no choice but to return to school, along with my sister.

The school bell rang. Didi left Baba's letter and my report card at the principal's office and went to her class in the 'girls' section', and I to my class and sat on the last bench, to be as obscure as possible. Our class was about to commence when the principal's peon entered the class and handed over a folded chit to the class teacher. I had been summoned to the principal's office. I followed the peon, like a lamb to slaughter.

Principal Banaji was a large-framed Parsi of Dickensian demeanour and girth. He was always dressed in a spotless white three-piece suit of a popular fabric called 'Duckwhite'. A watch on a gold chain was tucked in his waistcoat pocket. As I entered, he rose from his desk and swivel chair, a figure, larger than life, hovering over me with pince-nez glasses at the edge of his nose, in menacing sternness and silence. Not a word was uttered. I knew, from earlier episodes, what I was supposed to do—stretch out my hands, perpendicular to my body, parallel to the floor and with palms open. Principal Banaji picked up his long cane and swished it in the air, with the usual menacing gesture. Then the cane came down with lightning speed and fell on my palms, by turn. From my earlier experiences, being amongst those who had experienced the pain of the principal's corporal punishment, I had learnt to turn my palms slightly sideways, to divert the descending cane to the space between forefinger and thumb, hoping to make the excruciating experience less painful. It actually did not help, in practice.

By the time the mandatory four strikes per palm had ended, I had tears running down my cheeks, in humiliation and pain. The ordeal was over, not one word had been exchanged. Banaji went back to his chair and I shuffled out in pain, back to my classroom. My classmates were gleeful; we were at that cruel age; they all knew that I was returning from a 'Banaji caning', in humiliation. As I was trying to cross the room to return to my seat in the last row, the teacher gave a thudding punch on my right ear. My teacher was angry because he had not noticed my four-day absence but felt it was his right to whack me, for whatever I may have done to deserve the principal's attention. The rest of the day passed in a daze of pain and humiliation. The pain of the caning, which left deep marks on my palms, persisted for a while. Apparently, I was not missed in the class. We were at an age, and in a school, where I do not recall having even one really close friend. My friends were all from the neighbourhood where we lived, and of whom I have happy but fading memories with the passage of time.

On the way back home, I told Didi what had transpired. Strangely, Baba had not mentioned my misdeeds to either her or Ma. My second escapade remains a secret between my late father, our redoubtable school principal, Banaji, and me, to this day. I never discovered why my class teacher felt free to whack me!

A few other episodes from my school days may be worth recalling. On more than one occasion, my father suddenly came to our school, in the middle of the week, met Principal Banaji, collected Didi and

me from class and drove us home. More than once, Ma had these
sudden urges for a trip to our maternal grandparents' home in Patna.
The sheer excitement of skipping school and going on an unexpected
holiday and enjoying carefree days with hordes of cousins, the care
and affection of the elders, overshadowed missing classes.

Looking back, I wonder why I had never thought about a
few of our sudden visits to Patna and what may have triggered
these. A sudden holiday was a relief from the drudgery of school.
That there may have been other more complex triggers did not
come to mind, until I commenced writing. Considering the
happy childhood Didi and I enjoyed, any other cause for a few
of these sudden trips to Patna was not a matter which concerned
us as children.

Baba visited Patna only twice during his lifetime, both times
along with us, and seemed quite relaxed during just the few days he
spent there, mostly playing bridge with our elder cousins. He seemed
to enjoy more our annual holiday trips to Benares, especially the
morning oil massage on the ghats, which I also loved, followed by a
dip and swim in the Ganga.

The other place we went to, for short winter breaks, was a small
isolated bungalow on the riverside, in the Bund Garden, Poona.
The daily fresh catch from the river, delivered by the fisher folk, and
cooked by Ma, remains a very fond memory of our childhood.

One of the biggest celebrations, which I recall, was 15 August
1947, Independence Day. I have vague memories of the British
rule in India, from my childhood. The one incident I recall was
the appearance of British soldiers in our lane late one night, who
mercilessly beat up a crowd of young people, following a communal
incident. The sight of brutal beatings, which we witnessed from our
balcony, left a strong and vivid memory of violence.

We did not have a radio in our home. I recall visiting Baba's
elder cousin Tarakeshwar's home, in our neighbouring lane, and
watching the elders glued to a large radio. Much later, I realized they
were all listening to news of World War II, of which I had no clue

at the time. The elders read a daily newspaper in the morning, the *Free Press Journal. Blitz* and *Illustrated Weekly* were the other two favourites of Baba.

On 15 August 1947, my father took Ma, Didi and me for a horse-drawn carriage ride, around a spectacularly lit up, decorated and hugely crowded Bombay, towards the Gateway of India. Earlier in the day, a gathering was held in our school, speeches were delivered regarding Independence, and each student received a packet of sweets and a four anna coin (big money!), to mark Independence Day. The four anna piece was, soon thereafter, collected from us, to be sent to a relief fund for the refugees flowing into Delhi, following the partition of India and the creation of Pakistan. At the time, we did not comprehend the nature of one of the most traumatic events in the history of independent India.

In March 1951, the final results of our secondary school certificate (SSC) exams were declared. Didi and I had appeared for this examination. Passing this exam would qualify us to seek university admission. As expected, Didi had, of course, passed but I had failed, as I had not scored passing marks in Sanskrit.

I was sad but not remorseful. My parents must have been disappointed but may not have been surprised, considering my indifferent school performance. A cousin of ours, Shombhu, himself a good student, and who had just joined a medical college, used to come and spend time with Baba. Shombhu was arrogant and sarcastic, but Baba somehow had a soft spot for him. That evening, the school final results were declared, and he dropped by our home, as he frequently did. On hearing that I had failed, he suggested to my father that I was not going to amount to much in life and that Baba should invest in a small kiosk, selling betel leaf and cigarettes, in order to secure my future. Baba kept quiet, but Ma was visibly angry and very upset.

Didi got admission in Jai Hind College. I was left behind to prepare and get ready to appear in the supplementary exam, in October of that year. But Baba never lost hope. His attempts, earlier, to enrol me in a better-known school, had failed. His disappointment at my scholastic indifference, he never expressed.

He encouraged me to renew my efforts, for the supplementary scheduled in October 1951. During the summer break, Didi and I joined a shorthand and typing class, to fill our time. Didi went on to join college; I remember for the first time feeling downcast, a sense of humiliation and failure. To prepare for the October supplementary examination, besides additional coaching at home, Baba got me a part-time job in a small company, selling laboratory glassware, for science departments in schools. I have a vague recollection of my rather desultory stint with that company. Looking back, I think this kept me out of trouble and provided vague exposure to the rudiments of commerce.

The supplementary exam results were declared in December 1951. I had passed with middling scores in all subjects, including Sanskrit. I got admission to Jai Hind College, under the Bombay University. My sister was already in the first year of the four-year bachelor of science honours course.

The memories of my childhood days and growing up were uncaring but happy, although failure in SSC, as I look back, was a wakeup call. Ours was a typical Indian, middle-class home of modest means, but full of love and caring. Baba's stoicism and determination and Ma's enthusiasm and discipline were what moulded the character and achievements of Didi and me, for the rest of our lives. My failure in matriculation on my first attempt was the tipping point of the rest of my life.

The values imbibed, being born and brought up in an Indian middle-class family, are deeply ingrained. I recall what my father, a man of few words, told me, but sadly I do not remember the context.

My father's homily, that sustenance does not require subservience, has remained deeply ingrained in me and my outlook in life. Of course, it is not all that simple. Genes, upbringing, etc., play a critical role. One's childhood, upbringing and domestic environment play powerful roles in how we grow up and what we accomplish in our lifetime. Looking back, on more than one occasion, my deep sense of self-belief has moulded my actions and thoughts, while providing a great sense of inner pride and happiness to my parents.

Postscript

On 30 January 1948, we got the shocking news of Mahatma Gandhi's assassination, by Nathuram Godse, which triggered anti-Brahmin riots in Bombay. The names of Jawaharlal Nehru, Sardar Vallabhai Patel, Maulana Azad and their colleagues were at the top of my mind and a feeling of national pride seemed to have, somehow, grown within me. In the following years, I started expressing myself by hanging a large canvas portrait of Subhash Bose on our balcony, with an electric bulb on top of the frame and a thick floral garland around the frame, which became a fixture on every 23 January, for a few years. Someone remarked that it was the Bengali in me, though I had never been to Bengal and was not overly conscious of being a Bengali, other than speaking the language at home and weekend tutorials under my mother. In those days in Bombay, one grew up as a multilingual Indian. I inherited a sense of self-confidence from my parents and have never felt like an alien in Bombay, which is the most and the only cosmopolitan city in India, and has been ever since. I grew up playing barefoot tennis-ball cricket in the lane and spoke a mixture of Marathi, Gujarati, Parsi, Konkani, Hindi as well as Bengali.

Ma taught Didi and me to read and write Bengali at home on Sundays and during holidays. We had to write a one-page dictation without spelling mistakes every Sunday morning, due to which I regularly missed the first innings of our gully cricket. I was grateful that I had learnt to read and write Bengali, which helped me to read her weekly letters and write in the only language she was fluent in.

I have never suffered from any identity crisis as an Indian whose mother tongue happens to be Bangla, in various places around the world where I have lived and worked.

Transition from childhood to youth was marked by what I can best describe as budding 'patriotism', a comprehension of the transition from colonial rule to Independence.

As I take a step back into the memory lane, the milestones of my character-building included becoming a proud Indian with a mental vision of its future, an India made to rise by its bootstraps, through the call for self-reliance and building the 'temples' of a modern India.

The next phase of life was my education, first in India and subsequently in America, while conjuring a future of a resurgent India, in spite of the humiliation by the Chinese in 1962, the dependence on American aid, the PL 480 scheme and the demise of Pandit Jawaharlal Nehru.

Hopes and anticipation of the future at a certain age are difficult to be dented easily. The Green Revolution restored hopes and expectations.

I had also become conscious that India faced some almost-insurmountable hurdles, as a poor developing nation facing population explosion and a growing numbers of citizens condemned to the miseries of poverty.

During my postgraduate years in America, a few of us from India occasionally got together to chat about issues back home. On one of the occasions, we were joined by a recently arrived student from India. During our conversation, this young man suddenly declared that Nehru and socialism were destroying India. Instead of countering his statement, which I did not agree with, I lost my temper and told this new chap to immediately leave our company. He departed sheepishly; I immediately regretted the way I had reacted, but that was how strongly I felt at that time.

After returning to India, I began my working life, soon got married and, for the next few decades, enjoyed a wonderful family life and a professional career. As I grew older and continued to face the realities of independent India's short history, I did suffer from bouts of disappointment about how things could have been better, but my beliefs and optimism about the future of India did not falter.

On work assignments, my wife Connie and I spent time in America and Europe, but the question of settling down anywhere, other than India, was never an issue.

Over the decades, India has progressed, but neither sufficiently nor anywhere close to the nation's potential. I could not quite comprehend the politician's mindset, other than the insecurity of the profession, alongside the stranglehold of the bureaucrats and babus on the systems and processes, parts of which can be traced back to the days of the British Raj. Some prominent leaders attempted to modernize and bypass some of the hurdles, to let development breathe, with none or very limited success. I remember one of India's prime ministers failed in his attempts to introduce modern technology and reforms to accelerate progress as well as the ease of doing business, in the 1980s. These attempts were subtly sabotaged, by the 'system'. The 'reforms' of 1992 did let in some oxygen.

The themes which remained intact were the hurdles of ease of doing business in India, faced by the private sector, existing multinationals as well as potential foreign investors.

In spite of these travails, India remains the world's largest democracy, with an unfulfilled but ever-promising future. Fortunately, India's information technology (IT) service sector grew and thrived, almost by stealth. The famous Y2K 'threat' ultimately brought Indian engineering talent and knowledge of twentieth-century software and computer language to the world stage, and the prominence of India's global IT service brands grew.

In India, there are frequent references to research and development (R&D), innovation and especially the term 'frugal innovation', without appreciating that frugal innovation can only lead to fragile outcomes. There is, however, a buzz about twenty-first-century knowledge industries.

Like most Indians, I remain optimistic that we will get to where we should have, some day, in spite of the unending social, economic and political hurdles, and mind-numbing poverty and unemployment.

I must, however, admit that I was certainly more positive and optimistic in my young and professional days, because I was able to face challenges with the freedom and confidence I and many of my peers enjoyed. However, the slowness and energy-consuming outcomes were disproportionately disappointing, but not hopeless. Our generation's expectations did not allow the over 1000 years of foreign occupation, the history of the numerous Indian princelings and maharajas, to dampen our hope and energy and optimism about democratic India's future.

So as I conclude this chapter, in the silence of the COVID lockdown, by stating that my confidence has been reinforced by the fact that much has changed, and I am confident that much more will continue to change, under the succeeding generations, in one of the world's most diverse and largest democracies, of multiracial, multilingual, multi-religious people; because we are, above all, Indians.

School and University:
In Bombay and America

Didi may relate her own story some day; towards me she was always protective, diligent in her studies and a great help to Ma as we grew up. While we were growing up, I realized that Didi was the apple of Baba's eyes.

As I started college, my whole attitude and outlook changed, which I can best describe as remarkable, given my school episodes and indifferent attitude to studying. From indifference to studies in school and at home, I suddenly developed genuine interest in my studies. In retrospect, a few of our professors at Jai Hind College triggered my enthusiasm towards learning and excelling in my performance. I am also convinced that in the life of every child, there comes a tipping point, and parents need the patience to nurture children, no matter how hopeless things may seem at times.

Jai Hind College was established in Bombay in 1948 by a group of former faculty and staff of the Basant Singh Institute of Science and DJ Sindh College, of Karachi, who had moved to Bombay, as refugees, following the partition of India in 1947. The newly established college was well endowed by the Sindhi community of traders and entrepreneurs. Historically, the Sindhi diaspora had settled in all corners of the world, as successful entrepreneurs, and were known as generous philanthropists.

The academic challenges to Jai Hind College, which was, nicknamed, derisively, as a 'Sindhi College', were primarily from the older and well-known colleges of Bombay, such as, Elphinstone and St Xavier's. The faculty of the newly established Jai Hind College must have been quietly determined to challenge the upstarts and surpass the scholastic performance of the 'establishment'. We happened to be amongst the early batches of raw material, with whom to drive towards that objective.

In complete contrast to most of my schoolteachers, and my own indifferent attitude towards learning, the faculty of Jai Hind College were inspirational. In order to convert that inspiration into outcomes, they advanced their commitment through exceptional quality of teaching, kindling in us the sheer excitement of learning. My four years (1952–56) in Jai Hind College were mentally and intellectually transformative for me. A few of us were selected, by the senior faculty, for special tutorials after normal class hours, for deeper immersion into theory as well as repeating laboratory experiments, in different subjects, especially in the third and fourth years.

Didi and I usually studied together at home in the evenings and late into the night, after evening meals. We performed very well in our college tests as well as Bombay University examinations. In our second year, in Jai Hind, to my surprise and delight, I was the recipient of the Rotary Prize and Scholarship. My mother was more expressive of her happiness, less so my father, although he must have been pleasantly surprised and felt proud. In our fourth year, when the BSc final results were announced by Bombay University, Didi and I passed with flying colours and honours. As a matter of fact, I got a rank in the university. We were proud that the 'Sindhi College' had not only matched but, in many subjects, excelled its snooty peers. Ever since, Jai Hind College continues to occupy the top ranks in Bombay University. Over the decades, Jai Hind has groomed several well-known alumni in different professions and leadership roles.

I had already made up my mind that after graduation, I would undertake research towards a PhD degree in Bombay University.

My American Adventure

Jai Hind College, at the time, had no postgraduate research facilities. I applied and got admitted to the venerable Royal Institute of Science (RIS) in Bombay. I was also the recipient of the prestigious Homi Bhabha Fellowship. It paid for the fees and a small surplus provided pocket money. Didi decided to pursue a master's degree in organic chemistry.

The postgraduate session at RIS commenced in June 1956. I was excited, to settle down, to do my PhD research, under Prof. D.M. Desai, the doctoral guide assigned to me. My research project's objective was to explore the paramagnetic resonance of complex organic molecules, and use the data towards a novel correlation with molecular structure. Prof. Desai was, unfortunately, not a keen teacher.

Some weeks subsequently, a colleague of my father's suggested that I should apply for a fellowship to the University of Illinois, in the USA, and about which he had come to know from one of his relatives, who happened to be a postdoctoral fellow at Illinois. I had not the slightest idea about America, other than childhood memories of American comic books. Anyway, I sent in my application to the University of Illinois and, within a month, received a reply inviting me to join the department of food science and technology, to work towards an MS and PhD. The university also offered me a research assistantship, which would cover all the costs for my postgraduate education, as well as my boarding and lodging, besides all other incidental expenses. It was indeed a most generous and a very attractive offer, which I immediately accepted. My father, in his usual way, got down to getting for me an Indian passport, an American visa and an air ticket to travel to the USA. Baba was one of the most energetic and resourceful men I have known in my life. Didi also felt ecstatic. But Ma, once she realized that I would be away from home for five years or more, in a strange, distant land, was heartbroken and cried copiously. Baba had to arrange for our maternal grandmother to come to Bombay from Patna, to soothe and pacify my mother.

Didima soon landed in Bombay to 'take charge'. I recall a late-night conversation between Grandmother and my parents during which Grandmother floated the idea to get me married before I left for the USA, in order to ensure that I would be forced to return. Baba immediately, and respectfully, rubbished the idea, by saying: 'He is not even twenty.' I was eavesdropping and felt a twinge. What a fool I still was!

The next few days flashed by, in acquiring my Indian passport, US visa (both palms stained with black ink to take my hand prints, etc.) and finally buying an air ticket. The price of the air ticket was Rs 3782, which was quite a big amount at the time. Baba had arranged to borrow money for the ticket. At that point, Ma brought out from her almirah a briefcase-sized black metal cash box. We were aware of the cash box, but had never actually seen it in use. Ma unlocked the cash box and started to count the small denomination currency notes and heaps of coins. Apparently, she had been collecting bits and bobs of small change and notes since her marriage twenty-five years earlier. The small heap, in front of her, on the floor, after counting, added up to a few rupees less than Rs 4000. There was enough money for the one-way air ticket to the US and then a bit more. Those days, the Reserve Bank of India permitted overseas travellers to carry only $20 in foreign exchange, at the exchange rate of Rs 4 and 50 paise per dollar. Soon my TWA ticket to Chicago via New York was in hand. My parents, as well as I, felt reassured knowing that an acquaintance of Baba's, the chief of TWA in Bombay, had arranged for me to be 'looked after', on arrival in New York, as well as assisted in transferring to a domestic flight to Chicago. The day of my departure was fast approaching. I had to make a quick visit to Patna and Benares, to seek the blessing of my grandmother in Patna and elders in Benares. Given my poor school career, there were whispers from one of the elders in the Patna joint family, who loudly expressed serious doubts regarding my sudden scholastic transformation. But, for me, the visit revived fun-filled childhood memories. From Patna, I went to Benares, to our ancestral home, before returning to Bombay.

We used to, as children, visit Benares almost once a year during winter holidays, when my paternal grandmother, Surangini Devi, was still alive. Annual holidays to Patna and Benares were events we looked forward to. Baba's cousin, Tarakeshwar had retired from BEST and settled down in his ancestral home, which was next door to ours, in Benares. They did not have any children of their own but had adopted the eldest son of Tarakeshwar's sister. Tarakeshwar was very affectionate towards Didi and me. We have very happy memories of our closeness to Tarakeshwar and his wife, Nandarani, as we were growing up. He was a first cousin of Baba as well as a very close friend, and we lived in homes located in adjoining lanes in Bombay.

This was the last time I was to see Tarakeshwar in Benares; he one day peacefully passed away, in his sleep, while I was still away in the USA.

After my farewell visits to Patna and Benares, I returned to Bombay and got busy with the final preparations for my departure to America.

Baba took me to get my first made-to-measure suit (there was no other kind at the time), to be stitched by the then well-known Chatterjee Tailors, on Lamington Road. Baba also bought for me a pair of thermal undergarments, taught me how to knot a tie and also purchased a nice blue suitcase for my trip to the USA.

Friends and neighbours in our residential building got together and arranged a touching farewell party. Everyone seemed happy and proud, without quite grasping what it was that I was off to do in America!

Baba did all the last-moment running around, Didi felt sad and Ma frequently broke into tears. Recalling the events, I feel I was probably insensitive, wallowing in my own excitement and nervousness.

There are a couple of old photographs of my departure from Bombay, accompanied to the airport by family and a few close college friends, who came to see me off. In the photograph, I look rather callow in my new suit with garlands hanging around my neck.

Two pieces of last-minute advice from my mother, or rather promises I made to her, were that I would not eat beef (which meant I could only eat chicken or mutton) and not imbibe alcohol while in America. Baba just told me to not spit on the roadside. This was rather unusual as I could not recall being in the habit of spitting on the roadside. I guess it might have been a general caution to conform to the cleanliness of Western societies.

Ma's instructions were more specific. In order to adhere to the assurance promised, I did not drink alcoholic beverages until 1964, well after I joined Hindustan Lever, in 1962. Furthermore, my promise not to eat beef and pork was also not hard to adhere to, although I missed partaking of American fast foods like hamburgers. Pizzas with only vegetable fillings, though not popular, were reasonable, when available, substitutes for the real stuff. Plenty of milk, eggs, cheese, breaded fish fingers, as well as a variety of vegetables and potatoes, more than made up for culinary variety. Lamb 'curry' was inedible because of the strong odour. Chicken, those days, was considered a luxury.

Finally, on the night of 10 September 1956, the TWA super constellation flight from Bombay lifted off and I was on my first journey by plane to destination USA, a country about which I knew virtually nothing.

As the aeroplane was taking off, the first thought that came to my mind was a sense of irreversibility of the journey I had embarked upon. I had been feted over the past several weeks, and made into a sort of minor celebrity amongst our own small circle of friends, neighbours and relatives, all of whom had built up some unusual expectations of what might eventually become of me! That was when the enormity of the endeavour I had embarked upon struck me like a thunderbolt, as the engines of the plane strained and shuddered to gain altitude. While the 'Fasten Seat Belt' sign was still on, a strange feeling of panic arose within me. What if I failed to achieve what I had embarked upon? With a tinge of fear at the back of my mind, still fully suited, and my tie as knotted earlier that evening by Baba, I dozed off into a fitful sleep. I was next woken up by the announcement that we were about to land in Cairo. After landing, passengers were permitted to disembark and walk around the tarmac to stretch our limbs. After we took off from Cairo, we were served a breakfast of fried eggs, tomato, bacon, toast, butter, jam and coffee. Sitting next to me was a young Muslim gentleman and a first-time traveller, like me. He asked me what the origin of the red piece of meat on our dish could be. I instead suggested that he may request the stewardess for a fresh serving of breakfast, but without the bacon.

Although I had never eaten bacon, Ma's stricture was now in force. I enjoyed the eggs, toast and coffee but left the bacon untouched. The coffee was rather tasty. I had never tasted coffee before. The flight continued, stopping at Geneva, Athens and then Paris, where passengers were once more permitted to walk around the swanky air terminal. I still remember a display of a huge bottle of Chanel No. 5 in front of a backdrop, covered by a large mirror. I could see myself clearly in the mirror, my suit was badly crumpled and the collar of my white shirt had a visible black rim. Quite a contrast to the smartly dressed men and women purposefully walking past all around. The next long leg and somewhat longish stopover was Gander, in Northern Ireland. It was 3 a.m. local time, and passengers once more disembarked for a walk around the tarmac to stretch our limbs. I walked into the almost empty terminal building and came upon what looked like a twenty-four-hour café. As I walked into the café, it was empty, except for a solitary customer. That customer turned out to be Jack Lemmon, the famous, at that time, Hollywood actor. He seemed extremely pleasant as he greeted me. We introduced ourselves. I told him I had seen one of his movies, and we chatted for a while, until my flight was announced.

The last leg of the journey was across the Atlantic, before we finally landed in New York. I vaguely recall that immigration was fairly painless, but customs was not. One had to carry one's chest X-ray plate and medical certificates, to be submitted at the customs, and following which began a rather thorough search of the contents of my new blue suitcase. A burly customs inspector picked up my suitcase to place it on a desk and unlocked it. During this manoeuvre, the handle of my brand-new suitcase promptly snapped. The inspector helped in holding the handle together, by tying it tightly with a piece of rope, before unlocking the suitcase and rummaging the contents. I am, even today, not sure what he expected to find. He picked up a small photo frame, wrapped in a newspaper, with a picture of Lord Shiva in all his splendour, which was a gift from Ma, for my daily prayers. The inspector looked at the framed photo for a long time and then asked me, 'Who is this?' I promptly replied that it was my uncle, with a birth deformity. After hearing my response, he quickly and carefully wrapped the frame up in the newspaper and put the photo back, without asking any questions regarding Shiva's four hands and the water (Ganga) spouting out of his head. The search was over, the inspector gently closed my suitcase, put it on a trolley, and I walked into American territory. I was met by a local representative of TWA, who was to assist me, to connect to an onward domestic flight, for my last leg to Chicago. By this time, I was feeling quite ragged, after a forty-five-hour journey, adjusted for the time difference between Bombay and New York. Looking at my state, the kind man from TWA offered me a cup of hot black coffee, hoping it would perk me up.

After a few gulps, I felt a strange rumbling in my stomach. I excused myself and rushed to the nearest toilet and threw up into the closest sink, washed my face with cold water and felt hugely relieved and rejuvenated, ready to continue my journey. I thanked the TWA person who had met me, checked in and got into the connecting domestic flight to Chicago. After reaching Chicago, I collected my suitcase, with a broken handle, tied tightly with a string, and took a yellow cab to the Illinois Central Railroad station, for the last leg of my journey to the University of Illinois campus, 125 miles away, in the twin towns of Champaign–Urbana.

On reaching Chicago station, an African–American porter loaded my suitcase from the taxi on to his trolley. The cab meter read $3. I gave a $5 bill to the driver and waited for the change, wondering how much I should tip him. The cab driver drove off, shouting, 'I will keep the change.' He had correctly identified me as a new arrival. The African–American porter had watched the episode in silence. He guided me to the ticket counter, where I bought a ticket for Champaign–Urbana, and then I sought his help to send a telegram home to inform that I had reached Chicago. The porter took me to a Western Union telephone booth, from where I had to call the operator in order to send a message home. We then faced the accent dilemma. The operator and I could not understand each other. But she was extremely patient and helpful. I started spelling each syllable of my message, my name and our address in Bombay. It took the next forty-five minutes for me to convey the message 'arrived and safe' and my home address in Bombay to Western Union. The porter waited through all this, stoically. He seemed used to seeing foreign students on their first day in America. After I finished sending news of my arrival via Western Union, he took me to the station to catch the next shuttle, to Urbana–Champaign.

The porter picked up my luggage and placed it in the luggage rack and showed me to my seat. I took out my purse to pay him the porterage and a good tip because he had been so patient, waiting with me for more than an hour. He not only refused to take my money, but told me that on my first day in his country the cab driver had cheated me, and that should not have been my first experience of America. I was deeply touched. Here was an individual of great dignity, who earned his livelihood working as a porter with great patience and dignity. He had seen the cab driver not returning my change and he had patiently waited for over forty-five minutes, while I was trying to send a telegram home via a Western Union telephone; he had put me on the train and then refused to take what was due to him. He was a proud and sensitive African–American who, that day, gave me a deep sense of reassurance about the US, where I was to live for the next six years.

As the train started, the porter and I waved at each other, and I settled down taking in the lush fields and meadows, typical of the Midwest. There was only one other young couple in the compartment. We greeted each other with a nod.

The train journey from Chicago to Urbana–Champaign took about two hours. My plan was to get off at the station, take a cab to the address of an Indian couple, Dr and Mrs Bhalerao, with whom I was to stay for a couple of days, while searching for accommodation. As the Champaign–Urbana station neared, I must have seemed a bit anxious when the young man sitting across the aisle introduced himself and his wife, and asked if I was travelling to Urbana–Champaign for the first time. He happened to be an assistant professor at the university. Jet lag was obviously showing on me. I showed them the piece of paper with Dr Bhalerao's address. As I was getting down at Urbana–Champaign, the young man picked up my suitcase, with the rope-tied broken handle, and offered to drop me at Dr Bhalerao's residence in their car, which was parked in the station parking lot. I was overjoyed with relief and gratitude. The couple drove me to my address. I profusely thanked them. I was so overstressed with fatigue that I forgot to take down their names and address, and deeply regretted not meeting them during my years on the campus.

Vasant and his wife, Sulu Bhalerao, were related to a colleague of Baba's. It was getting dark. They showed me to a small spare room with a bed, a side table and a lamp, alarm clock and a straight-backed chair, alongside a cupboard. They asked me to join them for dinner in an hour. I partially unpacked my suitcase. The room was comfortably heated. Central heating and warm and cold taps were already common in America.

I briefly sat on the bed, suddenly feeling very lonely and sad, and shed a few tears, realizing the enormity of the challenge, of being by myself for the first time and far away from home, where I had grown up until then. I missed Didi, Ma and Baba.

Shortly, I was summoned to dinner by my host. Vasant was a visiting postdoctoral fellow at the university. He would be returning to his Nagpur academic job and home at the end of his two-year tenure. Dinner that evening was chapatti, lentils and a bean curry. Simple and tasty. The Bhaleraos were a very quiet couple and did not at all seem curious about me, and did not even try to have a conversation. We finished a quiet, silent dinner. After dinner, they bade me good night, and I went to my allotted room, changed, washed up, prayed briefly and was happy to get into bed, jet-lagged and totally exhausted.

Next morning, as per the schedule sent to me by the university, I went to meet the dean of foreign students, following which I went to the department of food science and technology to meet my doctoral adviser, Dr Robert McLaughlin Whitney. The fall semester had already commenced; I was ten days late.

I had a good night of sound sleep. I then washed up and put on my new woolly undergarments that Baba had bought, a fresh shirt and my only suit, which had regained some of its shape on the hanger overnight.

I joined the Bhaleraos for a silent breakfast of toast and coffee. Vasant hoped that I would soon find my accommodation and move on. I found this a bit abrupt and off-putting. I was yet to get used to the frank speaking ways of Americans. He offered to drop me at the office of the dean of foreign students, on his way to his own department.

It was a sunny and bracing autumn morning. The dean was very warm and welcoming. He informed me that there were 35,000 students at the University of Illinois, Urbana campus. The university's medical school was located in Chicago. He reconfirmed my monthly stipend, gave me an advance and informed me that all my education books and medical costs, etc., would be paid by the university, as part of the programme I had come under. He then gave me a list of addresses for graduate student accommodation which I should check, to find what suited me. He also provided me a map of the campus and drew the route to the building where I was due to meet my PhD guide and mentor, Prof. Robert McLaughlin Whitney. The dean of foreign students gave me his telephone numbers and said that he was contactable round the clock, if needed. He then recorded all the details regarding my address in India, passport, etc., and did not seem to be surprised that we did not have a telephone at our residence in Bombay. I thanked him profusely for the reassuring conversation, and wound my way that sunny morning, following the map he had given, through beautiful criss-crossing campus pathways, along the well-spread-out, manicured and wooded campus, towards my next destination.

Dr Whitney's office was on the upper floor of a two-storey red-brick building, with ivy creepers covering the outside wall. I walked in and was shown to Bob Whitney's office. Bob was bespectacled and middle-aged, with a receding hairline, brownish hair and a broad smile. He motioned me into his office, sat me down, lit a cigarette and started talking to me. The conversation made me feel at ease and welcome. After a very pleasant and reassuring mutual introductory conversation, he told me that even though I was a few days late, he had arranged for me to take three courses—one within the department, a second in statistics and the third in the biochemistry department. He then went on to briefly explain the outline of my research project, for master's degree, the number of course credits I would have to earn besides qualifying in French or German, one of which was a prerequisite for a PhD. I was next taken around, assigned a laboratory bench and a desk space and swivel chair, in a very large room, where there were already two other graduate students with their assigned desks and laboratory benches. This was the start of my postgraduate experience. Dr Whitney also informed me that when I was not attending classes in departments located in different buildings on the campus, I may return to my assigned desk and workbench, to study or work on my research project, for my MS degree.

Bob (everyone on campus addressed each other by first name) introduced me to other faculty members in the department. Prof. Stuart Tuckey, Emeritus Prof. Ernest Tracy, Prof. Ernie Herried, Prof. Joe Tobias and a few postdoctoral fellows from India, Egypt,

Greece, the West Indies and a number of American graduate students. The American graduate students were mostly war veterans from the Korean War. The same morning, Bob took me to my first class, across the corridor, being conducted by Prof. Stuart Tuckey. There were fifteen other students in the class and I thus began my first class, of my first course, at the University of Illinois, on 28 September 1956, twenty-four hours after I landed in America.

During the lunch break, I joined a few other students from the department and walked across to a central building, located at some distance, popularly called the Students' Union, the students' activity centre. I bought a couple of cheese sandwiches and a glass of chilled milk from the cafeteria. One important practice I learnt on my first day was that each person paid for himself only. A very good and simple American practice.

At some point in this narrative, I propose to describe my daily life, the courses I was taking and my MS research work. I may also digress from time to time to narrate a reasonable amount about my personal life during my years in the USA.

After about four nights with the Bhaleraos, I settled my accounts with them and shifted to a house on the campus meant to accommodate four graduate students. I was introduced to the place by one Nagesh Mhatre, a fellow student in the department I had joined. Nagesh was from Bombay and had come one year earlier. In time, we became lifelong friends, till he sadly passed away, in 2016.

In this new graduate residence, each student had an independent bedroom cum study, and shared a communal toilet and a bathtub with a shower head at the end of the corridor. A bit old-fashioned but I was glad to move into one of the vacant rooms. The Bhaleraos charged me $40, for four nights' board, breakfast and dinner. In my new accommodation, Nagesh showed me the ropes for getting around, for meals at the local cafeteria or in the Students' Union, etc. Winter was rapidly setting in, I had to abandon my woollen undergarments from Bombay, which were giving me rashes on my rapidly drying skin. My skin had already become even more dry than before, during my first week, as I continued having my usual daily baths—a childhood habit—until to my great relief, I discovered the famous Vaseline moisturizer at the local grocery store, which I have been using ever since.

After a few days of my reaching the campus, I was invited by a couple, Prof. and Mrs Chatterjee, who happened to be the Bhaleraos' neighbours, to celebrate Dussehra, with about ten other Bengali graduate students and a postdoctoral fellow and his wife, Dr and Mrs Ranjit Sengupta. Everyone was from Bengal, other than me. Prof. Chatterjee was the director of a well-known engineering college in Roorkee. He was in Urbana on a two-year visiting fellowship and so was Mrs Chatterjee, who had come as a visiting fellow in the department of mathematics. The Dussehra evening was quite cheerful. I was a bit of an outlier amongst the invitees, not only as a newcomer but also as a Bengali from Bombay. As the evening progressed, there was a lot of chatter all around and then one of the guests, Bishuda (Bisheshwar Gupta), a somewhat older graduate student, suddenly announced that he was well versed in palmistry. Some amongst the guests immediately lined up for Bishuda to read their palms. I have described Bishuda's eventful palm-reading elsewhere in this book. The evening was enjoyable. Mrs Chatterjee's menu was excellent, and I also became acquainted with the local Bengali crowd. In Bombay, I did not have any Bengali friends.

There used to be a few social events on the campus, usually during the short breaks between semesters. These breaks were a welcome relief for rest and recreation.

Nagesh was a happy-go-lucky individual and led a very active social life on the campus. It turned out that this left very little time for him to seriously attend to his studies and research. He was a warm and generous friend. Sadly, about a year after I started my graduate studies, it turned out that Nagesh had failed in a number of courses, disqualifying him to continue for his MS and PhD degrees at Illinois. His graduate adviser, Prof. Ernest Harried, arranged for him to get a place in the University of Oregon, in Corvallis, and we lost touch with each other for quite a few years after that.

I quickly settled down to serious studies and work on my research project, for my master's degree. One had to also be prepared for the weekly surprise tests by the professors who taught the courses I had enrolled for. Surprise tests are a unique feature in the American education system, which keeps one on one's toes all the time. I will not forget scoring a zero out of 100 in my first surprise test in the very first week of my arrival. I was totally shattered. Prof. Tuckey, who was teaching the course, told me that although my answers to his questions were all correct, they could have been condensed into one paragraph instead of the rambling four pages I had written. That put an end to my Indian habit of writing long-winded answers during exams.

It was a telling message. Then onwards, I learnt to write brief and crisp answers. My first test really shook me up, but it was an excellent lesson, which has stayed with me ever since.

I soon settled down to a daily routine and to a new pattern of a very busy academic life, with reasonable ease. The only contact with home in Bombay was a weekly aerogram letter addressed to Baba and Didi in English and to Ma in Bangla, and awaiting their weekly letters to me. Each of these letters took two to three weeks to be delivered at each end. This was the first time I was grateful that Ma had almost forced and taught Didi and me to read and write Bengali, starting with the beginner's alphabet, from a very early age, and progressing forward, stepwise, creating spare time throughout our school years. I remain very grateful for her strict and uncompromising Bengali lessons daily and a dictation every Sunday, although I had to regularly miss the first innings of our game of tennis-ball cricket.

In 1957, Ram, a new graduate student in plant pathology, and I got together, and we rented a one-storey bungalow, with a basement, a garden in the backyard and porch in front of the house and a driveway, on 906 West California, a quiet, residential street on the Urbana part of the campus. I learnt to drive using Nagesh's car, obtained a driving licence in my first attempt, following which I bought a second-hand 1950-model Ford, in 1957, for $100. The car made it convenient to drive around the sprawling campus, but was of less utility during the severe winters and heavy snowfall of the Midwest.

Our small house was cleaned and looked after, Monday to Friday, by our elderly landlord, Chuck Whalen. He also washed our laundry, in a washing machine, in the basement. The house was neat, clean and well furnished, consisting of two bedrooms with attached bathrooms, hot and cold showers, a well-equipped kitchen and a reasonably sized living room, with a large balcony in front. I cannot recall Ram and I ever locking the front door of the house, even when away on brief holidays.

Ram and I shared 906 West California for the next five years. We, and our families, remained close friends after returning to India. Ram sadly passed away in 2016, after suffering a stroke.

The academic year in American universities is made up of three semesters, with a couple of days' break between every semester and a longer break in summer and two shorter ones during Thanksgiving and Christmas.

My daily routine was to enjoy an early morning hot shower, quick breakfast, usually of buttered toast and chilled milk, followed by a ten-minute brisk walk to my laboratory. I prepared my research schedule for the day, as well as plans to catch up on the courses I happened to be taking in a particular semester. Next, I would walk down to the building where I was taking a particular course during a semester, and during breaks between classes return to my department and work at my research desk. I would meet Bob Whitney briefly every morning, and give him an update of the progress of my research work and generally talk with him about my courses. I had chosen German as the prerequisite foreign language. It so happened that my MS thesis was on a subject on which articles had been published mainly in German scientific journals.

I will now briefly relate my very early experience of undertaking 'research' in America. To begin with, I was trying to reproduce an analytical test, which I had to standardize. Papers of the original work had been published in German journals, and which I had to first translate into English, with the help of a fellow student, whose mother tongue, fortunately, happened to be German. My own German at this stage was rudimentary, although I eventually managed to pass the qualifying examination.

For my MS research, I had to reproduce and standardize the analytical procedure, which had been described in a well-known German scientific journal. The test was fairly long, consisting of a number of steps. Every evening, I had to prepare a fresh batch of analytical reagents to carry out the test, to reproduce the published results. Most days, when I returned home in the evening after classes, Ram or I would quickly slap up a meal of soup and toasted cheese sandwiches, washed down with glasses of chilled milk. Occasionally, Ram would cook sambhar and rice for dinner, with spices sent from his home. We tended to overeat rice and feel drowsy. So rice was usually avoided on weekdays. After dinner, we returned to our respective departments, usually around 7 p.m., to continue work for my MS thesis for a few hours. Every day, after finishing my experiments, I washed the glassware, cleaned up my work bench and walked back home. I would quickly fall into 4–5 hours of deep sleep and wake up early, to get ready for the day's schedule.

I recall three events relating to my research work and my interactions with my PhD adviser, Dr Bob Whitney, for the record.

The first event, I can best describe as 'searching for answers, before running for help'! As mentioned earlier, I was trying to reproduce a certain published but lengthy analytical test, which was essential to progress my research. The analytical procedure was slightly complex, but Bob Whitney and I agreed that reproducibility was a prerequisite to progress with my MS thesis. Every night I would repeat the analysis, and some nights, several times. The next day, I would sit with Bob and share with him my previous nights' experiments. But I kept failing to reproduce the published data. Bob would go through my laboratory notes carefully, ask me a few questions and suggest that I should continue repeating the tests carefully, until I was able to reproduce the published data.

I continued to repeat the test for several days and nights, but failed to reproduce the published data. Without reproducing the test, my MS research could not progress. I had to discover where I was going wrong! Bob had told me that as soon as I was able to find the error and reproduce the published test, I should call him, no matter what time of day or night it might be.

I still vividly recall that after having carried out the same experiment repeatedly for about ten days, one night while going through the pages of the data I had collected, I suddenly stumbled upon one step in the procedure which I seemed to have kept repeating incorrectly, every time, without being at all aware. I suddenly felt an unusual sense of relief and thrill. I repeated the now corrected test a few more times that night, with consistent and reproducible results, and experienced a deep sense of satisfaction. As I recorded the data of the rectified experiments, I realized, later, that it was the 'eureka moment' of my research career. I had discovered my own mistake and had reproduced the correct procedure, all by myself. The experience was thrilling, in its simplicity. Earlier, I had spent hours minutely scrutinizing the data I had collected every day before repeating the test, until the day when I stumbled upon my own mistake, which, until then, I had been consistently repeating. The time was 3 a.m. I was tired but overjoyed. I phoned Bob, as he had instructed, even realizing that he must be in deep sleep. Bob promptly picked up the phone, and I gave him the good news. He said he would drive across to the laboratory right away. Soon he walked in, with a broad smile, freshly bathed and beaming. We sat at my desk, and he lit a cigarette (those were the days before the link between smoking and cancer had been established).

I briefly explained the error in the test which I had been repeating. Bob was as happy going through the data as I had been overjoyed. From the very first day, when I had shown him my experiments and how I was unable to reproduce results which had already been published, he had become aware of that one step I was doing incorrectly. *But Bob said he wanted me to discover my own error!* It would have been easy for him to point out which step I was doing incorrectly. But he wished me to feel the thrill of discovering and correcting my own mistake. That was the beginning of my comprehending what curiosity, as a habit, was all about in research and exploration; it is something beyond ruggedness and persistence, one's enquiring mind thus evolves! The next morning, Bob presented me with a box of Kent cigarettes. The episode was simple, as I have described, but profound in the way that my sense of enquiry had been triggered.

It was during my time working with Bob Whitney that there were two other truisms he had shared with me, which are worth narrating.

One, how to honestly admit and then being able to say, 'I DON'T KNOW', about any subject or any issue one did not know; and the other was that, 'ALL HUMANS WHO FELT INDISPENSABLE, REST PEACEFULLY IN THE BACKYARD OF CHURCHES.'

Bob taught me that no matter how complex a subject may be, someone who truly understands a subject must be able to explain it, even to a lay individual, in simple but comprehensible terms.

I have, on purpose, digressed quite a bit from where I was trying to explain the start of my scientific research.

My MS research exploration thereafter progressed rapidly and, before I had even completed my first full year, I had successfully completed the required courses, passed German and submitted my thesis, to qualify for my MS degree, in 1957.

I soon moved on to the next phase, to complete a number of remaining courses required to qualify for a PhD, and then devote full time to the research work for my PhD thesis. It was in slightly more than four years when I fulfilled all the requirements to qualify for a PhD in 1960.

In addition to food science, I took a number of courses in biochemistry and microbiology. There were some famous professors and future Nobel laureates amongst the faculty of our university. As a matter of fact, John Bardeen of the physics department at Illinois shared the Nobel Prize with William Shockley, in 1957, for their discovery of semiconductors.

Amongst the professors whose courses I attended were famous microbiologists Salvatore Luria and Sol Spiegelman, biochemists John Clark, Bill Rutter, Ernie Gonsalves, Bob Henderson, Carl Vestling, William Woodward Hastings and Fin Vold, and food scientists Bob Whitney, Stuart Tuckey and John Herried. Each of them and a few others instilled in me the foundations of logic and reasoning and the joys of inquiry, leading to discoveries. The outcome was that my way of thinking and my sense of curiosity were moulded, and transformed, in the University of Illinois, and especially by Bob Whitney, for the rest of my life.

The US education system I was exposed to consists of deep learning and comprehension, repeatedly tested by a challenging series of discussions and 'surprise tests'. In Jai Hind College, Profs Keswani, Gurshahani, Khubchandani, Kotwani and a few others were similarly interested in building up scholarship through the comprehension of knowledge as opposed to rote memorizing to pass examinations. Sadly, the reasons for my complete lack of interest in studying in school may have been due to the absence of teachers who enjoyed teaching!

What Bob Whitney did to initiate me into research had been triggered by my college teachers in Bombay—to instil a sense of curiosity and comprehension. These qualities shaped the rest of my life. Bob was proud the day I was invited to become a member of the prestigious scientific research society Sigma Xi. He sadly did not live to witness the prestigious Distinguished Alumni Award conferred upon me by the University of Illinois, in 2004.

Not All Work and No Play

Madhu Sahashrabudhe, Bhimsen Rao, John Colmey, Ray Speckman, Harold Graham, Bob Brezensky, Kegeaki Aibara, Wassef Nawar, Pol Paulson, Mike Style and Nick Papadopoulos were my contemporaries in the department either as postdoctoral fellows, working on various sponsored projects or graduate students, like me. Besides India, others were from the US, Japan, South Africa, Egypt, Denmark, Greece, the West Indies, etc. The staff and students gathered around the communal coffee kettle twice a day, once at mid-morning and again during mid-afternoon, for a break and informal conversation, every day of the week. Some of us also met socially, once in a while. A number of my colleagues and I smoked pipes, which was more economical compared to cigarettes. I had started smoking during a flu epidemic, when patients were kept in isolation, except for two half-hour daily breaks, individually, in a TV room, which had a vending machine for soft drinks and another one for cigarettes.

My small circle of Indian friends comprised either graduate students or members of faculty in different departments of the university.

Ram and I shared a house, as I have already described, and we became very close friends. Our small circle of Indian friends included Mohan Kokatnur, Shripad Wagle, another Ramchandran, Vellathil Chacko, Hemant Sathe and Chenelu. Mohan Nair and his wife Vijayam were and have remained close friends, besides the Indo–Swiss couples Claudine and Channapragada Rao as well as Maggie and Soli Mistry. Our ladies' circle of women graduate students included Lalitha Rao, Tara Rao, Saroja Iyer, Asha Amin and Kheyali Nandi. Asha was a frequent visitor to Urbana, from Cincinnati, where she was a graduate student.

During the semester, none of us had spare time, for either meeting or socializing. During the short inter-semester breaks of a couple of days, we tried to catch up. During the longer break in summer, a few of us went on driving holidays across America. Our smaller and intimate friends' group met more frequently, to cook and enjoy Indian meals. We met mostly at our house, which Ram and I shared. We had a large open balcony, ideally suited to relax and 'shoot the breeze' as the Americans call it, during the long summer afternoons. Few of us owned cars; gas, the American term for petrol, varied between 19 and 20 cents per gallon, during the 1950s and '60s. There were frequent 'gas wars' between different petroleum companies, and prices sometimes dropped to 15 or 16 cents a gallon, when we would rush to fill up our car tanks. Most of the campus cafés and shops were within walking distance of where we lived. Prenz Café, around the corner, was a favourite for beer and pizza. I usually ended up having a coke and crisps. In most of the eateries non-alcoholic drinks were available, and only a few dishes were free of pork and beef. For gatherings at our home, Mohan, our master chef, once in a while prepared a decent Indian meal or a vegetarian pizza (from packaged ingredients available in the local grocery store). Such summer evenings were very relaxing and enjoyable.

I was sometimes invited by and met the Bengali graduate students and postdocs. I had first met them at a get-together, only a few days after joining the university, to celebrate Dussehra, which I have narrated elsewhere. The Bengali group usually met at the home of Dr Ranjit and Mrs Manju Sengupta. Abdur Rahman and Sultana Alam, from erstwhile East Pakistan, were a part of this group. The Bengali gatherings were devoted to exchanging stories and gossip, mostly about Calcutta, and sharing excellent Bengali food prepared by Manju Sengupta. I was the only Bengali-speaking Indian from outside Bengal. Subir Kar, a graduate student at the University of Wisconsin, was an occasional and welcome visitor to Urbana. He entertained us for hours on end with his mellifluous rendering of Rabindra Sangeet. Subir was of large build, with an insatiable appetite for all kinds of food. But Subir's weakness for eating in excess was forgiven, as he would sing and entertain the group for hours on end with songs accompanied by his folding harmonium, which he always carried with him.

The Indian lady students—Tara, Lalitha and Saroja—stayed together, while their friend Asha, who was an occasional visitor from Cincinnati, became a part of the group. The ladies were choosy about whom they befriended but also very hospitable. Ram and I were amongst the very few frequently invited to join them for dinner. Ramanathan, another graduate student, used to be smitten by Tara. While Tara did not quite discourage him, she made him run many errands for her, such as changing the flat tyres of her second-hand Nash car and accompany her to the local movie theatre, etc. Ramanathan and Tara had returned to India well before I did, and went their separate ways.

During my time in Urbana, I began to take interest in the local Indian students' union. The annual highlight was a grand India Day celebration, organized by a committee of Indian graduate students. The large central hall of the students' union, where national day festivities took place, was jam-packed with students from all over the world, whenever there was an event. On India Day, usually, an entertainment programme was followed by visitors walking along food stalls set up by different groups of students. National days of various countries were celebrated here, and the audiences were entertained with their national songs, dances and cuisines. In 1958, we performed one of Tagore's well-known dance dramas on India Day. In 1959, I took the lead and organized a shadow play, accompanied by the musical rendition of selected episodes and songs from the Ramayana, accompanied by drums, cymbals and a few other musical instruments, lent to us by the very helpful music department of the university. These summer events were something all the students eagerly looked forward to.

During the 1950s, other than a handful of southern states, where segregation was legally in force, the rest of America used to be a reasonably liberal society. Most of the graduate students, many of whom were supported by the US Army's Veterans Scholarship, were married and had their own families. Young undergraduate boys and girls, during weekends, parked their cars in secluded spots of the campus or visited drive-in cinemas, in search of privacy.

Most Indians were graduate students and of such an age that they considered the ways of the American undergraduates during weekends unusual public display. For Indian graduate students, the pressures and challenges of academic life were sufficiently daunting to keep all of us fully occupied without distractions.

Amongst social activities, in addition to the India Day, there were the Dussehra get-together and Diwali celebrations. These events

had to be squeezed into the breaks between semesters, and not as
per the almanac. The Bengali students soon also started celebrating
Saraswati (the goddess of learning) puja, which was held in the local
YMCA. The *bhog* offering to the goddess was also cooked in the
YMCA kitchen, the previous night, by one of the most enthusiastic
architecture graduate students, Abdur Rahaman, from Dhaka. The
previous evening, besides cooking bhog, the volunteers would make
the arrangements for the puja in the main YMCA hall and install
a clay image of Saraswati, especially imported from Calcutta every
year. The priest, a graduate student from the University of Wisconsin
familiar with the rituals, travelled all the way, every year, to perform
the puja the following morning. The celebrations included a grand
community lunch of the bhog, enjoyed by Indian graduate students
on campus as well as some curious Americans and students from
other countries. Word got around that everyone was welcome.

Thanksgiving, for the year's good harvest, is the biggest family
event and a national holiday in America. It is held every year on
the third Thursday in November. All American students went home
to celebrate with their families. On university campuses, foreign
students used to be invited by the local 'families', to the late Thursday
afternoon special Thanksgiving lunch of turkey and cranberry sauce,
besides several side dishes. The late afternoon lunch was always
preceded by offering a silent prayer of thanks, by the head of the
family. I attended Thanksgiving lunch once and enjoyed the host's
warm hospitality.

On summer weekends, Ram and I would sometimes drive
125 miles to Chicago, to enjoy an Italian pizza or a Chinese meal.
Ram, a Tamilian Brahmin, became a non-vegetarian in America, while
I stuck to my dietary stricture and no-alcohol promise to my mother.
In American cities, European immigrants as well as immigrants from
other nationalities, such as Chinese, Indians, Africans, seemed to prefer
to live in ethnic enclaves. So for pizza, the place in Chicago one had
to go to was Little Italy, and so on. During my stay in the USA and
frequent visits to that country in the course of my working career,

I never experienced any racial restrictions or restraints, but I did become aware of subtle American social mores over the years. Campus towns were too idyllic to give a real feel of American multiracial society.

Ram and I hosted occasional dinners at our home to celebrate a close friend's successfully completing the coveted doctoral degree, for example. Our dinners were never lavish but always great fun. Alcohol used to be inexpensive; most of our friends drank beer. Teetotalers had to always be careful, to ensure their fruit juices or soft drinks were not 'spiked'. Once in a while, during semester breaks, we got together for long overnight sessions, playing bridge. During these card sessions, those who imbibed spirits gradually slackened their concentration and started losing. One of our elderly friends, teetotaler Bhimsen, had an irritating habit of chiding fellow players, and he invariably collected most of the winnings at the end of our overnight bridge sessions. On one winter weekend, while our late-night bridge session was in progress at our home, one of the participants began to surreptitiously spike Bhimsen's orange juice with low doses of vodka throughout the night. Early next morning, at the end of our bridge session, the participants started dispersing. My housemate Ram offered Bhimsen a ride home in his car, since it had been snowing quite heavily during the night. Bhimsen had, as usual, won a fair bit of cash and said he preferred to walk to his apartment, which was reasonably close by. He was as yet unaware that he had consumed a large quantity of fruit juice spiked with vodka throughout the long night. Ram and I stood at our window as the bridge players began walking across our snow-covered front porch. Suddenly, we watched in horror Bhimsen slowly sinking down on his knees and then passing out, on our snow-laden front porch. Ram and I grabbed our overcoats and rushed out to rescue Bhimsen. We lifted him, with some difficulty, pushed him on the rear seat of my car and drove him to his apartment. Once we reached his house, lifting him out of the car and carrying him over the steps into his apartment proved to be extremely strenuous. We put him down in his bed, fully clothed, took off his shoes, covered him with a quilt and returned home. We both felt a bit guilty at the

turn of events of the previous night! Subsequently, Bhimsen refused
to either meet or greet all those in our card group for several weeks
after the incident.

Midway, during my time in Urbana, I met a newly arrived Bengali,
a graduate lady student enrolled for a master's degree in psychology.
Over time, we got to know each other well and became close friends.
Sadly, our close friendship had to end when she subtly tried to
pressure me to promise to marry her after we returned to India. This
I was not prepared to do, and our friendship was very short-lived. In
India, Didi had become friends with Narendra, a handsome young
Maharashtrian and a student of dentistry, in Bombay. Ma and Baba
were not agreeable to the proposition of my sister marrying a non-
Bengali. Baba had been busy searching for a suitable Bengali match
for Didi. Didi and Narendra got married in 1961 against our parents'
wishes. Baba and Ma were, apparently, devastated. After many years,
Ma eventually became reconciled, but Baba suffered a heart attack,
deeply disappointed by his dearest daughter marrying against his
wishes. He recovered from the heart attack, but never reconciled
for close to twenty-five years with Didi and her family, until shortly
before he passed away.

While the spring, summer and autumn were gorgeous, not
describing life during winter, in a small town in the Midwest of
America, will be amiss. During the winter months, temperatures
would drop dramatically, and for days and weeks remain well below
zero along with frequent and often heavy to very heavy snowfall,
and occasional snow storms. The Champaign–Urbana facilities for
clearing the snow on campus streets were usually very effective, but
would be often overwhelmed! Besides having appropriate winter
clothes, overshoes and snow boots, and snow chains over car tires,
one had to be very well prepared to face the winter. The relief was
that all the buildings and homes were very well heated. In spite of
all these defences, slipping and taking a fall was not infrequent. The
saving grace was that the walk from our house to my laboratory
normally took about ten minutes, but on windy winter nights, and

steady snowfall, the short walk could take up to half an hour or more and felt like an ordeal. Returning to our house early in the morning, back from the laboratory, I would take a short break at the round-the-clock doughnut shop. A hot and fresh cherry-topped doughnut, washed down with a tall glass of chilled milk, made it all feel very endurable. Being young, of course, helped.

Memories of summer days remind me of gentle and carefree 12–14 hours of daylight, while the changing riot of colour of the maple leaves heralded the joys of autumn. Looking back to those years, I have wondered whether this clear change of seasons was at the core of the happy and productive lifestyles of Americans and their work ethics!

I have digressed quite a bit. To delve into some of the private and social aspects of life of Indian graduate students I thought would be worthwhile in order to provide a somewhat broader picture of life on an American campus. I lived in Urbana for close to six years. My only objective was to complete my MS and PhD successfully, although there were sufficient avenues for social balance and relaxation.

An Unusual Encounter

Most of the graduate students and postdoctoral fellows in our department in Urbana, Illinois, were married with families, except three of us. Horace Graham from Jamaica, Yasuo Azuma from Japan and I. All my fellow students and postdoctoral fellows in the department were a friendly lot. The incident, for which I have digressed, relates to Mike and Shirley Stiles, from South Africa. Mike was a fellow graduate student in our department. After completing his PhD from Illinois, Mike and Shirley emigrated to Canada and settled down happily there. While in Urbana, Illinois, I counted Mike and Shirley amongst my close friends. During our occasional and idle chats, the issue of segregation in South Africa as well as in the US cropped up. It was during one of our usual conversations that Shirley mentioned that her father was planning to visit them in Urbana. Shirley's dad was, at the time, governor of Witwatersrand and a well-known political figure, as well as a prominent white supremacist in South Africa. It was during the governor's visit to Urbana that Shirley and Mike invited me one evening to join them for dinner, and also to meet Shirley's dad. I was very hesitant, for obvious reasons. Mike and Shirley must have anticipated my reluctance, but assured me that they were sure I would enjoy meeting Shirley's dad over dinner, at their home. I accepted the invitation and went on the appointed evening to the Stiles' home for dinner.

I was introduced to a very distinguished-looking, tall, grey-haired gentleman: Shirley's dad. We engaged in the usual pre-dinner small talk, and soon the four of us sat down to dinner. The governor right away told me that he had been informed of my hesitation to accept the invitation to dinner that evening. He went on to add that yes, it was true that he had never sat at the same table with any coloured person before. But that was because he was part of and supported the official policy of apartheid in South Africa. But when Mike and Shirley talked to him about their friends in Urbana and especially wished to invite me, to meet him and have dinner with them, he was quite pleased, and anyway, he was not visiting America as a politician. The environment around the table soon thawed, and everyone felt more relaxed. The governor chatted away all through dinner on various interesting subjects, but nothing on South Africa. The evening was quite enjoyable, but did not influence my views regarding the horrors of segregation and the policy of apartheid in South Africa. My friendship with Shirley and Mike remained happy, and as close as it had been before. Living in Urbana–Champaign and even during our travels during the summer holidays, I had not seen or experienced segregation in practice.

After completing PhD and postdoctoral work at the University of Illinois, we had all moved on. Over the years, I lost touch with most of my contemporaries. This still saddens me, when I recall my very happy years as a student in Urbana. However, I did keep in close touch with Bob Whitney after settling down in Bombay. We regularly exchanged letters, till he was sadly killed in a car accident some years later, while on a holiday in Florida. When Connie and I got married in 1967, Bob sent us a wedding gift, a beautiful silver bowl, from him and his family. Bob must have been slightly disappointed that I had not returned to America and the job at the Washington University and settled down in the US. But, he was also very proud of my professional progress in India. Connie and I travelled to Urbana to attend a memorial service at the university, held in Bob's honour and memory. I had been invited to deliver an address at the service. I recalled my very happy memories as a graduate student and postdoctoral fellow under Prof. Robert Whitney and my eternal gratitude to him, and the University of Illinois, for my achievements in India. The memorial service coincided with the annual university homecoming, and one of the Big Ten football tournaments. Homecoming is an American institution of alumni get-together. During our visit, I introduced Connie to some of my former professors and a few of my contemporaries. Memories of my student days in America will forever remain deeply etched in my mind. The last occasion when I visited Urbana was to accept the prestigious University of Illinois International Distinguished Alumni Award. It was a happy and proud moment for me, to deliver the acceptance speech at the formal award function. I sadly missed the late Prof. Whitney.

In Search of the Illusive

I learnt a few valuable and lifetime lessons during my initial months as a graduate student at the University of Illinois. Within nine months of joining, I had completed the required course work, for an MS degree, in 1957, with good grades, and completed typing my research thesis draft. I had bought a portable Remington typewriter to save cost. When the final draft was ready, I had copies professionally printed for submission. Incidentally, I followed the same procedure for my PhD thesis, three years later. The successful completion of my MS, in less than a year, was a confidence booster for me, and my course grades established my reputation as an excellent graduate student.

My second and third years, in Urbana, passed in a blur, with loads of course work, surprise tests and exams, alongside a challenging PhD research problem. My experiments to isolate and identify an elusive molecule(s) and its structure turned out to be very complex.

The research project which I was engaged in was funded by the US Army's Quartermaster Corps. Vacuum-packed powdered milk rapidly turns stale once the vacuum is released, prior to use. The milk from reconstituted milk powder, invariably, tastes unappetizing, caused by rapid oxidation of certain chemical entity(s) in the milk powder. The problem was to search and identify the suspect molecule(s), establish the chemical structure(s), and then eventually, find means to block the oxidation pathway. The process of searching for the molecule(s) responsible for the off taste and flavour turned out to be very challenging. I had to design an ultra-high-vacuum device and then get it built by the campus glass-blowing specialist. The glass-blowers built an excellent contraption as per my design. The contraption was built for a very high vacuum distillation and provided with receptacles to collect the distillates in liquid nitrogen chilled (minus 183 degrees Celsius) for analytical investigations. The analytical procedure included, at the time, liquid and gas chromatography, ultraviolet and infrared spectroscopy, as well as nuclear magnetic resonance (NMR) spectroscopy. The ultimate identity of various fractions had to be tested organoleptically, by a panel of tasters, to pinpoint the molecules responsible.

I drove down every morning, in a pickup truck, with a large insulated liquid nitrogen container, to the chemistry department's liquid nitrogen plant, to have the container filled with liquid nitrogen and drive back to our lab, before I could commence the day's experiments. To attain, stabilize and sustain ultra-high vacuum in the extraction unit itself was very time-consuming. After the distillates were collected, they were subjected to separation and analysis, mentioned earlier. Reproduction and reconfirmation of the composition, structure, etc., used to be a day-long process and frequently, lasted through the night as well.

The analytical data gathered over several experiments suggested a molecular structure, apparently not reported in the published literature.

In due course, I successfully completed all the courses required, prior to submitting my PhD thesis. The completion of all the courses set me free to devote full time to my research project. For the next year and a half, I spent the whole day and a good part of the night in my laboratory, repeating the experiments, establishing reproducibility and frequently, discussing the analytical data collected with Bob Whitney. The final phase of the research was the most exciting of my time in Illinois. Looking back, I felt extremely happy that I had chosen a future devoted to science and exploration.

Bob Whitney was a fairly well-known name in the field of physical chemistry, and his erudition and knowledge in other branches of chemistry and biology were also extensive. Our long discussion of data collected, after a number of experiments, raised challenging questions, suggesting that we may be searching for a structurally novel molecule, while our analytical results suggested a few reported structures, but not an exact match. From time to time, I walked across to the famous Noyce Chemistry Laboratory building on the campus, to seek advice from some of the professors in the department of organic chemistry whom I had come to know— among them was the future Nobel Prize winner Prof. Hal Corey, and Prof. Charles Gutovsky, head of the new NMR department.

For quite a while the exact structure of the molecule causing oxidative deterioration of milk powder remained elusive. In the winter of 1960, on a weekend, I was briefly resting on the living room sofa of our warm, comfortable home, with Tchaikovsky's 'Swan Lake' playing on my record player. It had been snowing continuously and the air outside was thick with snowflakes. I had my lab notebook on my lap; I had been going through all the data I had collected, once more, while searching for the novel carbonyl molecule and its possible structure. The molecules in the distillates collected every day were all known, except for the one. Basically it had a carbonyl configuration.

I had already dozed off on my sofa while Swan Lake Ballet hummed in the background. Subconsciously, my thoughts must have been wandering, or I was probably fast asleep and dreaming of the elusive molecule. I suddenly woke up with a start, and tried to recall what I had been dreaming about in my fatigued mind. In retrospect, the picture of floating molecules in my sleep may not have been as strange as this narrative may convey. I was excited and wrote down, as best as I was able to recall, the 'phantom' floating structures, possibly an outcome of my tired and exhausted mind! The next day, I sat down with Bob and related to him my previous day's experience, but Bob persuaded me to explore the possible 'structure' some more. Soon thereafter, Bob and I were able to narrow it down to a well-known carbonyl molecule, but with what looked like an additional double bond. I repeated the experiments and analytics spectroscopy tests several times over the next few weeks, to confirm reproducibility of the analytical data, as well as ways to block the unusual double bond in the possible precursor molecule, which was attacked by oxygen once the vacuum in the storage containers was released. It could possibly be one of the by-products in the spray-dried milk powder. The issue of devising ways to block the formation of the molecule would have to be explored by another graduate student, after me.

Bob and I spent days going through all the experimental and analytical data I had collected during the previous two years. Bob had deeply ingrained into me the habit of patience, perseverance, commitment to enquiry and uncompromising reproducibility of results. These were deeply embedded in my mind for the rest of my life.

Bob informed me that I was now ready to write my PhD thesis. I was quite pleased but a little apprehensive as well. I started typing the first draft on my old Remington portable typewriter. It is a fairly common and sensible practice to first chalk out the broad structure of the thesis, which I did and discussed with Bob; example, the list and sequence of chapters, broad content of each of the chapters, and finally the discussions and logic of the outcome and its novelty, all with the supporting and appropriate data. It took me a few weeks to produce the first draft of my thesis, with Bob regularly helping to edit the chapters while going into painstaking details as my adviser. It took the next couple of months for the final draft to be ready. The university printing department then printed the required number of copies, and my PhD thesis was ready for submission.

As per procedure, Bob Whitney arranged an official university examining committee, consisting of faculty members of the chemistry department, forwarded to them a copy, each, of my thesis and fixed a date for my final PhD oral examination.

The following days, I remained quite anxious, waiting for the final day for my PhD viva. On the appointed day, the committee of examiners assembled in Bob's office first to discuss amongst themselves, while I waited, nervously, for their call. Next, I was summoned to Bob's office, where the examining committee had assembled. PhD oral examination in the USA, as I expect in most universities, is quite a serious and formal procedure. Bob was seated at his desk, the committee members, who of course knew me, as I had taken courses under them in their departments, were seated around in a semicircle next to him. I remained standing in front of the large green board on the wall of Bob's office. Given the formality of the event, everyone in the room was formally attired in suit and tie. Each member took turns to ask me questions pertaining to my thesis as well as a few in their own area of research interest. This questioning by each member went on for more than an hour. I had to frequently explain my answers by drawing graphs on the green board. I recall gradually gaining confidence as I responded to a succession of queries. Bob did not utter a single word throughout this viva process. At the end, Bob requested me to step outside and wait. That wait was not very long but seemed to be endless. In reality, it happened to be only a few minutes. Bob emerged from his office with the usual twinkle in his eyes and a broad smile, shook my hand and congratulated me and for the first time addressed me as 'Dr Ganguly'. He then invited me back into his office, and each committee member stood up to shake my hand, by turns. I joined Bob and the committee members for a cup of coffee and biscuits and felt euphoric receiving their compliments regarding the work I had presented in my PhD thesis, and my interaction with them at the viva.

I had completed my MS and PhD, in somewhat of a record time of less than four years since arriving at Urbana. The next day, Bob handed over to me an appointment letter as a postdoctoral fellow on a one-year tenure, with a handsome annual salary, for those days, of $25,000. I suddenly found myself very well endowed, compared to the $130 per month stipend, which I had received as a graduate student. By then, I had already saved a reasonable sum from my stipend in the bank and now I thought I would save more than enough after a year as a postdoctoral fellow. Enough to plan a holiday and travel to Bombay to see my parents and sister almost after six years.

Postdoctoral Fellow and Return to India

During my postdoctoral year, Bob Whitney one day informed me that there was a position on offer for me, as assistant professor at the University of Washington, in Seattle, on completion of my postdoctoral year.

On completing my postdoctoral year, I packed up, warmly thanked Bob and the rest of the faculty members of our department, bade goodbye to friends and took a train to New York. After spending a few days with Nagesh and his new wife, Lee, I departed on the *Queen Mary*, from New York to Southampton, and then spent a few weeks travelling across Europe by train. I returned to London and boarded the SS *Canton*, from Tilbury, reaching Bombay after sixteen days.

It was during my second year in Urbana, in 1957, that there was an outbreak of flu in the Midwest; it was called the Asian Flu. I took ill and was put in an isolation room of the campus infirmary. The infirmary was rapidly filling up with students who had been infected. No visitors were permitted. After the first few days, each patient was allowed a short daily break, in a TV room, alone. The TV room also had a cigarette-vending machine. After the first week, I was bored out of my mind, with the slow pace of recovery. One day, during my break, I put a quarter in the vending machine and pulled out a packet of twenty. I recalled how I had at a very young age bunked school for a few days in Bombay and wandered aimlessly along the streets near the school. I had bought a packet of bidis with my pocket money and had also smoked, a rather daring act for the time! In the university infirmary, out of sheer boredom and loneliness, I suddenly started smoking Kent cigarettes. Considering that I had been a non-smoker until then, I ran through the packet of twenty cigarettes during the rest of the day. Nobody seemed to mind. It was still a few years before scientists raised the alarm regarding the link between smoking and cancer. Following my first cigarette, I became a regular and heavy smoker. I finally quit smoking in 1973.

High school education in America, at the time, used to be aptitude-driven in primary and secondary schools, until 'graduation' from school, in which everyone qualified. Of those who next join colleges and universities, a large number fail and have to leave either in the freshman or sophomore years. The survivors mostly complete the remaining two years and graduate.

Very few pursue postgraduate studies in the US. Early- or mid-career work break for business studies has become more popular during the last fifty years. The foreign graduate students at the university were mostly on scholarship, based on exceptional undergraduate performance records. Courses and publishing an MS thesis used to be mandatory to qualify for PhD. Postdoctoral research then reinforced one's biodata, for faculty appointments. I enjoyed my one-year postdoctoral experience of exploring independently, publishing papers, etc.

My postdoctoral project was to investigate the nature of its 'native structure', the pure β-lactoglobulin was subjected to gentle and gradual unfolding, by heating to different temperatures. The gradual unfolding stages of the molecule were monitored by a technique known as electrophoresis. Electrophoresis was discovered by Prof. Arne Tiselius, a Nobel laureate, at the University of Uppsala, in Sweden. On my way back to Bombay, I visited Uppsala to meet Prof. Tiselius. On the appointed date, I went to Uppsala, and he welcomed me very warmly. Over coffee, Prof. Tiselius explained to me what led to his discovery of electrophoresis. He had to define and pursue his hypothesis separating proteins on electric field and design experiments to prove it in practice. A novel discovery is indeed the ambition of every budding scientist who is seriously pursuing a research career. Subsequently, Prof. Tiselius took me to the university cafeteria; we sat at a table, where seven other Uppsala professors, also Nobel laureates, were enjoying their daily morning coffee break. What a memorable day! I wish I had a camera with me. In my suppressed excitement, I even missed collecting their autographs! My Uppsala trip, in 1961, remains deep in my memory.

In the course of my postdoctoral research in Urbana, I had tested the gradual unfolding of β-lactoglobulin molecules under very carefully monitored conditions, and was able to reproduce a set of similar unfolding results. The results suggested that the tertiary structure of the molecule was held in place, primarily, by hydrogen bonds. This was already known. But we were also able to detect a set of weaker bonds, called Van der Waal's forces, whose presence could be novel. In addition, the unfolding results also indirectly suggested that there may be a third type of bond, even weaker than Van der Waal's bonds. By that time, my postdoctoral assignment was nearing a year. Bob and I drafted a manuscript of my postdoctoral research for publication. I had already started preparing for my visit to my parents and sister in Bombay.

Ram, my housemate of five years, had already gone back to India, soon after completing his PhD, a few months earlier.

In retrospect, my close to six years at the University of Illinois had indeed been eventful, happy, fruitful and exciting. Time seemed to have flown by. I was indeed fortunate to have been a student of Bob Whitney, who was an inspiring guide and mentor, all through my time in Urbana. I had made many new friends, driven a fair bit in summer breaks around America, studied and worked diligently, and had a great time. During these six years, my only contact with Ma, Baba and Didi was the weekly exchanges of air mail letters.

During short breaks between semesters, and in the summer, my social life on and off campus had also been relaxing, except for one incident involving a car accident. On a particular winter day, I had borrowed Ram's car to run an errand. I was accompanied by our good friend Mohan Kokatnur. I had to drive a short distance to a nearby town. It had been snowing all day long, while the temperature had kept dropping. The road was covered by snow, over a hard layer of ice. Under these conditions, one had to drive with even greater care than usual. We reached a junction where I had to take a turn. As I slowed the car and came to a stop, our car slowly skidded, sliding into the lane of oncoming traffic. The first oncoming car crashed head-on into our stationary car. This accident took place well before the days of cars having seat belts and air bags. Fortunately, both the front doors of our car were thrown open under the impact; Mohan was flung out by the impact and landed on a bank of snow piled across the roadside. I was very badly shaken, after banging my head hard on the windshield, but was able to step out of the driver's seat on my own. While the other car's front was badly dented, ours looked like a total wreck. Soon, the traffic police arrived in their patrol car, with sirens and flashing lights, to record the accident and take down individual statements, etc. Both cars and passengers, of course, were covered by car insurance. Ram's wrecked car was soon towed away, to clear the road. It was a total loss and I would have to pay the towing charges separately. The occupants of the other car seemed shaken, but were able, after a while, to drive away in their car. Next day, our accident was reported prominently in the campus newspaper, the *Daily Illini*, with a photo of the wreck. I prayed and hoped that no one would do me the 'favour' of sending a cutting of the news to my parents in Bombay. Ram generously said that he did not wish to be reimbursed for his old car, and I soon thereafter got rid of my old Ford as well, since I was planning to return to Bombay, in another few months.

A couple of months after the accident, during my postdoctoral year, I received a summons to appear in the local court in connection with the accident. The passengers in the other car had apparently sued for damages of $60,000, claiming that their pregnant daughter, who was in their car, had a stillbirth following the accident. The summons made me very nervous. I did have car insurance, for a cover of $30,000 and if I had to pay the rest, I feared I would have to work longer in America, to earn the money, and which would delay my return home by at least another two or three years.

The company, with whom I was insured, had appointed a lawyer to defend me. The case lasted three days, and the claim was dismissed. My insurance company lawyer had produced one witness—a paediatrician from Chicago—who produced reports of previous stillbirths of the lady travelling in the other car involved in the accident. The judge finally ruled that there was no case for compensation. After three very grim and nervous days, I felt hugely relieved. Bob Whitney had sat along with me through those three days the case had lasted. He seemed as relieved as I was. Bob was a mentor in the true sense of the term.

I got back to my research and daily routine once again, and to the preparations for my return to Bombay. On the day I was due to leave Urbana, I felt sad. I had got used to living in Urbana, learnt many valuable lessons, in more ways than one, and felt enriched by many wonderful and exciting new experiences, in the University of Illinois. Bob Whitney must get all the credit for my becoming a researcher and the transformation of my thinking. Some months later, I sent him a letter, explaining that I needed to stay back in India; he must have been disappointed but appreciated my domestic obligations. We continued to correspond regularly, and Bob and Mrs Whitney sent us a lovely silver salver gift when Connie and I got married, in 1967. Some years later, on a holiday in Florida, Bob was most unfortunately killed in a car accident. I was deeply saddened. A few years later, I travelled to Urbana along with Connie and had the honour of delivering a brief eulogy at a special memorial service held in memory of Dr Robert Whitney.

During my postdoctoral year, I received communication from the Indian embassy in Washington regarding the annual visit of a Government of India S&T (science and technology) delegation to the USA, to attract Indians who had completed their studies back to India. The Indian consulate in Chicago sent invitations to Indian graduate students on US campuses in the Midwest, to meet and interact with the visiting Indian S&T delegation in Chicago. These meetings were meant to provide an opportunity, to mutually explore, what returning scholars might wish to pursue on their return home as part of the 'Scientists Pool' scheme of the Government of India.

One was free to choose any institution in India, to continue the work they were engaged in. The offer included a monthly stipend and accommodation at the chosen institution. Individuals were free to explore permanent opportunities in academe or industry, as the case may be.

In the summer of 1961, I met that year's visiting Indian delegation, headed by Prof. M.G.K. Menon, in Chicago. A number of other Indian graduate students, from campuses across the Midwest, had also travelled to Chicago to meet the delegation individually. In my allotted thirty-minute time slot, I had an amicable and pleasant interaction with Prof. Menon and his team. I informed them that I was planning to return to India in a few months' time, but that I already had a job offer at the University of Washington to return to. Before the meeting concluded, I was offered a position as a 'Science Pool Officer' in India at any institution of my choice. What it meant was that I could join any government-funded laboratory in India, pursue my research interests and receive a stipend of Rs 450 per month and accommodation in the institution. Before the conclusion of the meeting, I was handed a signed offer letter and the contact details, to follow up, after I returned to India. This was the Indian prime minister Jawaharlal Nehru's brainchild, to reverse India's brain drain. The offer provided an anchor to returning scholars, to explore more permanent opportunities of choice. As I look back, this was indeed a great initiative on the part of India, to at least dent the impact of the 'brain drain'.

On the scheduled date, I bade goodbye to Bob and my other colleagues and departed from Urbana, for my first halt, in New York, where I was to meet my old friend Nagesh, and his wife, Lee, and spend a couple of days with them. I had sent ahead the bulk of my possessions in a large black wooden trunk, to be loaded on the ship for the last leg of my journey from Tilbury to Bombay in a few weeks' time. My farewell visit with Nagesh and Lee was very enjoyable. That was the first and only time Nagesh took me to the Playboy Club in New York and Lee, Nagesh and I also stood in a line to watch the first Rolling Stones concert in New York in 1962.

After a couple of days in New York, I embarked on an exciting transatlantic trip to Southampton on the *Queen Mary*. The trip turned out to be four days and three nights of almost non-stop parties, dance and music. I did go to my cabin, briefly every night, for a shut-eye and change of clothes. I was still a teetotaler, so staying awake was not a problem! I also understood that non-stop jollity would also become tiresome after a while.

At the end of the exciting and hectic transatlantic trip, we disembarked from the *Queen Mary*, in Southampton. My childhood friend and schoolmate Biju was at the Southampton dockside, to welcome me. We were meeting after quite a number of years, and felt delighted and happy—we reminisced endlessly of our childhood years. Biju had moved to London after completing high school and was working as a computer servicing technician in the city. I spent a few days as his guest, on this my first visit to London. From London I travelled on a short tour of Europe, before returning to London and then embarking in Tilbury on the SS *Canton*, for the final leg of my journey to Bombay. Biju lived in a rented flat in London. London was my first unhappy experience of a cold and wet city, without running hot water or central heating in Biju's flat. His flat had a large lantern-like contraption into which coins had to be dropped for the gas heating to start and continue until bedtime. The heater radiated enough heat to warm one room and was usually placed in the bedroom. In the kitchen and living room of the flat, one had to wear heavy sweaters and socks to protect from the damp chill. While cooking meals, the kitchen also warmed up a bit. I was disappointed when Biju informed me that the occupants were permitted to bathe only once a week, in a communal bathroom, located on the top-most floor of the building. I began to feel miserable, without my daily shower, and twice during summer, and pleaded with Biju to find a way for me to have a quick bath.

On my second day in London, Biju stole up to the communal bathroom, filled up the bathtub with warm water, and told me to be very quiet and stealthily walk up, have a dip, dry myself and quickly return to the flat, without making any noise at all. I felt refreshed after a bath, even in a bathtub. I quietly cleaned the tub, dried myself and padded my way back, stealthily, to Biju's flat. The landlady caught up with what we were up to almost immediately and sternly warned Biju not to repeat such an unauthorized act in the future. Biju, by nature, was overwhelming in his friendship and hospitality, and we spent a great deal of time chain-smoking and reminiscing about our young and carefree years.

I spent the next couple of weeks travelling to Sweden, France and Germany, before returning to London, to bid goodbye to Biju and embark on the sixteen-day trip, by the SS *Canton*, to Bombay.

On the final leg of my trip, I was impatiently looking forward to meeting Didi, Ma and Baba, after close to six years. During the early days of this trip, my spirits were temporarily dampened, as our ship entered the Bay of Biscay, and the upheaval caused by the towering and rough waves, through which our ship had to navigate, was the most off-putting experience of the voyage.

For the next three days, the ship's dining room remained virtually empty, for breakfast, lunch and dinner, except for the presence of another passenger and me. All the other passengers were confined to their cabins, experiencing endless bouts of sea sickness. Coincidentally, I happened to be sharing a cabin with my old friend Subir Kar, from Wisconsin. He loved to consume enormous quantities of any food. It was a sad spectacle seeing him unable to get off his bunk for three days, while he was feeling deeply distressed just thinking about the number of meals he was missing. At the end of three days, the ocean calmed down, and the dining hall filled up once again with relieved and cheerful passengers.

The ship's first stop was Port Said, before crossing the Suez Canal. The dockside was crowded with a large number of hawkers, alongside magicians and conjurers. There was much ship-side bargaining by many of the passengers. That was the only stop during our sixteen days' trip to Bombay. While on the ship, I met and got to briefly know a young Canadian woman dressed in an Indian sari. Elaine was travelling from Canada to India, in search of her Kashmiri roots. Although she did not know anyone in India and did not have any contact address, she seemed quite confident to fend for herself. During the course of our conversation, I volunteered that my parents would be happy to give her temporary shelter for a few days in Bombay, before she travelled on her search to Kashmir. Elaine eventually spent a couple of weeks as a guest of my parents, and then set off in search of her roots. She sent us letters from time to time, describing her travels, but the letters stopped after a while. We heard no more from Elaine, until a few years later. She had married a local and settled down in a village called Batlagundu, in Andhra Pradesh. After some years, her husband passed away, and we stopped getting any more letters from her and lost touch.

On the sixteenth morning, the SS *Canton* gracefully docked in Bombay. The passengers were requested to wait, while our luggage was being unloaded, and after that we were to disembark, identify and collect our luggage. I was looking out for Ma and Baba, from the third level of the ship. There they were, waiting amongst many who had come to receive their near and dear ones. From where I was standing, my parents looked very much the same as when I had left for America, except that in the meantime, they had been estranged from Didi, who had married Narendra against their wishes. Ma and Baba both had jet-black hair when I departed for the US six years back, which had turned completely grey. While still staring down at them, I decided that I would not leave them on their own in their advancing years and return to America. On the way home, I was told for the first time that Baba had two cardiac attacks, about a couple of years ago, but had since fully recovered. I had been kept completely in the dark.

Meeting them after such a long absence was a hugely joyous moment. We drove to Kakad Estate in Worli, to their new flat, which Didi had persuaded Baba to buy and move from our old home in Tardeo. Sadly, Ma and Baba were not prepared to talk at all about my sister. The next day, I found my way to Didi and Narendra's home in Khar. I was delighted to hold their newly born daughter, Shilpi. I felt overjoyed. The severance from Ma and Baba was indeed very sad for both Didi and me, and would take several years to heal. After some years, I was at least able to persuade Ma to meet Didi and her family. Sadly, Baba finally reconciled a few months before he passed away, in 1991.

A Job in Bombay

After returning to India in 1962, I comfortably settled down, in my parents' apartment, at Kakad Estate, to my old ways and days. My dormant taste buds were, as if, rekindled by Ma's culinary spreads (at breakfast, lunch and dinner, as well as snacks in between). The new flat was a spacious, one-bedroom apartment. There was a sofa-cum-bed in the living room, which served as a comfortable bed for me at night. I started getting to know our new neighbours and renew contacts, with my old college mates, spending more time with Didi's family in Khar and with Baba's youngest brother, Prabhat, in Andheri. I was in no great hurry to explore my appointment as a 'Pool Officer'.

I cannot recall the reason for my first trip to Delhi, after returning from the US, to meet Manubhai Shah, the minister for industry in Pandit Nehru's cabinet. Apparently, someone had briefed the minister about me. When I met him, the minister enquired if I would be interested in setting up some industrial venture, as an entrepreneur, in the state of Gujarat, which happened to be his home state! I was somewhat surprised by the unanticipated suggestion of the minister. The minister said the government would consider start-up funding, once I had prepared a project proposal and came back to meet him again, soon. I thanked the minister and returned to Bombay, somewhat bewildered by the unexpected proposal. After introspection, I concluded that I really did not have any entrepreneurial inclination, and had never given any thought to the idea before. I wrote a polite letter to Mr Manubhai Shah, thanking him for his proposal, and regretted that I was really not quite suited to pursue his generous proposition. So I moved on, and sometimes wondered what it would have turned out to be if I had given some serious thought to the idea! It was generous of the minister and I was grateful. But becoming an entrepreneur honestly was not one of my strengths.

While in Bombay, I met up with one of my contemporaries from Urbana, Tejen Sen, who had returned earlier. Tejen had got a job, heading the Indian subsidiary of an American chemical company. He was, temporarily, staying in a hotel, before moving to a suitable company accommodation. We met regularly, on most evenings, at my home or at his hotel. Both Tejen and my other friend Subir, who after returning from Wisconsin, was appointed to the faculty of the recently established IIT in Bombay. Subir was a very frequent visitor, as he loved to eat, and ate enormous quantities of the dishes cooked by Ma.

Asha Amin, my friend from Cincinnati who was back in Bombay, also visited our home frequently. After a few years, Asha got married and settled down in Khar. We have remained very good friends.

After a couple of months of my return, I decided to explore what I might do if I were to live in India. I had travelled to Karnal in Punjab to take up my appointment as a 'Pool Officer' at the Indian Council of Agricultural Research (ICAR) laboratory, on a stipend of Rs 450 per month. The institute had well-equipped laboratories and decent accommodation. The employees were friendly and welcoming. I decided to continue the work on my Illinois postdoctoral project, exploring the tertiary structure of β-lactoglobulin. I usually ate my meals at a nearby Punjabi 'dhaba'. After a few weeks, I started feeling restless and nostalgic and regularly started looking up job advertisements in the scientific journals and daily newspapers. I went back to Bombay for a short break. My friend Asha put me in touch with our mutual friend from Urbana, Tara Rao, who had returned and was working in Bombay. One day, I called her and went across to her office, to catch up over a cup of tea. After returning to India, Tara had joined the market research

department of a company called Hindustan Lever, of which I had
never heard. While we were reminiscing, I told her that I had come
to Bombay to make up my mind about what I wished to do, and
that I was also keen to pursue my research interests as best I could.
After listening, Tara got hold of an application form, and told me
that Hindustan Lever had just set up a new R&D department, and
insisted that I should explore R&D opportunities in the company.
Tara insisted I fill up the application form while we were having
tea in her office, and leave it with her. The application form was a
four-page affair. In spite of my doubts about a company of which
I had never heard before, I filled up the form and left it with Tara.
After a few more days at home, I returned to Karnal.

Some weeks later, I received a letter from Hindustan Lever,
referring to the application I had filled in and left with my friend
Tara, to come to Bombay and appear for an interview in their office,
on a particular day and time, at Scindia House in Fort, Bombay. The
call for the interview did not excite me, but the first-class return rail
fare to and from Bombay did. So, once again, within a couple of
weeks, I found myself back home, in Bombay, in June 1962. Baba
was still working full-time at Tata Power, and both he and Ma were,
as usual, overjoyed to have me home. I was getting used to the lazy
life of relaxation in Bombay. I continued to smoke, quite heavily, but
as is our custom, I never smoked in the presence of my parents.

On the appointed day, I took a taxi from Kakad Estate to the
Hindustan Lever office in Scindia House, at Flora Fountain. I was
ushered into a room and joined a number of other interviewees
already waiting in the room. We were being served tea, offered
cigarettes and were welcomed by one Mr Ullal of Hindustan Lever,
personnel department. After we had briefly introduced ourselves,
it did strike me as a bit unusual, as all the other interviewees were
engineering graduates. As the interviews commenced, Mr Ullal
escorted the candidates, one at a time, to meet the panel. When
my turn came, I walked into the interview room, where the panel
introduced themselves. The panel was chaired by Jim Davies, the

vice-chairman of the company. The other members of the panel were Dr K.S. Basu, personnel director, V.G. Rajadhyaksha, general factory manager, and one Dr Patel, who introduced himself as a psychologist. My interview began with each member of the panel starting a conversation by turn. The only question to which I had to plead ignorance was when one of the panel members asked me what I knew about Hindustan Lever, as well as the names of some of its well-known products.

I honestly pleaded complete ignorance regarding both. My ignorance must have intrigued the panel, although they were aware that I had been away for a long time! It was also obvious that I had not made any effort to find out anything about the company where I was being interviewed for a job! After a while, my interview was over, the panel thanked me, and I left the room. Mr Ullal informed me that I had to wait a bit longer. Some more tea and a few cigarettes later, and after all the candidates had been interviewed, Mr Ullal came in and announced that three candidates, Sashi Gupte, Prem Chadha and I, had been asked to wait and meet the psychologist, one by one. The others were thanked and Ullal settled their bills. After a while, each of the three of us, by turn, interacted with the psychologist, Dr Patel. I found my conversation with Dr Patel bordering on the farcical, but did not tell him so. Finally, it was all over. Mr Ullal settled with each of us our train and taxi bills, along with three days of lodging and boarding charges. Since none of the other applicants smoked, Mr Ullal gifted me the tin of fifty Gold Flakes, out of which I had already smoked three. I lazed around at home for a few more days before returning to Karnal.

While I was still in Karnal, I got a letter from my old friend Dr Ranjit Sengupta, whom I had met and got to know in Urbana, where he was working as a postdoctoral fellow in the chemistry department. His letter was an invitation to travel to Calcutta (Kolkata), to appear for an interview for the post of a lecturer in chemistry, at the newly established Kalyani University. After returning from Illinois, Dr Sengupta had joined Kalyani, as the head of the chemistry department. The prospect of joining a university excited me. I travelled to Calcutta by train, and appeared for the interview by a high-powered selection committee of two well-known academics. Following the interview, I was offered, on the spot, the post of a senior lecturer in chemistry in Kalyani University, at a salary of Rs 390 per month, which included three increments, but was less than what I was already earning as a pool officer. Notwithstanding, I felt the offer of a senior lectureship was exciting. I joined Kalyani University, travelling from Karnal via Bombay and Calcutta. On reaching Kalyani, I found the place desolate, and immediately felt disenchanted looking at my new surroundings. I realized that I had acted in haste. After a few days, staring at empty laboratories and the barren surroundings of Kalyani, I put in my resignation and returned to Bombay. For the first time, I found myself at a loose end, as to what I wanted to do next! However, my status as a pool officer remained valid and, after a few days in Bombay, I was planning to return to Karnal.

While I was still in Bombay, I received an appointment letter from Hindustan Lever, offering me a job as a 'management trainee', at a salary of Rs 750 per month. If I were to accept the offer, the letter went on to ask me to report to V.G. Rajadhyaksha, the general manager of the company's Bombay factory in Sewri. Mr Rajadhyaksha was one of the members of the interview board. The appointment letter was a complete surprise, since I had almost forgotten about my interview at HLL. My decision to accept the HLL offer and present myself at the company's Bombay factory was under the impression that I was joining their R&D department, located temporarily within the factory premises. On the appointed date, VGR (as Mr Rajadhyaksha was referred to) greeted Sashi Gupte, Prem Chadha and me, in his office, and handed over to each of us our daily schedules for the next three months.

It was at that very moment, on receiving the training programme, that it suddenly dawned upon me that I had been selected to undergo a two-year training in manufacturing, etc., and if successful, would be appointed as a manager in the technical arm of the company.

I recalled that at the interview, I had more than once mentioned that my primary interest was to pursue a career in R&D. Obviously, there had been a mix-up between what I had presumed I was being selected for and what I had landed myself into. Sashi and Prem were both engineering graduates, and the training programme fit their qualifications perfectly. I was very disappointed and there was no one I could think of, from whom to seek advice, in order to extricate myself from the situation I found myself in!

On the first day, Prem, Sashi and I were together, taken for a walk around the rather large and spread-out Bombay factory, manufacturing soaps, washing powder, toiletries, hydrogenated vegetable oil, etc. At lunchtime, we went to a cafeteria 'for junior managers'. The vegetarian meal was served in metal trays and at a modest price.

It was more than clear that I had ended up being selected for the wrong job. I was at a loss, thinking how to deal with my awkward situation! The first day passed quickly, and sort of in a daze. I did not know Sashi and Prem at all, since we had met only once during our interview. The next day, as per the programme, Sashi, Prem and I went our separate ways. I was supposed to spend the next two weeks in the central chemical testing laboratory, headed by one Dr S.M. Patel, who was himself a PhD from Stanford. Dr Patel had just become the head of the laboratory, as I found out later. He had succeeded one Dr Gopal Hattangadi, a chain-smoking Indian, trying to imitate English accent, dress and mannerisms, quite common, at the time, amongst covenanted (God's own chosen!) staff of British multinationals in India. The urge to ape the British was strong, especially amongst the Calcutta Bengalis, Boxwallahs as they were called, and their faux English accent was jarring to the ears. Dr Patel was assisted in his role, in the central laboratory, by two 'junior' managers (the lowest rung of management), Pai and Subramanyan, who shared a glass-partitioned cubicle. According to my training programme, I was supposed to first meet these two gentlemen. I noticed that the dress, which distinguished junior cadre of managers from 'other ranks', was their white full-sleeved shirt and white trousers. When I knocked and entered, Pai and Subramanyam were having their mid-morning tea, served on individual metal trays, with a tea cozy-covered stainless steel pot and other accoutrements. They sent for another tea tray, for me. They were courteous, reserved and rather formal. I discovered later that this stiff demeanour was an acquired trait, amongst most native managers—another colonial hangover in Indian subsidiaries of multinational companies. This 'imitating the foreigners' faded over the years, with the emergence of a more self-confident generation of young Indians.

After tea, Subramanyan took me across to introduce me to their boss, Dr Shankarbhai Patel. Dr Patel walked me through my schedule for the next two weeks, in the central laboratory. Shankarbhai Patel was a soft-spoken but dour individual. The first thing he told me was 'forget all your PhD stuff and learn what the real world is all about'. It immediately put my back up.

Dr Patel asked me to start by relearning titration, which we had learnt in our high school days. His whole demeanour was off-putting. My next two days went by in a blur. Much later, I silently thanked Dr Patel; he had by his behaviour and comments, helped me to make up my mind. I was completely unsuited as a management trainee in HLL. I had realized that from the very beginning, during the interview, and what followed had all been a terrible mistake on my part, and which I had to undo right away.

At the end of my second day in the demotivating central laboratory of HLL's Bombay factory, after returning home, my parents were keen to know about my second day at work. I told them that taking the job had been an awful misunderstanding, entirely on my part. I had, therefore, decided to resign. The best alternative under the circumstances would be for me to return to the USA and take up the offer as assistant professor at the University of Washington. The news must have been a great disappointment for Ma and Baba, but they did not show or express their real feelings, and actually Baba was most encouraging of the idea of my returning to America. Apparently, joining HLL as a management trainee was a highly prized job in India. As a matter of fact, that very evening, Baba also encouraged me not to waste any more time and get back to doing what I was really interested in, even if it meant settling down in America.

The next day, I did not go to the Sewri factory and instead sent a letter of resignation addressed to the personnel department, in the head office of HLL. I also wrote to the University of Washington that I planned to join shortly, to take up my appointment as assistant professor. It was already close to six months since I had returned to India, and I hoped a few more weeks would not really matter.

I spent the next few days at home, eating Ma's home-cooked food, having an afternoon siesta and occasionally going to see a Hindi movie. Before the end of the week, I received a letter from HLL, requesting me to visit their head office at India House, the following Monday at 11 a.m. The letter was signed by the same Mr Ullal who had looked after us on the day of the interview. I presumed that HLL wanted me to complete certain formalities, following my resignation. On the following Monday morning, I went to HLL head office and met Mr Ullal. At this point, a bit about Ullal would be appropriate. Ullal was a junior (assistant) manager in the human resources department. He wore a full-sleeved white shirt and white trousers, with a tie around the collar, which seemed to be a sort of uniform. Other than their shapes and sizes, 'Indian Officers' in multinationals were more or less indistinguishable, dress-wise. Amongst the women employees, a majority were Parsis, Goans and a scattering of Anglo–Indians, who had not yet emigrated. Majority of the secretaries, stenographers and receptionists were women. At the time, there were also a reasonable number of male secretaries, mostly Tamilian Brahmins, who were considered to be very able and reliable in their jobs. In the head office, ground-glass-fronted cubicles were provided for covenanted (senior) managers, and large open-plan space for the desks of the junior managers, clerks and secretaries.

Ullal had his desk in the open-plan hall, on the fourth floor, where I had met him first. A distinguishing feature of Ullal, was a large round vermillion religious mark, on his forehead. On the day I was summoned, following my resignation, Ullal greeted me most pleasantly, offered me a chair, across his table and asked me if I would like some tea. It was not a very crowded floor. Ullal did not smoke, but he remembered I did. He opened a new tin of Gold Flake cigarettes and offered me one. Those days smoking in the workplace was considered normal. Ullal helped light my cigarette and then started talking to me, almost in a whisper. He told me that by suddenly resigning as I had and walking away, I had upset a number of very senior people in the company. Be that as it may, I had been summoned to see the vice-chairman of HLL, Jim Davies, who had chaired the interview committee. Ullal also cautioned me that the VC was extremely angry and would be giving me a serious 'dressing down' for rejecting what Ullal described as the very coveted HLL management traineeship, and which was considered, in India, to be a 'God's gift'. He also pleaded with me not to get upset by the anticipated dressing down by Mr Davies, as he called it, and, ideally, not to react in any way whatsoever. By this time, I had started feeling tense and lit my second Gold Flake. In short, Ullal also whispered that the 'dressing down' was supposed to be a preamble to rejecting my resignation, and, at the same time, not letting me off either, for my misdemeanour, as Ullal put it. I was, shortly thereafter, summoned by the VC's secretary and ushered into Jim Davies's office. The vice-chairman was a tall and well-built Englishman. He kept standing, looking out of his window, while I too kept standing. In a short while, he turned around and as we kept standing, he launched into an angry diatribe about my despicable behaviour in submitting my resignation and demanded an explanation from me.

As forewarned by Ullal, I was reasonably prepared for the onslaught I was now facing. I politely explained that when I joined, I was under the mistaken impression that I was being interviewed for a position in the company's R&D department, and only discovered my error after joining. To his credit, Mr Davies heard me out. He then told me that if I were so keen to abandon a prized career of an HLL management trainee and wished to join R&D, HLL would recruit me in the R&D department, as a junior manager (Ullal's rank) and, as far as the VC was concerned, he said he was done with me. He then picked up my letter of resignation lying on his table, tore it up and dumped the pieces into his waste-paper basket. He then picked up his telephone and talked to someone. I presumed this was the signal for me to leave. Ullal was waiting for me outside. He was obviously relieved that I had not come out of Jim Davies's office in a huff. Ullal handed me a fresh letter of appointment which had been obviously kept ready, for the post of assistant research scientist, at the same salary of Rs 750 and similar perquisites. He also had a cup of hot tea waiting for me on his table. We sat down, without exchanging a word. He handed me the tin of Gold Flakes, to keep. I lit a cigarette and, although quite upset by the rude behaviour and tirade of Jim Davies, I felt strangely relieved that I could now stay on in India, as I had resolved, while standing on the third deck of the SS *Canton*, some months ago, looking at my parents waiting to receive me.

The idea of setting up an R&D unit in India was the brainchild of Sir Ernest Woodroofe, who was then the Unilever director responsible for worldwide R&D. Soon thereafter, he went on to become the chairman of Unilever Plc and member of the special committee, in succession to a Lord Cole.

Lever Brothers (India) had commenced its business importing Sunlight soap in 1884 from Lever Brothers, UK. The Indian company was a 100 per cent subsidiary of the parent. Sometime in the 1930s, Hindustan Lever was created by merging Lever Brothers with Hindustan Vanaspati Manufacturing Company as a fully owned subsidiary of Unilever Plc & NV, the Anglo–Dutch company, which had been established in 1926. The history of Hindustan Lever and Unilever are well known, and I do not intend to digress into the details. Indian publications and Indian business considered multinationals the leftover scars of colonial rule. Multinationals were seen as unnecessary and untrustworthy by politicians.

HLL was, and remains, one of the most, if not the most, respected publicly quoted companies in India. It continues to hold a pride of place in Unilever Plc, for the quality of its management integrity and impeccable professionalism, although, due to restrictions and hurdles faced by foreign companies in India in the post-Independence years, the rewards to shareholders remained very modest for long. In the 1960s, India faced a serious shortage of food grains and was overly dependent on imports, compounded by a depletion of foreign exchange, which became a major hurdle for importing raw materials on which the consumer product companies were critically dependent. This persuaded Unilever, and particularly Sir Ernest Wodroofe, to invest in R&D in India, to urgently explore import substitution by local raw material, for the survival and future of Unilever's Indian business.

To set up the Indian research unit, Sir Ernest Woodroofe, had recruited Dr S. Varadarajan. Dr Varadarajan did his PhD, under Sir Robert Robinson, at Cambridge University and then went to America as an assistant professor at MIT. Incidentally, Vasant Rajadhyaksha, the general manager of the Sewri factory, had also qualified for his degree as a chemical engineer from MIT and had been recruited from there. The role of R&D in HLL is indeed a fascinating story of entrepreneurship.

Ullal had already arranged for me to meet Dr S. Varadarajan in his office at Scindia House. Dr Varadarajan was expecting me, and I was ushered in to meet him as soon as I reached his office. SV, as he was popularly known in the company, is a sparse man, and appeared dishevelled in a tie and cotton suit, the dress of more senior-ranked managers of the time—but his dress and appearance remains the same, even as I draft this piece, almost fifty years later.

SV sounded gentle and soft-spoken, speaking almost in an inaudible whisper. When I first met him, he did not seem too pleased by having to 'accommodate' me. Subsequently, I came to hear that this was because he had not directly recruited me, as he had all the other scientists in R&D. However, he welcomed me politely, as a fait accompli. After a brief conversation, he asked me to report to Dr K.K.G. (Govind) Menon, who was the head of the biochemistry department of HLL R&D, on the following day, in Sewri.

It turned out to be an unexpectedly eventful morning. I returned home with my tin of Gold Flake (hidden in my briefcase), gifted by Ullal. My parents were overjoyed when I informed them that HLL had offered me another post in R&D, which was to my liking. I would continue to live in Mumbai and rejoin HLL in their R&D department the following day. As was the custom and tradition in India, I never smoked in the presence of my parents or other elderly relatives. So I hid Ullal's gift of the second tin of Gold Flake in a safe place and wrote another letter to the University of Washington apologizing for the change in plans. I never found out what the head of department at Washington University may have made of my letters!

The next morning at 9 a.m. I reported to Dr Govind Menon in the temporary quarters of the R&D unit, in Sewri. Govind always wore a bow tie, which was in vogue amongst the senior ranks in universities in the West, but it also seemed to suit him. He had started working in India as a scientist, in Bombay's Haffkine Institute, and then went to Canada, to do his PhD at the Banting and Best Institute. Both he and his wife, Tara, returned to India after completing their PhD. Govind joined the recently set up HLL R&D division, as head of the biochemistry division. Senior managers in HLL are designated 'covenanted', and within the covenanted cadre at the time, there used to be three levels of seniority, all very British— steps by which managers progressed, based on their performance and their potential, over time. Govind Menon, with his years of experience and achievements, had joined as a senior scientist.

Besides Govind, SV had also recruited an excellent group of organic chemists—Dr N.V. Bringi, Dr G.V. Nair and Dr S. Ravindran, physical chemists; Dr Bibhuti Mazumdar and D. G Srinivasan, chemical engineer; Dr S.S. Kalbag; they had all done their PhD and postdoctoral in the US and Canada, other than the chief perfumer Nimbalkar, who had a specialized talent. There were quite a few junior staff members. I discovered that all my colleagues were designated as either scientist or senior scientist. I was the sole assistant scientist. I was allotted a smaller desk, in the biochemistry department, as if to fit my junior rank. These were the petty symbols of status. All others had glass-partitioned offices. Sitting in the open never bothered me.

The research division was temporarily housed in a very large, corrugated, tin-covered warehouse, provided with partitioned offices and research benches, etc. The warehouse was within the premises of the Bombay factory. A false ceiling had been fixed in the warehouse, which insulated the premises from some of the heat. The department also housed a reasonably well-stocked library, headed by an excitable Bengali, Shantanu Majumdar. Soon after I joined the department, biochemist Dr Girish Mathur and analytical chemist Dr R.L. Bhasin joined the division as scientists. Even though I was the junior-most amongst all of my colleagues, in the midst of the British hierarchy, there prevailed an American informality in the R&D department.

At lunch, while all my colleagues went to the dining room meant for covenanted managers, I continued to have lunch in the junior manager's canteen. I was happy to meet Prem Chadha and Sashi Gupte, once again, over lunch. News of my resignation episode had already spread in the Sewri factory, and I felt a touch of chill in the canteen, in the midst of the other junior managers.

After a long while, I discovered that the episode of my resignation and rehabilitation was, apparently, without precedent. Mr Rajadhyaksha (VGR), the general factory manager, was very upset that I had resigned without the courtesy of either meeting him or taking his leave. Subsequently, even when our paths crossed in the factory, he did not acknowledge my greeting, or speak to me, for a very long time. After some years, and as time passed, we became good friends, but that is a different story.

In 1962, when I joined the R&D division, HLL was building a new dairy in the small rural town of Etah, in the state of

Uttar Pradesh. R&D was working on a number of milk-based product development projects, such as a baby food formulation, 'instant' processed cheese, ready mixes for Indian, milk-based sweets, etc. Govind Menon and I worked on the development of milk products while Girish Mathur, who also reported to Govind, pursued an exploratory project on skin pigmentation. Dr Varadarajan was keen for us to develop 'instant' processed cheese (no locked-up capital, to age cheese stock, etc.). Eventually, our efforts failed, in spite of novel approaches. The consistency was all right but the taste and flavour could not be mimicked. I also resumed my earlier work in Illinois, on the tertiary structure of β-lactoglobulin.

On the home front, Baba was still working with Tata Hydroelectric Company and we happily lived, in the flat, at Worli. The only dark cloud was the refusal of Ma and Baba to reconcile with Didi and her family, although I continued to meet my sister and her family frequently. A number of friends visited us in Worli, in the evenings and on weekends. Tejen Sen continued his daily visits and my other friend Subir Kar, now a professor of IIT Bombay, came frequently, especially to savour Ma's Bengali cooking.

In 1962–63, we came to know that a distant cousin of Ma, Nilima and her family, had come to live in Bombay. Her husband, Sasankha Bhattacharya, was a doctor in the Indian Army and they had two schoolgoing daughters, Connie and Annie. Their army quarters were located in the Santacruz army cantonment. After we got to meet and came to know them, Lt Col Sasankha Bhattacharya (or Mesho—generic Bengali for maternal 'uncle') and Baba seemed to enjoy chatting with each other whenever we met. Ma and her cousin (Mashi) enjoyed recalling and tracing family ties, and both loved cooking tasty dishes. Connie and Annie used to attend school in Bombay and were very quiet and gentle. I have digressed at this point into our private lives, but this needs some explaining.

In the 1960s, India was short of almost everything, such as food grains, automobiles, telephones and almost all consumer products. After returning from the USA in 1962, I had applied for a telephone connection at my parents' Worli flat, for which

I had to deposit Rs 5000. I was informed, subsequently, that it would take 10–11 years to be allocated a telephone connection. A telephone was eventually allocated ten years later. The waiting period to make a deposit and buy a car was even longer. Only two brands—the Ambassador and the Fiat Millicento—were manufactured in India. No imports were permitted. In 1963, Lt Col Sasankha Bhattacharya was allocated and bought a Fiat, after a brief wait, from the defence forces priority allotment. In 1964, he was transferred to his next posting. He knew that we had also booked to acquire a Fiat, but had a long wait ahead of us. He kindly offered to sell us his almost-brand-new Fiat for the same price he had bought it for and used for just a few months. We gratefully accepted his kind offer. At the time, we did not have any idea that in three years' time, Connie and I were going to be married, in 1967. I seem to be running ahead of my narrative.

I was happy with my job and work in Hindustan Lever Research. Prem Chadha, Sashi Gupte and I became good friends. Sashi Gupte got married to Meena within a year of joining HLL as a management trainee. He was reprimanded, because management trainees had been cautioned not to get married during their two-year probationary period. Sashi eventually left HLL after a few years. Sashi and Prem were confirmed as covenant managers in June 1964, and I was also covenanted on the same day. After confirmation, Prem got married to Kusum; we became close family and personal friends. Prem, very sadly, passed away unexpectedly in 2016.

A covenanted manager in HLL was entitled to a number of perquisites, including a company flat. I chose a two-bedroom apartment in a building named Panorama on the old Golf Course, Pali Hill, Bandra. My salary and allowances also increased substantially, part of which I used to furnish the new flat. Ma, Baba and I shifted to Panorama, after locking up the Worli flat. The flat also had an allocated parking space, for our newly acquired Fiat Millecento. The distance to Sewri and back was a slightly long drive and I was one of the very few, or maybe the only one of the newly covenanted managers, owning a car. The covenanted managers were entitled to be picked up from home and dropped back every day. I preferred to drive our own car.

In R&D, my projects were progressing well. The infant feed formulations were tested on experimental rats in our laboratory's small animal house, in a section of the R&D's cavernous warehouse. After the safety and nutrition tests, the Baby Food was commercially manufactured in the newly commissioned dairy plant at Etah, and soon launched in the market. Our attempts to make instant processed cheese did not succeed. But I had discovered a novel interaction between α-casein and β-lactoglobulin in milk, when heated to a certain temperature, which led to the formulation and launch of a well-known instant Indian sweet mix powder, as well as a new patent. Menon and Mathur's work on skin pigmentation led to a novel and patented breakthrough discovery, and eventually the famous and successful global brand Fair and Lovely. There were other significant successes over the years by other colleagues, very notably for import substitution and a significant commercial benefit towards HLL's import substitution efforts led by Dr Bringi. The R&D unit thus played a leading role in import substitution of imported basic raw materials used by HLL and the company's business growth and business performance.

In early 1966, I was seconded to TJ Liptons, the newly acquired instant tea plant, in Agrapatana, next to Newaraelia, a well-known hill station in Sri Lanka. Unilever's Lipton team, from New Jersey, USA, which was seconded to Sri Lanka, was led by an American senior manager, who had moved, with his family, and settled in a sprawling bungalow in Newaraelia. I and a fellow scientist from Unilever Research, Colworth House, in the UK, were boarding and lodging at The Club, in Newaraelia. I was one day, sotto voce, very politely, told in a whisper, by one of the bearers of the club, that I was the first coloured person to stay at The Club, and this was in 1966! Newaraelia is a picturesque range of hills covered by tea gardens. The climate is salubrious and perfect for tea gardens to thrive. Our work brief, frankly, was not clear. Lipton had just acquired a German-owned instant tea plant. We presumed that we were expected to master the process of tea extraction, concentration and spray-drying in the company's Agrapatana factory. During our stay, each of us was provided a rented Ford Zephyr car to get around. The arrangement for comforts and conveniences seemed somewhat over the top. A Lipton agency called Bosanquet and Skrine, in Colombo, provided the services.

During the weekdays, there wasn't enough work to keep us busy. It almost felt like a paid holiday on a hill station. We spent evenings playing billiards at The Club. For our spare time, we had requested for a cricket set and nets, which were sent over by Unilever. We practised at the nets, set up on the sprawling grounds around the instant tea factory. On weekends, my English colleague and I drove down to Colombo, and stayed at the Galle Face Hotel, before returning to Newaraelia on Sunday evening. In the factory, the lovely tea flavour and aroma during the instant tea manufacturing process seemed to be wafting everywhere except in the instant tea powder being spray-dried. My colleague and I drafted a report on the Agrapatana instant tea process, and the general state of the technology which Lipton had acquired from the Germans.

After a couple of months' secondment, I returned to Bombay. Soon thereafter, I was asked to proceed to the US on my next secondment, to the TJ Lipton R&D, situated at their headquarters building, in Englewood Cliffs, New Jersey. I was unaware that my short stint at CeyTea, in Sri Lanka, had turned me into an instant tea 'expert'! During the next three months, in the USA, I stayed at the Lexington Hotel, on 52nd Street in downtown New York. Monday to Friday, I travelled by bus, to and from Englewood Cliffs. It turned out to be a most exciting and enjoyable experience. In Lipton's R&D department in Englewood Cliffs, where I worked, all the scientists and staff were Americans and most of them happened to belong to the Jewish faith. Lipton was apparently a very prized Unilever acquisition. Gardy Barker, its president, ferociously guarded his autonomy. Any visitors, including board members from Unilever, were supposed to seek his prior permission to visit Englewood Cliffs. Apparently the excuse was supposed to be a requirement of some American anti-trust law!

Englewood Cliffs in New Jersey is a picturesque location, and I enjoyed working in Lipton's R&D laboratories. Occasionally, I would reach office early and enjoy a hearty breakfast of fried eggs and bacon, in the company canteen. Normally, I also had lunch in the canteen. However, once or twice a week, a few of my R&D colleagues and I drove down to one of the local restaurants, for a famous American two-martini lunch, with a side of the famous 'American cheeseburger'. The two-martini lunch was much in vogue in the 1960s. After such outside lunch breaks, getting back to work was a formidable challenge. Since my student days in America, I had enjoyed working in the laboratory late into the evenings. At Lipton, USA, my assignment was to explore the intractable problem of finding ways to prevent or minimize the loss of flavour while extracting tea solids from tea leaves in hot/boiling water, concentrating the extract, followed by freeze-drying the concentrate, to produce instant tea powder. In other words, whether I could discover how to extract tea solids at a lower temperature, rather than in boiling water. I began my search making a list of known hydrophilic organic solvents with low to very low boiling point. Among the shortlist of such hydrophilic solvents, acetone fit the bill. However, acetone by itself could not extract any tea solids from black tea leaves. One late evening, at the end of a series of experiments, as was the usual practice, I started tidying up my work bench and washing the used glassware. While I was pouring the contents in the beakers down the sink with the tap running. Suddenly, the contents of one of the beakers being poured turned a deep purple colour. This was one of my Eureka moments. I recorded some rough notes. It was quite late.

Next morning, I reconfirmed that a mixture of water and acetone, in a certain ratio, could extract all the tea soluble solids, along with flavour and taste molecules, at room temperature. The aqueous residue left, after distilling off the acetone at 60 degrees Celsius, contained most of the water-soluble tea solids and significant amounts of the taste and flavour components. This residue, after freeze-drying, tasted significantly better than traditionally concentrated and spray-dried tea powder. The company immediately applied for a number of patents in my name, but which were the property of the company. My time in New York turned out to be very productive, successful and enjoyable. On weekends, I spent time with friends, watched movies occasionally and ate at different restaurants. I enjoyed lunch, on weekends, in one of the numerous Jewish delis, especially the Matzo soup and pastrami sandwich. I had a very enjoyable and productive visit with TJ Lipton's R&D in America.

I then returned to Bombay, with a brief stopover at the research division in London, to meet the research director, Dr John Collingwood, and some of his colleagues in Unilever House. I was always very well cared for during all my visits to London in the research division.

In late 1966, I was once more seconded, briefly, to the research division in London. This short secondment included visits to Unilever R&D laboratories in Colworth, Port Sunlight, Welwyn, Vlaardingen, Duivan, St Denis and Hamburg. I was not aware at that time why I was being sent on these visits, and frankly, I was not curious.

I had promised my mother that I would not eat beef or drink alcohol, as a student at the University of Illinois in Urbana. I had my first glass of beer in 1964. After my promotion as a covenanted manager in 1964, I was invited to frequent parties at Dr S. Varadarajan's home, along with my other colleagues in our division. I slowly learnt to enjoy not only beer but gin and tonic as well. During my secondment to the research division, on most Friday evenings, my colleague John Hubert and I made brief stops at different wine bars, which was fashionable in the 1960s. I usually returned fairly late to my hotel room. Thankfully, the two-day weekend allowed a restful Sunday, to recover for the week following. Times have changed; in the 1960s, it was usual in Unilever, UK, for a visitor to be frequently invited out for lunch, which commenced with a pre-lunch dry sherry, or gin and tonic, followed by white and red wine, during lunch. It was fun while it lasted but gradually disappeared, and finally, drinking at lunch was restricted to only special occasions.

The most important event in my life happened in 1966. In November 1966, Sasankha Bhattacharya (Mesho), whom I have mentioned earlier, was visiting Bombay and was invited to stay at our home, in Panorama. He had come to meet a young prospective match for his elder daughter, Connie. I drove him one evening from Bandra to Churchgate, to meet the prospective match. It is a long drive from Bandra, so we got chatting on the way. I waited for him in the car, while Mesho went to meet the young man. On the way back, I asked him what he thought of the prospective match. His response was somewhat vague. Later the same evening, he raised a proposal with my parents, if I might be the suitable match for his daughter!

After returning to Panorama, Mesho, Ma, Baba and I had our dinner and I retired to my room to smoke and relax, while Mesho, Ma and Baba kept chatting. As I came to know later, it was during the after-dinner chat that Mesho suggested the possibility of a match between Connie and me. Connie and I are distant cousins. Ma and Baba subsequently discussed whether this may pose a hurdle, with my maternal grandmother Hironbala, who assured them that such a match between 'distant' cousins was absolutely permissible. Earlier, there was a similar proposal from another one of our distantly related families for their daughter. In that case, I had my reasons to decline. She has since been happily married, with grown-up children and grandchildren of her own, and we have remained family friends.

Connie and my wedding was fixed for February 1967. Sadly, in the meanwhile, her paternal grandfather took seriously ill and passed away. Our wedding was then rescheduled, for 26 April 1967. Connie would have preferred an even later date in June, when she would have finished her BA final exams. We were married according to traditional Bengali Hindu rituals, on 26 April 1967, in Calcutta. The feasting continued for a few days. Our parents were very happy. I had committed to an arranged marriage. I had met Connie as a fifteen-year-old schoolgirl, five years earlier, and now we were husband and wife. It turned out to be a happy coincidence, which our children recalled, during our fiftieth wedding anniversary party, in 2017. Throughout our married life, Connie remained as beautiful and statuesque as on the day of our wedding. She was the best thing of my life. In the most shocking tragedy of a lifetime, Connie passed away on 28 October 2019.

After our wedding, Connie and I had a short holiday in Darjeeling. Ma, Baba, Connie and I returned to Bombay by train, in air-conditioned comfort. Air-conditioned train travel in India those days used to be very comfortable and leisurely, with excellent meals and all other services. On our arrival in Bombay, we were met by a small group of our friends, some of whom were our neighbours— Bulbul Bose, Tripti Chatterjee and Sunanda Majumdar were at the station to welcome us back, and of course were curious to meet Connie, whom they had heard so much about from my mother. It was sad that Didi could not participate in my wedding, as my parents remained adamant about their estrangement from her. We then returned to our home in Pali Hill.

It was also during 1967 that Hindustan Lever's research division moved from its temporary quarters in the Bombay factory to a sprawling, 16-acre spanking new facility in Andheri. The main building contained laboratories, offices, a well-stocked library and an auditorium. There were separate buildings for the pilot plant and another one for the animal house.

I had in the meantime been covenanted and re-designated as a section manager and had my independent laboratory and research assistants. Elizabeth Mulley, Shanbag and Anawkar were the research assistants, and Dhige and Pillai the technical assistants. The research assistants at the laboratory were very well qualified, dedicated and excited about the goals of their research projects. The new premises hummed with activity; the new library was modern and well stocked and well managed by Shatanu Majumdar, the large pilot plant was headed by one of India's outstanding chemical engineers, Dr S.S. Kalbag. Dr Girish Mathur and I were in charge of the animal house. I was also responsible for organizing the Saturday seminars. The weekly seminar was usually delivered by one of our colleagues, on a subject of the speaker's choice. Frequently, we invited outside speakers as well. At that time, in India, we worked for five and a half days a week. One of the external speakers I had invited was Prof. Jayant Narlikar, the well-known Indian astrophysicist, who happened to be a friend of mine. He chose to speak on black holes. Since it is supposed to be an esoteric subject, my colleagues were apprehensive. As it turned out, Prof. Narlikar delivered an extremely clear and comprehensible talk on black holes, and all of us felt delighted and satisfied, considering that the subject was almost totally alien to all of us. It reminded me of Prof. Bob Whitney's adage that if an individual has genuine comprehension of his/her subject, he/she should be able to clearly explain it, even to a lay person or audience.

In December 1967, Bombay and surrounding areas were severely rocked, in the middle of the night, by a major earthquake, with its epicentre several miles away in one of India's largest man-made water reservoirs, the Koyna dam. All the occupants of Panorama and the surrounding area quickly ran out of our buildings, to seek safety in open spaces. Luckily, the overall damage in Bombay, as a result of the earthquake, was inconsequential, considering the severity and the intensity of the earthquake at 6.9 on the Richter scale, and the aftershocks that followed.

In September 1968, Dr Varadarajan confided in me that I was to be seconded to Unilever's research division, Vlaardingen Laboratory in Holland, as section manager of one Dr Jan Van Roon's section, and Dr Van Roon would be in charge of my section in Bombay.

A Future Foretold

I have written or co-authored three books on technology, science and management, mostly drawn from my working experience, spanning over years. I have lived long and am fortunate to have witnessed some important events, such as the end of colonial rule and India's independence, man on the moon, Arapa Net, the foundation of the IT age and the Green Revolution in India, amongst others. What determines longevity remains a matter of speculation. However, the fact is that many people are living longer, compared to previous generations. All well and good, as long as one is in reasonable health, mentally and physically. My parents lived into their 80s and led reasonably active lives. But why this topic now? I used to entertain my daughters, during their childhood, with stories of my own childhood, growing up with Didi in Bombay, our holiday visits to Patna with Ma, where my maternal grandparents lived and to Benares, the home of my paternal grandparents. The short winter breaks in Poona were also a source of many stories. With the passage of years, Connie and our daughters, Nivedita and Amrita, urged me to take a crack at writing something light and entertaining for a change. Whether it would blend with the core theme I had in mind, will have to be assessed. So here goes. What follows is in no chronological order, but switches from event to event, and may provide some relief rather than weaving events, which unfold logically.

Let me begin with an episode concerning longevity, in the first-third of my life. At the time, I was living in a small campus town, in the Midwest of America, doing research and studying for a postgraduate degree. After living and growing up at home in Bombay up to the age of nineteen, the long journey to a completely new and alien surrounding, the feeling of loneliness, being away from home and the enormity of the challenge, to have to successfully achieve my goal, weighed heavily on me. I have earlier referred to the incident one autumn day in October 1956, when oak trees shed their leaves, and the chill in the wind signalled the oncoming Midwest winter, I was invited by a Bengali couple who were visiting faculty, to a gathering of Bengali guests, most of them belonging to Calcutta, besides two from Dhaka, to celebrate the Bengali festival of Bijoy Dashami.

As the most recent arrival on the campus, I was meeting the hosts and invitees for the first time. We briefly introduced ourselves. I did not realize at that time that not only Bengalis tend to linguistically congregate abroad, most other Indian communities do as well. Having grown up in Bombay, such community congregations were something of an enigma, although we did take part in the annual Durga Pooja festival in Bombay. Over time, linguistic associations amongst people of Indian origin have grown amongst the large communities of Indian Americans. It is interesting that, of late, many such associations have forged strong affiliations with political parties back in India. The vast majority of Indian Americans try to hang on to their Indian roots through their linguistic congregates, and try to retain Indian values, culture and religious rituals.

Back to the Bengali get-together on that cold 1956 October evening. While drinks and snacks were served by our hosts, the evening gradually thawed. Guests in small groups excitedly discussed political events in India. To liven up the evening, one Bishuda offered to read the palms of those of us who were ready to volunteer. Having one's palm read and eagerness to know about one's future is a common Indian pastime. It is probably more universal than most of us are willing to admit. While in America, my friends and I spent many pleasurable evenings holding the anxious hands of Caucasian girlfriends and spinning tales of future events. Amateur palm reading is mostly about good tidings, with a few downsides thrown in to seem authentic. In contrast, Bishuda seemed serious and claimed to have studied palmistry, as a hobby, in Benares, the holiest of holy Indian cities and probably the home of 'Hindu futurology'! He was a comparatively older person. Bishuda wore thick spectacles, was corpulent and displayed a scholarly disposition. The ladies were the first to extend their left hands (the right one for men, for some reason, which I have not discerned until now) that October evening.

Bishuda studied the left palm of each of the women, by turn and with great concentration. In a mellifluous voice, he related certain events from the past, which surprisingly turned out to be reasonably accurate, and then forecasted a few events in their future. By now, the guests were getting more and more drawn towards Bishuda. As the evening progressed, we gathered in a tight circle around Bishuda, the initial scepticism was now replaced by an atmosphere of suppressed excitement. We began holding out our hands, awaiting his benign attention. The smell of good Bengali food, being cooked by our hosts, kept wafting from the kitchen, while progressively, an anxious silence descended amongst the rest of us, while Bishuda continued reading each individual palm by turn with intense concentration. Someone else's future is of only limited interest to others, so each of us waited patiently our turn. Suddenly, the reverie and bonhomie of the evening was disturbed when the right palm of fellow student Shafique Ahmed was under Bishuda's scrutiny. Shafique hailed from Calcutta and was already well advanced in his graduate studies and research for a doctorate, in metallurgy. He was hoping to complete his PhD in the next couple of years. Bishuda, without any preamble, just announced that Shafique would be unsuccessful in completing his doctoral degree, but tried to soften this life-shattering blow and went on to add that this would not prevent Shafique from enjoying a successful professional career in America. Bishuda's forecast fell like a bombshell. Shafique was naturally shocked and did not wish to have his palm scrutinized any further. We had all come to the US to study, earn our degrees and not fail. Bishuda had just dropped a big brick. But none wished to argue with a self-proclaimed astrologer and a palmist from Benares. My turn was next. I reluctantly extended my hand, but my heart was no longer anxious. Bishuda took my right hand in both his hands, pressed it from various sides, and appeared to study it with intense concentration while I held my breath.

The tight circle around Bishuda had already started to drift. A few still hung on to every word of Bishuda's. As earlier, he started off reasonably accurately, mentioning a few events, from my past and some regarding my parents and Didi. I was impressed. Then to my great relief, he said that I would successfully complete my studies in America. Following which Bishuda suddenly fell silent. He asked me how old I was. I had just turned twenty. He went on studying my palm in silence for several seconds, suddenly broke out in a sweat and said, in a loud voice, that I would die at the age of thirty-seven, following a heart attack. This was heard with a collective gasp around the room, and those who had slowly slunk away once again crowded around Bishuda. I could feel an air of growing hostility towards Bishuda in the room. Shafique was sulking. More than seventeen years, to the age of thirty-seven, seemed a long way away. I did not feel overly concerned. But our host and hostess of the evening, both of whom were senior visiting professors and a very gentle couple, appeared not amused. Our hostess had hurriedly announced that dinner was ready, which was a clear signal for Bishuda to end palm reading. The mood in the room hung heavily. Palm reading had ended, ruining the evening. However, soon after, the excellent Bengali dishes were laid out on the dinner table. The aroma lifted our spirits somewhat, and at the end of the evening, we thanked our generous hosts and departed, in a reasonable frame of mind, although everyone seemed to avoid Bishuda.

In the following months in Urbana, Bishuda and I came to know each other a bit. From time to time, I would ask him to check my palm to see if any shifts had taken place, to change his prediction regarding my longevity! He seemed reluctant to read my palm, although he did reconfirm that I would live only up to thirty-seven years of age. Memories of my first October evening out in Urbana gradually faded as I tried to adapt to the severe Midwest winter and heavy snowfall, right until April, the following year. In time, Bishuda's palmistry forecasts faded from my thoughts, except that, in the following year, Shafique, whose academic record was very good, was asked to leave the university, as the progress of his research was judged to be unsatisfactory. The Indian campus community and the Bengali group in particular were stunned by the rather shocking turn of events. Indian students had a reputation of performing exceptionally well, and the failure of Shafique was a rare reversal. Some of the Bengalis from the evening get-together avoided Bishuda after Shafique left Urbana. One bleak winter evening, Bishuda dropped into our apartment for a chat. He said he was hurt that many of the Bengalis felt that he was responsible for Shafique's failure and departure. I tried to console him and told him naively that he was only reading what was in Shafique's palm, and what else could he have honestly done! I also took the opportunity to request him once more to check my palm. But the usually ebullient Bishuda looked distinctly downcast and said that he had stopped reading palms and predicting people's future, at least for the time being.

The Bishuda story moves on, to ten years later. After completing my time in America, I had returned home, found a job, got married to Connie, and we were living happily in a company-rented apartment in Bombay. My parents also lived with us.

Out of the blue, one day, I received a picture postcard from Bishuda posted somewhere in Turkey. I had lost all contact with Bishuda after my return to India. He was apparently returning from the USA via an overland route from London. On the way, he planned to travel through Iran, Uzbekistan, Afghanistan and Pakistan, before reaching India. His postcard said that he hoped to keep in touch during his trip, but did not expect me to reply, as he would be constantly on the move and hoped to meet up with me in Bombay, on his way to Benares. I had almost forgotten Bishuda. Bishuda's postcard triggered memories of that fateful evening in October 1956.

I suddenly remembered his forecast regarding my longevity. I was now thirty-two, and suddenly became conscious that I may have only five more years to live! Bishuda's palmistry forecast was not fit to be shared, either with my parents or with Connie. I suddenly felt deeply guilty that I may be leaving Connie behind, as an innocent widow, and my inconsolable parents in five years, which seemed not only short but also very unfair.

After a couple of more postcards from Bishuda, the last from Afghanistan, they stopped as suddenly as they had started. I must admit that I felt relieved. Almost after a year, one evening, our doorbell rang. There was Bishuda standing at our door, looking almost the same as he did ten years ago, bespectacled, corpulent and bedraggled. I was, of course, delighted and surprised to be face to face again with my palmist friend from America, Bishwasbandhu. My parents were always glad to meet my friends, especially those who were my contemporaries in America. It was right away decided by my mother that Bishuda would have dinner with us that evening. For obvious reasons, I was not keen, although I was curious to know where he had disappeared during the past one year. Bishuda had apparently run out of money and also lost his passport and travel documents, in Afghanistan. He was, as a consequence, detained by the authorities in Afghanistan as well as in Pakistan and, in addition, had to do odd jobs, to keep body and soul together, and save for his excruciatingly slow passage back to India. It was quite a story and it could have only happened to someone like Bishuda.

Bishuda's travels and travails were listened to with fascination by all of us; my mother seemed especially full of empathy for the harrowing time faced by Bishuda. Soon, dinner was served; some special dishes had been prepared in a hurry by Ma, to welcome one of my contemporaries from America. We all sat down to enjoy a convivial meal and chat of old times. There was no provocation, whatsoever, for Bishuda to suddenly start talking about his expertise in palmistry. Before I could stop him, he guffawed and said that although he had predicted that I would only live until thirty-seven years of age, in all probability, he could be wrong. Suddenly, a stunning silence descended upon our dinner table. My mother, who was usually gregarious, as well as a generous host, got up and left the table. My father continued to be polite. My wife, Connie, was very quiet by nature, therefore I could not judge how she felt. Ma did not return to the table until Bishuda left. The rest of us continued eating and moved to other topics. It was fairly late by the time Bishuda left, without being able to bid farewell to my mother. After he had left, my mother reappeared and was very angry at what she described as the crass insensitivity of our guest. She added that we were never to invite Bishuda to our home again! My father was in an introspective mood, but did not, as usual, utter a word. Connie remained totally silent. Ma's final wish that evening was that Bishuda should have been detained in Afghanistan indefinitely.

As I recount this episode and revise the manuscript for the umpteenth time, it is now almost fifty years later. My thirty-seventh birthday had passed uneventfully. Connie and I happened to be living in Europe, on a secondment. After that fateful evening of his visit to our home in Bombay, I lost touch with Bishuda.

The preoccupation of Indians with astrology is fairly well known, and most tourists in India are unable to resist palm readers. It used to be a normal practice in India to have a child's horoscope cast soon after birth. Palm reading is fairly widespread in India. A 'palm reader', or palmist in Indian English, goes through establishing his credibility with his client, by reciting a few salient events from the client's past, to build confidence in his predictions regarding the client's future. Then there are those who are supposed to have studied 'scientific' astrology, perusing vast numbers of books on the subject, from the West as well as Indian scriptures. These 'specialists' consider themselves several notches above, as compared to the run-of-the-mill hotel lobby or roadside palm 'reader'. In brief, palmistry is well and alive in India.

A good friend of mine, Kishen Khanna, a tall, handsome and jovial Punjabi, started his professional career as a chemical engineer and later went on to become a very successful businessman, fabricating and selling polymer pipes, for various applications. Soon after I moved into a company apartment, in 1964, my friend and neighbour Dr Kalyan Bose introduced me to Kishen in early 1964, when I was still a bachelor. Our mutual interest in chilled beer and day-dreaming about the future had gradually forged the bonds of our friendship. Kishen and I were still bachelors when we had first met; Kalyan was already happily married and had a wonderful, dry sense of humour, which he kept sharpening during the last forty years since we had become friends. Over the years, Kalyan never tired of repeating stories of his student days in Germany, making sure that there was a new twist of surprise every time he narrated some of the same events.

On one such beautiful summer evening, Kishen, Kalyan and I stood gazing at the sea from my hilltop apartment's balcony. A gentle breeze made the beer taste even better as we gossiped aimlessly. Out of the blue, Kishen wondered if I would like my palm read. I had never mentioned the Bishuda episode in the USA to either of them. Bishu's forecast that I would live only up to age thirty-seven came flooding back to me and, without alluding to the October 1956 episode, I said: 'Why don't we talk about something else?'

Kishen: 'But are you not curious about your future?'

Ashok: 'I am, but I don't trust palmistry.'

Kalyan: 'But Kishen is no ordinary palmist; he has been studying the subject seriously for the past several years. Besides, he does not offer to read palms readily. Ashok, if he has offered to read yours, I would not spurn the offer lightly.'

Our conversation had suddenly become a bit more serious. The sun had set and there was a golden glow of dusk, which is a very mellow part of a summer day's end in Bombay. I replenished our beer and looked at Kishen and Kalyan, wondering if this was some sort of a pre-planned fix.

I asked Kishen, 'Why do you wish to read my palm?'

Kishen: 'I have been watching your facial features. There is something which I cannot quite describe, but I wish to explore it further, by reading your palm, if you will permit me.'

I told him about my early experience with Bishuda, in America. However, being a Leo, I am prone to succumb to flattery. And that is how this second episode of palm reading began.

Sunlight had slowly faded; however, there was always a residual glow, after sunset and before dusk. We put down our beer glasses on paper napkins, making sure that the condensate did not stain my polished tabletop. We were at an age when surroundings mattered little during our student days, and which was being gradually replaced by a degree of neatness. The transit from living with parents to hostels and shared accommodation, and then in one's own apartment, progressively improved neatness. Incidentally, this unplanned transition is a good grounding and somewhat prepares one to, hopefully, live in harmony, after marriage.

Kishen took out his handkerchief, first wiped his hands dry, then vigorously wiped my right palm, while we both picked up our beer mugs with our left hand and took large gulps. Kalyan watched us stoically, beer mug poised in midair. We had stopped talking and the evening suddenly became sombre. Kishen was pressing and folding my right palm, apparently to 'read' the 'lines' on it. From time to time, he would flash a quick glance at my face. By now, I had become a willing participant, and wondered if Kishen had chanced upon Bishuda's 'death at age thirty-seven' line on my palm. Kishen kept staring at my palm in silence, for quite a long time, and not touching his beer. From time to time, Kalyan replenished our tumblers, ensuring that 'astrologer' and 'subject' (or victim) remained undisturbed. There was pin-drop silence in the room. It had, by now, grown dark, the lights in the balcony were switched on. Suddenly, Kishen announced, 'Your palm is both fascinating and interesting.'

Ashok: 'Whatever do you mean? Do say something specific.'

Kishen: 'No more today. It's become dark and I can only read a palm during daylight. Why don't we meet tomorrow, but start a bit earlier?'

I had now grown keen and readily agreed.

The three of us again gathered on my balcony the next afternoon. The summer sun was strong, and the air hot and humid.

Without much ado, Kalyan poured our three tumblers of beer and
Kishen and I got down to the palmistry business, with my right
hand extended, wiped by Kishen once again. Kishen's scrutiny
continued in silence, for the next hour or so, while the sun was
still bright. He wrote down some notes on a pad, with a sharpened
pencil. What he was writing, I could not see.

Finally, Kishen announced that he was done. He had a rather
strange beatific smile on his chubby face. Our beer had become
warm while Kalyan kept sipping and replenishing his glass. The
condensate had wet the paper napkins on which Kishen and my
beer glasses remained untouched. Kishen said, 'I am now going to
describe events, which you will only believe when they come to pass.'
I was, of course, curious. Kishen said: 'I'll forecast one thing for
certain now, and the rest when I have had more time to analyse my
notes, at leisure.' By this time, both Kalyan and I were on the edge
of our seats. Firstly, Kishen forecast the year and the month I would
get married. The year he forecast was three years away. I felt a bit
disappointed. He next predicted a promotion in my workplace in
the year following my marriage. I told him if either or both of them
turned out as he forecasted, I would gift him half a dozen bottles of
beer, and a deal was struck before the evening concluded.

With the passage of time, Kishen's palmistry forecast receded
from my memory, but our friendship grew. As it turned out, Kishen's
forecasts of both the year and month of my marriage and promotion
were accurate. As a part of our deal, I offered Kishen six bottles of
beer. However, Kishen said, 'Hold it, there is much more.' Before
I could respond, he reeled off six other events, into the future,
spanning the next thirty years. Each of the events took place, one
by one, and I stopped being surprised by the absolute accuracy of
Kishen's forecasts. Looking back to the time when Kishen had made
the six predictions, each had seemed so outlandish and improbable
that I did not take them seriously. Kishen had made notes of each
of the events and from time to time, and through the years and the
six events later, reminded me that now I owed him a brewery. While
I was more than convinced about Kishen's astrological forecasts,

thankfully, I never took them literally. Connie never took palmistry seriously. But each of Kishen's forecasts came to pass.

Some years later, Kishen and I happened to be sitting next to each other, on a flight to Delhi, where we were to attend the wedding of the son of a mutual friend, who happened to be a senior cabinet minister in Indira Gandhi's government. The minister, until then, had not won an election, not even to his college union, but he happened to be exceptionally clever and wise. He remained Indira Gandhi's most trusted lieutenant during her lifetime. The minister was beholden to Kishen, for predicting his meteoric rise in politics, tempered only by Kishen also telling him that he would experience some serious setbacks as well, in his lifetime.

After our flight for Delhi had taken off, the stewardess commenced serving the evening meal. Kishen and I continued to chat. I told the stewardess, I did not wish to be served the evening meal. Immediately, Kishen perked up and wondered why I was not having something to eat! I told him it happened to be my birthday and on the way to the airport, I had a nice meal, prepared by my mother. Immediately, Kishen took out his pen and pad, looked at his watch, did what looked like some number juggling, and shortly thereafter, told me a piece of information which was extremely sensitive, and to which only Connie and I were privy. I was honestly taken aback. It so happened that I was going through a tricky phase with one of my bosses, and which I had shared only with my wife, and here was Kishen, quite out of the blue, telling me about this same issue. I am certain it was not mind reading, as I was not even thinking about the subject. I recall a few such similar incidents, which Kishen talked about and which convinced me that he was on to something serious with his palmistry. In the years which followed, there were a number of other events which he had forecast, and which came to pass. I was convinced that there may be some aspects of astrology, although it was a subject which I did not trust, which I could also no longer entirely ignore.

As our daughters, Nivedita and Amrita, started growing up, on lazy evenings, at home, they would pester me to narrate the stories of

Kishen uncle's astrology forecasting. Could I persuade Kishen uncle to read their palms as well? This did not happen. Although he cast, at my request, the horoscope of Amrita, he did not predict her future, as he had done for me.

I had shared the stories about Kishen and his palmistry with my wife, Connie, soon after we were married. Connie was instinctively averse to palmistry, etc., which she considered to be occult. Although Kishen continued to be a good family friend, Connie steadfastly refused to have her palm read and strongly dissuaded our daughters as well.

Over the years following, Kishen and I both moved on, and were less frequently in touch. I had an acquaintance, a venerable and much older gentleman, who had retired after occupying senior positions with the government, besides becoming India's envoy to the UK, USA and UN, and finally as the principal adviser to Prime Minister Indira Gandhi. The gentleman's interest in astrology happened to be unusually intense. During one of our frequent social encounters, I told him about my good friend Kishen. He found my experiences with Kishen so fascinating that he gently insisted that I arrange a meeting for him with Kishen. I tried to persuade Kishen, who somehow kept avoiding meeting my friend. Over the years, Kishen had moved on from his interest in palmistry. After much persuasion, eventually Kishen suggested that I arrange to send him the horoscope of my friend and he would then consider what further he may do. My elderly civil servant friend was quite delighted, and promptly sent me a copy of his horoscope, which I then handed over to Kishen. After several months, I received a letter from Kishen, and in the envelope he had also enclosed my friend's horoscope, with a note. Kishen had been extremely busy with his business and conveyed apologies for the inordinate delay, and gave instead the name and address of another astrologer, who might be able to help. In a footnote, Kishen also wrote that this may not be necessary, since the person whose horoscope I had sent to him may have passed away in the meantime. I was stunned by the revelation. Kishen had no way of knowing who the horoscope belonged to, and hence was in no position to know that my civil servant friend had indeed died suddenly, just a couple of weeks earlier. This incident hardened Connie's resolve, even more resolutely, to shun astrology.

I must, however, conclude on the theme of astrology on a happier note. Herwig, a colleague in Unilever, and I were good friends. Herwig and his wife, Anèl, came to Bombay on a short holiday. They were staying at a five-star hotel. No five-star hotel in India worth its name was without a resident astrologer in those days. This was before the days of resident yoga teachers and Ayurveda masseuse. Anèl was keen to have her fortune read by the hotel astrologer. I dissuaded her and promised to introduce her to my friend Kishen, whom I trusted. Since a face-to-face meeting and palm reading was not possible at the time, I asked Kishen what was the next best thing we could do. 'Send me her date, time and place of birth, if she can remember,' was Kishen's response. Anèl wrote all this information on a piece of paper and sent it with a self-addressed envelope, and I forwarded it to Kishen. Well after Herwig and Anèl had gone back to their native Vienna, an envelope arrived addressed to me, from Kishen. Inside was another sealed envelope with Anèl's name and their Vienna address, on the cover.

Connie posted the sealed envelope to Anèl. We forgot all about the incident, until a few years later, when Connie and I went to Vienna for a short holiday. We were pleasantly surprised to see Herwig and Anèl at the airport, since receiving guests at airports and railway stations is a very Indian custom. We were, of course, pleased to see them, since it had been a while since we had last met. They drove us to our hotel. After we had registered and checked in, the four of us settled down to have a cup of tea together. While we were drinking tea, Anèl told us about the letter from Kishen, which we had posted to her some years earlier. Anèl told us that Kishen had listed events from her past which he had no way of knowing, having never met her, and which had absolutely bowled her over. Even some of the future events which Kishen had predicted had already come to pass, and both she and Herwig were absolutely convinced of the powers of astrology in general, and said that Kishen's mastery of it was stunning. All the while I was watching Connie's expression, which remained inscrutable. Finally, the Kresslers left, so that we could rest. Going up the elevator, I asked Connie what she thought about Anèls story. 'There may be something in all this, but I have no wish to know the future. It takes all the fun and surprise out of life!' she said.

I am at a stage in life when astrology no longer holds any interest. Kishen's predictions were most unusual, as all the subsequent events he had forecasted have come to pass. I was always surprised by the sheer coincidence of the actual events as they came to pass but besides his forecasts, I have also been very fortunate. There are people in India, a few of whom I happened to know, amongst the great and the good, who would not take any major decisions without consulting their astrologer. But I must also admit that I have never been able to put that evening with Kishen and Kalyan in 1964, and our subsequent encounters, entirely out of my mind. Since that summer evening of 1964, life has moved on, my friend Kalyan sadly passed away and I have almost lost touch with Kishen.

At the end of it all, life is what one makes of it.

Assignation Europe

In 1968, I was transferred on secondment to Unilever research laboratories, Vlaardingen, in Holland, and following that, in 1970, to the research division, in the Unilever head office, in London. In preparation for our departure from Bombay, we had to vacate Panorama. Ma and Baba moved back to their flat in Worli.

Connie and I departed for Amsterdam, via Frankfurt, by an Air India flight, on 31 December 1968. We were booked into the Hotel Central, in Rotterdam, where we stayed for the next one month, before moving into a Unilever flat, in Schiedam.

The morning following our arrival in Rotterdam, I was picked up from the hotel and driven to the Unilever laboratory, in Vlaardingen. The laboratory building was a massive, new, multistorey building, with modern and well-appointed offices, laboratories and a fairly large auditorium. The new structure blended into the existing structure very well. Vlaardingen had a very high reputation in the world of science.

Dr Jan van Roon, head of the protein section, handed over to me charge of his department on the same day. For the first time in my career, I now had a secretary, one Ms Mariejan. I did not know what her role was until Jan van Roon explained to me that she was supposed to arrange my weekly schedule and my appointments with other divisions, etc. There seemed to be a certain formality in all matters, which I was not accustomed to, and which I soon abandoned. The scientists in the protein section included Pete Smits, Frans Dorsman, Piet Holoman, Jan Hoffman and Jan Vingerhood, as well as a few research assistants. The Dutch have a sort of European formality, which I was not familiar with. Van Roon advised me that I also needed to be sensitive to the hierarchy at the workplace. My new colleagues did not show it, but they must have been curious about my antecedents, although they must have also been well briefed by Jan van Roon. I soon discovered that although the Dutch tended to be formal, they were also warm and friendly. The Dutch are also extremely discrete. I cautioned Jan that I did not have a secretary in my section in Andheri before he left for Bombay the next day, to be posted in my place, for the next three months. And that the Indian R&D set-up was tiny compared to Vlaardingen.

After Jan completed his three-month secondment in Bombay, and returned to Holland, Connie and I were invited and we met his wife, Pia, and Jan, at their home and became good friends during the rest of our time in Holland. As a matter of fact, within a very short time, we made a number of good friends with the families of my colleagues, including Cees and Gre Okkerse, Jan Van Gils and his wife, Ono Korver and Mrs Korver, Jap Hannewijk, our division head and several others. The only other Indian scientist working in Vlaardingen at the time was Bobby (Ramanujan) Iyengar. Bobby and his wife, Sudha, came to Hotel Central to meet Connie and me the day after we had reached Rotterdam. Over time, we became very good and lifelong friends.

Although the Dutch are fluent in English, they greatly appreciate if foreigners make an attempt to pick up their language and make an effort to speak at least a smattering of Dutch during conversations. Although Connie and I never formally learnt to speak Dutch, I became quite used to mixing Dutch and English in my conversations.

After staying a month at Hotel Central, Connie and I had become reasonably familiar with the city streets in the central parts of Rotterdam and some of the eating joints, including a small Surinamese restaurant which served Indian chicken curry and chapattis. We enjoyed Dutch as well as popular Indonesian cuisine. Parts of Rotterdam were still being rebuilt after the devastation of

World War II. The Rotterdam Central Station was located close to
Hotel Central, and we sometimes took a train and ventured out to
Amsterdam on weekends. Soon, Unilever arranged for us to move
to a two-bedroom furnished apartment in the town of Schiedam.
Schiedam is the next station after Rotterdam and two stations to
Vlaardingen. After settling down in our apartment, on one balmy
Saturday morning, we walked down to the local Schiedam police
station, to register our temporary presence in their city, as was
required under the law. In the police station, Connie and I sat across
an expressionless policeman, with a typewriter in front of him, who
then began, politely, asking us a series of questions, to fill the form
for record. He noted down the details of our passports, local address
and then wanted to see our marriage certificate. We had been, of
course, married as per Hindu laws and in those days one did not
bother about a marriage certificate. The policeman seemed to be
bewildered, pondered thoughtfully for a while, and then asked me
what we wished him to put on record; mind you, all this while,
speaking only in Dutch. I was a bit cheeky in my young days, and
suggested that he may consider recording that we were living in sin.
Connie was very embarrassed, and the dour policeman did not think
that what I had suggested was very funny either. Instead, he recorded
'living together', and brought our interview to a satisfactory close.

Our flat in Schiedam, at 664 Gravelandseweg (pronounced
Shravelandseweg), was very pleasant, large, well-lit and nicely
furnished. We stayed happily there, for over a year. Mr Kooij of
Unilever visitors' department was most helpful in our smooth
transition from the hotel to the flat, in every way possible. There was
a supermarket located on the ground floor of our apartment building,
and was convenient for Connie to shop, especially considering that
we had arrived in the middle of the Dutch winter, which can be
quite severe. On weekends, Connie and I would frequently walk to
downtown Schiedam. The weekly farmers' market used to be lively.
We loved shopping for fresh vegetables and flowers, and although
everyone spoke Dutch, we could still communicate well. Over the

following weeks and months, we built up quite an active social life, getting to know many of my Dutch colleagues and their families. We frequently invited some of my Dutch colleagues and their spouses for dinner at our apartment, and in turn were invited to their homes. Connie's basic Indian dinner menu was declared very tasty and much enjoyed by our Dutch guests, and the word got around. Invitations to the Gangulys were looked forward to.

In 1969, a number of visitors from India (Hindustan Lever) came to Holland, and we invited them to our place as well. Very frequently we met our friends Sudha and Bobby, and looked forward to South Indian lunches and dinners at their home. Quite often, the four of us drove on day trips or overnight, to other European cities, and especially during long weekends in the summers. Connie and I frequently reminisced about that memorable year of ours in the Netherlands. Sadly, Bobby passed away after he retired and they had settled down in the house they had built, in Bangalore. We remain in touch with Sudha and chat frequently. Didi and her husband, Narendra, visited us and enjoyed a holiday during the summer of 1969. Their visit coincided with the Dutch, or rather European, annual holiday summer month of August, when offices and factories come to a virtual standstill. My Dutch salary used to be generous, and we had reasonable savings. We booked a holiday, for the four of us, on a ten-day Thomas Cook Bus Tour of Europe. We have very happy memories of that holiday. To my pleasant surprise, I also received one extra month's salary in August, which was the holiday bonus, and about which I was unaware.

During my time in Vlaardingen, I got to know one of my colleagues, Prof. Van Dorp, an internationally well-known scientist. He was acclaimed for his pioneering work on a family of hormones called prostaglandins. Although our areas of scientific interest were different, Prof. Van Dorp was very curious and interested about India. He was also keen to meet Connie and mentioned to me that some of our colleagues had talked of the dinners at our home. We invited Prof. Van Dorp and Mrs Van Dorp, for an Indian meal at our apartment. Both of them very much enjoyed their first taste of Indian cuisine. So after dinner, as the Dutch did, we spent the rest of the evening chatting about India and Europe, over helpings of chilled beers, coffee and snacks. The Dutch custom is to settle down, to alcoholic drinks, coffee and snacks, after their meal, well into the night. An evening, thus, can stretch well beyond midnight, or one is invited for an after-dinner evening.

In the course of the evening, Prof. Van Dorp enquired of Connie how she spent her time while I was away at work! After he learnt of her interest and that she had graduated in history, Prof. Van Dorp asked her if she would like to spend a few hours a week at the University of Leiden, internationally famous for its history and Sanskrit departments. Soon thereafter, Prof. Van Dorp introduced Connie to one Prof. Galstein, a Sanskrit scholar at Leiden University. Connie was invited by Prof. Galstein, who introduced her to some of the faculty in the history department. Connie spent time in Leiden's famous library, sometimes, three times a week, and enjoyed the experience. To get to Leiden University, Connie travelled from Schiedam to Leiden, via Rotterdam, on some days, or by a direct train and then returned in the evening. The Dutch are normally very friendly, and would get chatting with the sari-clad Indian lady on the train or while she walked home from Schiedam Station.

Connie was understated and quiet by nature, even after we were married. One day, while we were walking, Connie confided in me that our time in Holland and London during that year and a half (1968–70), had very strongly bonded our arranged marriage. That statement has remained embedded in my mind forever. Our year in Holland, our holidays, weekend trips to various European destinations and social interactions with the Dutch, followed by the exciting period in London during 1970, were memorable indeed.

In the summer of 1969, the new laboratory building of the Unilever research in Vlaardingen, in which we were already working, was formally declared open, at a grand ceremony in the lovely new Opera House of Rotterdam, named the Doolen. It was a grand party for which all employees of the laboratory, and their spouses, were invited. There were many diverse entertainment shows going on simultaneously, and a large spread of food and drinks had been laid out, within easy reach. Walking around, watching the various entertainments, Connie and I also saw, for the first time, topless dancing girls, with a tinge of shyness. Even at the time, Holland was, and still remains, very liberal in matters concerning sex, opiates and euthanasia, none of which seems to have harmed them in any way—as a people or as a society. The Dutch are pioneers in adopting voluntary euthanasia, under well-laid-out legal and medical, procedures. A nation of 16 million, the Dutch are extremely hard-working people with Calvinist ethics, although they did not appear to be overly religious. Holland's colonial history is less edifying, when they had a small presence in India, Ceylon, Indonesia, Surinam, etc. During World War II, Holland was occupied by the Nazis early on, and large numbers of Dutch Jews were sent to concentration camps. The story of Anne Frank's diary is, of course, well known. Even when we developed quite close friendships with a few of our colleagues, any talk about the war tended to be avoided. In contrast, their dislike for Germans and the English is not very subtle. All in all, we immensely enjoyed our stay in Holland. I had no way of knowing that I was to return in 1990, as a director of Unilever Plc and NV, having offices and residences in London and Rotterdam!

In 1969, during my first three months in Vlaardingen, as section manager, proteins, I very closely and informally, interacted with colleagues in my section, and took great interest in their research projects. My informal ways were welcomed and adopted readily. I also continued my own research, on the tertiary structure of β-lactoglobulin. Although Van Roon's way of working expected me to sit down with my secretary, Mariejan, on Monday mornings to plan appointments and meetings for the rest of the week, I dispensed with this practice, and interacted with my colleagues at their work benches spontaneously, as and when necessary, and encouraged them to walk into my office whenever they wished to. Very soon, my colleagues adapted and enjoyed the informality, and it had a positive impact on the work environment. My colleagues got used to my ways of wandering into their laboratories, instead of formally planning and holding weekly meetings in my office. Sadly, during my stay, my secretary Mariejan was left without much to do. For example, if I wanted to make use of the spectroscopy division's services in the same building, the first time I contacted them, and the scientist in charge, Dr Ono Korver, whom of course I did not know then, in person informed me rather stiffly that I had to wait until the following week and fix an appointment to meet him. I put down my phone, went up to his spectroscopy department on the fourth floor of the laboratory, knocked on his door and barged in to introduce myself. I then told him that my sample for analysis could not wait until the following week, and that I needed spectroscopic analysis of my sample right away, and could he kindly help?

Dr Ono Krover's first reaction was to be taken aback by my intrusion and by my unconventional forthright request. After this incident, we became very good friends, and one day he confided in me that he had not met anyone like me before, recalling this first encounter. Further embarrassment on that first encounter was avoided by the appearance of one of his English colleagues David Frost, while I was talking to Ono. David always had a jolly smile and pleasant demeanour. He understood the situation instantly and suggested that if I left behind the sample I was carrying, I could pick up the spectra later that afternoon. Ono, David and I also became good friends, and the reports of my impromptu and informal ways soon spread across the laboratory, and was, surprisingly, welcomed as being refreshing!

Every Friday afternoon, a seminar used to be held in the large and brand-new auditorium of the laboratory, called the 'Aula'. These seminars were known in Dutch as the 'Fridag Midag Lessing, in der Aula'. During my year at Vlaardingen, I was invited to deliver a talk one Friday. I chose, for my talk, the work I was doing, exploring the tertiary structure of β-Lactoglobulin. Besides my talk, which

I delivered in English, my rather feeble attempts to interject my smattering of Dutch in my introduction was greatly appreciated. At the conclusion of my talk, I received huge applause, mainly for my feeble attempts to say a few words in Dutch, which left me wondering how well my hypothesis and results had been received!

In April 1969, Jan van Roon returned from Bombay and I handed back his section to him. Van Roon had enjoyed his time in Bombay, but was happy to be back. I had befriended my fellow scientists in the section, and convinced them during those three months, while I was in charge, not to shut down their experiments at 5 p.m. sharp. The Dutch normally planned their evening family meals between 5.30 and 6 p.m., and watched a very popular Dutch cartoon on the TV, with their family, during dinner. I had a habit of working late in the laboratory, and offered to complete some of their experiments when they left for the day. I returned home fairly late in the evening, after which Connie and I enjoyed our dinner together. My colleagues may have felt that I was staying back to complete their experiments after they had left for the day, which was not so, because I used to be busy with my work as well. After the first couple of weeks, some of them started returning to the lab after dinner, to complete their experiment, which they would have started earlier in the day.

The majority of the laboratory employees stayed within a small radius of the lab. Jan van Roon shared with me later that I had started a practice working after hours, which was not the 'Dutch way'. I responded, in good humour, that since I was not a Dutch, it didn't matter. I think Pia, his wife, was much relieved to get back to their daily routine once Jan had returned from Bombay. My laboratory colleagues were too Dutch to show how they may have felt about my unorthodox and informal ways at the workplace. But we became good friends. I met many of them, in 1990, and the years following, during my monthly visits to Vlaardingen, as a director of Unilever.

After Jan van Roon returned from India, for the next few months, I had another assignment, reporting to senior scientist Cees Okkerse, in the same division, which was headed by Jap Hannewijk. By then,

I was reasonably known across the Vlaardingen laboratory, but I did not realize that my smattering of Dutch and my habit of working hard and long hours were also quietly admired, in a silent, Dutch sort of way. My new project was to study and then prepare a report on the commercial uses of whey proteins.

During the course of my work on the project, Cees and I became very close friends, and those memories were rekindled, happily, in 1990, when Cees was one of the R&D management committee members. During the last two months in Holland, in 1969, I was transferred from Vlaardingen to the Unilever NV head office, in Rotterdam, reporting to the deputy head of Unilever research, Dr Han Petri. During our stay in Holland, I became aware that there was a not-so-subtle 'rivalry' between the Dutch and the English 'parts' of Unilever. So while Dr John Collingwood was a member of the Unilever board, and the executive director responsible for Unilever research, engineering, safety, etc., Han Petri had the designation as deputy head, reporting to John Collingwood but supposed to be looking after the 'Dutch interests'. I could never fully fathom the undercurrent between the Dutch and the English, until I was appointed to the Unilever board in 1990. I had, by then, become more aware that certain cultural differences between the Dutch and the English were indeed historic, but subtle!

In the Rotterdam headquarters of Unilever NV, I had a large office, secretarial assistance, but did not have any specific tasks assigned to me, although my new title was that of 'assistant to the deputy head of Unilever research', Dr Han Petri. I was not happy more or less whiling away my days in the Unilever NV head office. Very frequently, Han Petri would drop into my office for a chat. He was a nice and friendly person. Petri and his family had taken a shine to Connie and me. It was all very nice, but I remained miserable without the pressure of tasks. After the exciting months working in Vlaardingen, the last two months in Rotterdam turned out to be a bit of a let-down. It took a very long time for the penny to drop, as to why we had been sent to Holland for that one year in 1969.

During the 1969 Christmas holidays, we moved to London for the next leg of my secondment to the research division of Unilever, at its Blackfriars head office. During the first few days after we moved to London, Unilever had arranged for us to stay at the Royal Court Hotel on Oxford Street. Unilever had also arranged for us to go across to see an apartment in Dolphin Square, in Pimlico, near Victoria. The apartment belonged to a Unilever manager, Maurice Fitzmaurice, who was moving to New York for a six-month secondment, and his apartment was available for the duration of our stay.

The first time Connie and I went to the Dolphin Square flat, Maurice showed us around the flat. His larder was surprisingly well stocked with Indian spices of a well-known Indian brand, Patak's, popular in the UK. Maurice also told Connie that Patak's delivered orders home. His interest in Indian spices went back to his childhood years, growing up in India. His father used to be the mint master in Nashik before Independence. Maurice and his fiancée were warm and friendly, and they both seemed keen to invite Connie and me to join them for the Boxing Day dinner at his fiancée's home. It was a very enjoyable dinner, in the midst of a bleak, sooty and grey winter day of 1970 London, and we were made to feel very welcome, by the host and the other guests.

Soon, Maurice left for New York, and we moved into his apartment in Dolphin Square. Once we settled down, we realized that Dolphin Square was one of the posh London addresses consisting of blocks of flats, with modern facilities, for the well-to-do English owners and few other occupants.

During our stay in Dolphin Square, we found out that the facilities included a warm water swimming pool, barber shop, health club, etc., for residents. My assignment in the research division of Unilever House in Blackfriars began in right earnest in the New Year. It was the time of the UK miners' strike, during Prime Minister James Callaghan's government. Compared to Holland, my salary dropped a bit in England, and may have had something to do with purchasing power parity or cost of living! Connie and I were happy and contented after settling in Dolphin Square. We soon realized that Connie was with child. Especially in the bleak winter with the faint odour of boiled cabbage along the corridor of our flat, Connie experienced regular bouts of morning sickness. My childhood friend Biju, from Bombay, happened to be living and working in England at that time. He had married one of his English colleagues, Betty, and they lived in Southend-on-Sea. Biju was employed as a computer service engineer with ICL, and became virtually a daily visitor to our flat. As in his childhood, Biju had retained his vim and vigour, and frequently rescued Connie from cooking dinner. Biju loved to cook, and always expertly put together a quick meal in our kitchen, joined us for dinner and then dashed off to attend to clients, before returning home. After a couple of months, Biju one day announced that he had saved enough money to invite us to their home, to spend a weekend. We spent a very hospitable and enjoyable weekend with Betty and Biju, at their pretty home in Southend-on-Sea.

During our stay in London, Connie and I frequently walked across, for our evening meal, from time to time, to one of the 'Indian' restaurants, on Tottenham Court Road. Those were the days of red and green velvet-covered walls, of 'Indian' eateries, owned and run mainly by Bengalis from Sylhet, in soon-to-be Bangladesh. They started their careers as cooks on cargo vessels, which were manned by Bangladeshi Khalashis, and were rumoured to have jumped ship, in some UK port or the other, and started a new life.

My colleague John Hubert and I shared an office in the Unilever House research division. I got into the rhythm of preparing notes on various topics, working on other assignments and visiting Unilever laboratories, in the UK and in Europe, on behalf of Dr John Collingwood. A couple of days after starting work in London, I was requested to meet a manager in the personnel department of Unilever. He informed me about my salary and London allowances. The cheeky fellow then went on to caution me that I should live within my means, going on to say that people from 'your part' of the world tended to get carried away and spend beyond their means while in London. His unsolicited homily instantly irritated me and I retorted by telling him to mind his own business, and also informed him I had worked in several places around the world. I went on to tell him that I doubted if he had ever stepped out of London, and still had the temerity to give me unsolicited advice! I then walked away and returned to my desk. Subsequently, I learnt from the research division secretary, Rosemary Wilkins, that the personnel chap had complained to Dr Collingwood about our exchange the previous day, and, in turn, had got told off by the research director, that he deserved every bit of what I had told him.

On behalf of the research director, I frequently had to visit the Unilever R&D laboratories, near Bedfordshire, Welwyn Garden city, near London, Port Sunlight in Manchester, Vlaardingen and Duiven in Holland, Hamburg in Germany and one in St Denis, outside Paris. I kept happily busy, and enjoyed my work.

Most evenings, if the weather was amenable, Connie and I would go out for a walk around Pimlico, occasionally take in a movie or a play (we saw *Hair*) and usually have dinner at a nearby restaurant. Weekends were relaxed and restful. The division secretary, Rosemary, asked me if my wife and I would like to attend a performance at the Royal Opera House the following Saturday! Connie and I witnessed the performance of Tchaikovsky's 'Swan Lake Ballet', by Rudolph Nuriyev and Dame Margot Fonteyn. Rosemary had handed me the pass for two, for the Unilever Box at the Royal Opera House. It turned out to be an exquisite and memorable evening. Besides the novelty and privacy of the Unilever Box, the superlative ballet performance by the most famous artists was a once-in-a-lifetime opportunity.

During the interval, a trolley was brought into our box, with canapés, mini sandwiches, along with a bottle of champagne in an ice bucket and two flutes. Connie did not drink alcohol at the time, but I happily had a succession of flutes of champagne. Witnessing 'Swan Lake Ballet' at the Royal Opera House was the high point of our stay in London. We also visited a number of museums and art galleries, on weekends. The months in London passed quickly.

We were not aware that Connie was with our first child until she started feeling a bit unwell. There was a GP living in one of the flats of Dolphin Square. One morning, Connie was feeling more than a bit under the weather, so I requested the GP to visit. After examining her, he declared that her morning sickness was normal in pregnancy, and added that all was well, and I should really start doing all the housework and allow my wife to rest. Connie and I were delighted at the news, although it took a while for Connie to feel physically better. Mrs Lassiter, who worked as a cleaning lady for Maurice, continued to come in every morning. After arriving, she would first make herself a cup of coffee and smoke a cigarette in the kitchen, and then get down to some cursory cleaning and dusting around the flat. In her state, Connie did not like the smell of food. Biju dropped by a few times during the week, cooked a quick meal and had dinner with us.

Most evenings, we used to eat pre-cooked meals or walk down to nearby restaurants, on evenings she was feeling better. Betty and Biju, and their infant son, came and spent a weekend with us, and we all somehow squeezed into our small flat. We also met one of Didi's and my old college mates, Zarin, and her husband, Ghulam. They had settled down and made their home in London. We enjoyed meeting them a few times while we lived there. Zarin was a superb cook. I remember eating a very tasty biryani meal cooked by her.

We also had visitors from India from time to time. Dr Mohan Mulky, who worked at the Colworth House Unilever Laboratory, came home to have a chat with me before he moved to India, to join Hindustan Lever's R&D division, as head of the toxicology department. A wonderful and a very knowledgeable scientist, Mulky sadly passed away a few years back. Dr Varadarajan, HLL research director, also dropped in on one of his trips to the UK. He had visited us in our flat in Schiedam the previous year, when we were in Holland.

By the middle of 1970, we had spent, altogether, eighteen months between Holland and England. It had been a wonderful work experience, we had made new friends, travelled on holiday across Europe, and while in London, Connie was carrying our first child as we got ready to return to Bombay.

Where to Spend Your Life?

Connie and I are on one of our usual annual visits to London. It is a rather chilly but sunny morning, and we are in our cozy one-bedroom apartment, in Chelsea. The flat now belongs to Amrita. Later in the morning, we will go for our daily walk in Kensington Gardens.

The title of this section takes me back to 1962, while I am still in the USA. I informed Bob Whitney that I planned to go to India, after having been away from home for close to six years. Bob saw the point, but since he had initiated getting me a job offer, as an assistant professor, at the Washington University in Seattle, he assumed I would be back in time to take up the post. I must have responded in the affirmative. Bob asked me if I was happy living in the US, and reminded me that there would be a green card awaiting my return. As I have mentioned elsewhere, eventually, I had decided that I would settle down in India. I wrote to Bob about my decision to remain in India and the reason which had led me to the decision, and conveyed my apologies. Bob sent me a very nice reply, saying that he fully understood my reason for staying back. Being a gentleman, he never shared his possible disappointment that I had decided to not pursue my academic interests and settle down in the US.

The next episode was in 1969, when Connie and I were temporarily living in Holland on my secondment to Unilever's Dutch R&D laboratory. One of my closest friends used to be Cees Okerse. Cees was one of the two Dutch senior technical officers in the Unilever Research Division, with office in the Vlaardingen Laboratory. Although he was senior in rank to me, we both reported to Dr Hannawijk, the head of our division. My assignment was progressing well; Connie and I were happy, living in friendly Netherlands and with our growing social life. Cees and his wife, Gre, were amongst our very close friends. After we had been in Holland for six months, I was requested by Cees, one afternoon, that we both meet Dr Hannawijk in his office. Jap Hannawijk was an extremely polite and friendly person, but we met infrequently, as and when my work required such a meeting.

At the scheduled time, Cees and I went to see Dr Hannawijk in his office. After exchanging pleasantries, he informed me that the Directie (pronounced Direkshee in Dutch), directors of the Unilever R&D laboratory in Holland, where I was on secondments from India, wished to offer me a very senior position, to head a larger group of scientists, and wanted Connie and me to live and settle down in Holland. This offer was a complete surprise, and took me a while to comprehend. The prospect of a whopping promotion, of course, was very enticing. I said that I would need to discuss the proposition with Connie. After the brief conversation, and in the usual formal Dutch way, both Hannawijk and Cees stood up and shook my hand, giving the impression that a deal had been struck!

Before returning home that evening, I had phoned and briefly mentioned this to Connie and shared the events of that afternoon with her. While job-wise it was exciting, it also meant that we would have to live and permanently settle down in Holland. It did not take us much time to conclude that we would prefer to live in India, notwithstanding the material attractions of living in Europe, and especially the Netherlands.

The next morning, I met Jap Hannawijk and Cees Okerse, first to thank them for their generous and very exciting offer of a very senior role in Vlaardingen. However, Connie and I wished to return to India. They appeared, visibly disappointed and wondered if they could help us, in any manner, to convince us to settle down in Holland. I explained to them that we were grateful for their generous offer and that we were enjoying our stay in Holland, but wished to return to live in India, for personal reasons. Jap and Cees both understood what I was trying to convey, but still expressed their disappointment honestly, as the Dutch are very open and frank.

There was a similar episode in 1986. I was the chairman of HLL at the time. I received a call from my contact director, Patrick Egan, to visit London at short notice, to see Floris Maljers, the Dutch co-chairman and a member of the three-member Unilever Special Committee (the Dutch and the UK co-chairman and a third member,

An evening out in the rain

With wife, Connie, and daughters, Nivedita and Amrita

Starting life in Holland, 1969

The golden jubilee, 2017

PM Dr Manmohan Singh introducing the author to President Obama

With Sharad Pawar in the 1980s

Business leaders meet with J.R.D. Tata at Hotel Taj, 1984

With West Bengal CM Jyoti Basu

With Pranab Mukherjee and Murli Deora, 1983

Presenting a copy of my book *Business-Driven R&D* to
President K.R. Narayanan, 1999

The author, as president of BCCI, hosts a lunch for UK
PM Margaret Thatcher in 1984

Investment Commission, with Ratan Tata, Deepak Parekh and
PM Dr Manmohan Singh

The Unilever Board Plc and NV, 1991, at the global headquarters at
Unilever House, EC4, London

(*L to R*): V.G. Rajadhyaksha, Prakash Tandon, T. Thomas
and author A.S. Ganguly—HUL (HLL) chairmen

The author with Mother Teresa and T. Thomas at Ashadaan, Mumbai

the vice-chairman) wished to see me, if possible, the next day. This unusual request, out of the blue, intrigued me. Even my boss Patrick Egan, a personal friend, did not know the reason for the sudden summons. I travelled to London overnight, and after freshening up at my hotel, went across to Unilever House in Blackfriars, to meet Floris, in his sixth-floor Unilever House office. After exchanging pleasantries, Floris explained the reason for the urgency of his request. He wanted me to consider taking up the post of head and director of Unilever research in Vlaardingen, and move to Holland, along with my family, at the earliest. I did not have the slightest hesitation to politely inform Floris that I was not keen to take his kind offer, as I was quite satisfied with my present job, in Bombay. I thanked him for the offer and politely declined. I explained to Floris the reasons why I was happy in my role as the chairman in India. Floris tried to gently, but unsuccessfully, persuade me for a while. I then enquired about my future in Unilever, after the Dutch assignment he was proposing, Floris said he did not know and honestly told me so. Our brief meeting concluded pleasantly.

In April 1990, soon after I joined the Unilever board, I had to meet Sir Michael Angus in his office. He briefed me of my emoluments and perquisites as a board member, as well as a generous pension I would be entitled to following my retirement. The fork on the path was a happy development.

In May 1990, Connie, Nivedita and Amrita joined me in London. For a few weeks, we stayed in one of the service apartments of the Grosvenor House Hotel. Unilever helped us to choose a very nice and conveniently located residence in London. Sir Michael Angus seemed keen that we should buy a house in the country, to really enjoy living in the UK, especially, as he put it, compared to having to live in apartments in crowded cities. He further suggested that the UK would be a good place to settle down, eventually, after I retired from Unilever. While I tried to imagine the scenario of a bucolic country retreat, with gardening on weekends during the English summers, which seemed uplifting, I did not think of the cold and frequently wet winters. However, Connie brought me down to earth, and we chose an exclusive, well-serviced and sprawling apartment on Sloane Square and, unusually for London, with an attached garage in the basement. Connie also shared with me that she was not really keen on gardening. Most of my English colleagues lived in the countryside and commuted to London by train during the weekdays—they were picked up at the station, and driven to Unilever House every morning and driven back, in time for their train, in the evening.

In 1995, it was Connie's good sense and gentle persistence which helped us acquire a one-bedroom flat in Cramer Court, in Chelsea. We moved in there briefly, after I retired from Unilever in 1997, and before we returned to Bombay and our flat in Pemino on Altamount Road.

A Fork in the Road

In July 1970, we returned to Bombay from London, and moved back into our old flat in Panorama, on Pali Hill. Ma and Baba moved back to Panorama, from Worli. The rest of the year 1970 also turned out to be eventful.

Within less than a month of our returning to Bombay, and my rejoining my old post as section manager in research, I was summoned to the head office, to see Vasant Rajadhyaksha, the chairman, and T. Thomas, the technical director of Hindustan Lever. Dr Varadarajan, who informed me about the meeting, did not tell me what the meeting was all about, and I was not anxious either. I was intrigued, but not overly concerned. Incidentally, Thomas had visited Vlaardingen for a day in 1969, while I was working there on secondment. I had not met him before, in India. My first rude encounter with Thomas (he was known within the company as TT) was during his visit to Vlaardingen. Connie and I thought it would be proper to invite Mrs Thomas and him for dinner to our flat in Schiedam. When I had conveyed a message of invitation, during his visit to the Vlaardingen laboratory, he phoned me back, and rather rudely declined our invitation. Later on, I was also told that when asked if he would like to meet me, by the head of the laboratory, TT had flatly said that he did not wish to meet me. In the meanwhile, TT may have talked to Mrs Thomas, who, we found out later, used to be his saving grace. I was surprised when TT called me back the same morning, and told me that he had changed his mind and that Mrs Thomas and he would come to our flat in Schiedam for dinner that evening. It may also have been because of the presence of Mrs Thomas that we had a surprisingly pleasant evening and dinner with them at our flat. Mr and Mrs Thomas invited us out for dinner the next day, in Rotterdam, where they were staying at the Hilton. That evening also turned out to be quite friendly and pleasant, but did not help erase the memory of my first impression of Thomas, the previous morning, at the Vlaardingen Laboratory. I was told that like many in Unilever, he felt at the time that R&D was a waste of time and money, but later changed this view regarding the critical role of R&D.

I have, very early on, narrated the episode of my resignation two days after joining HLL in 1962, as a management trainee. Vasant, at that time, was the general manager of the Bombay factory. He was, obviously, very annoyed with my abrupt behaviour, and our paths had not crossed at work since then. Subsequently, VGR had moved on from the Bombay factory, was appointed as the technical director in 1968 and soon succeeded Prakash Tandon, as the chairman of HLL. TT was then appointed as technical director, succeeding Mr Rajadhyaksha.

Given this background, I was not very keenly looking forward to meeting Chairman Rajadhyaksha and Technical Director TT. In retrospect, I happened to be at a stage in my life when I did not feel either anxious or overly concerned about what the meeting with the chairman and technical director was all about. It was not my sense of overconfidence, but that was the way I happened to be, and have remained ever since, without being conscious of it. I am glad I was not even aware of these traits in my character.

By the time I reached Hindustan Lever House, I admit, I did start feeling a bit anxious. I was soon ushered into the chairman's office, where VGR and TT were seated. It turned out to be a pleasant but matter-of-fact—although, an entirely unexpected—conversation.

VGR spoke most of the time, with occasional inputs from TT, while I listened. In summary, Vasant told me that in their view, it was time for me to move on from R&D to manufacturing. Such a move would give me wider experience of the business; they would advise me to think seriously about their proposal. However, they also made it very clear that any decision was entirely up to me, and also added that my future career prospects would be entirely dependent on 'whether I swam or sank' as the chairman put it, if I decided to move to manufacturing. I listened to this most-unexpected proposal in stunned silence. What they told me had landed upon me out of the blue. I had to carefully assess what VGR and TT were proposing, and requested for time to think. Soon they bade me goodbye, while requesting to let them know my decision before the end of the week. With that, this unusual, most-unexpected conversation was over.

I returned to Andheri, deep in thought on the drive back. I related in detail what I had been told by VGR and TT to Dr Varadarajan, who did not seem to be surprised. Apparently, he seemed to have been aware of the reason I had been summoned by the chairman. I never actually found out, but surmised that the feedback from Holland and England, regarding my work there in 1969–70, as well as the fact that I had not accepted the offer of a senior position, and for Connie and me to settle down in Holland, may have had something to do with the unfolding scenario I have described above. But frankly, I had no way of knowing the reason, either then or thereafter.

After returning home that evening, I described the proposal of the chairman to Connie. As always, she was very supportive, but she also said that the decision had to be entirely mine, since I was much better placed, and she knew almost nothing about HLL. Connie also encouraged me, by adding that she would be very happy, whatever I decided, going forward. Given the day's events, which I have described, and the fact that the chairman and technical director had given me a choice, I realized that it was rather important for me to decide my response with care. This was a new fork in the road.

I met Varadarajan first thing next morning, and informed him that I would be happy to accept the offer of the chairman and TT, to move to manufacturing. It was a deeply wrenching decision for me, to give up my love and passion for research, but I had given thought to a number of potential outcomes in the future, in the context of the previous day's conversation in the chairman's office. In 1970, I had a reasonable understanding about HLL and Unilever, and decided that life had to move on. This was probably the most crucial decision I was to take during my career with HLL!

Manufacturing and Beyond

After speaking to Varadarajan, I sought an appointment and went to meet TT, the technical director, in the head office, and conveyed to him my decision. He then informed me that I would be joining the Bombay factory, as the 'laundry packing manager', to start in manufacturing. I was asked to first meet K.P.V. Menon, general manager of the Bombay factory, and after reporting to him, take up my new assignment. My job role was, hierarchy-wise, a step down in my career, but that did not bother me, since I had made up my mind that I had to move on, and that was that. My salary, grade and perquisites remained as they already were in R&D. Everything moved so fast that I did not even have time to bid goodbye to my colleagues in research.

I was taken around for a conducted tour of the factory, by Susim Datta, senior production manager, who was a couple of years senior to me in the company, and to whom I would be reporting in my new role. We are about the same age. The next day, I took formal charge of the laundry packing department from Mr Thombre, who was to move to another department in the factory. The laundry manager's office was a large wooden oblong, box-like structure, surrounded by glass panes and situated in the middle of the shop floor. From this raised office, one could see the Sunlight and Lifebuoy soap production lines. From heading as section manager in R&D, where I had three people reporting to me, I was suddenly in charge of the largest, labour-intensive department in the Bombay factory, with approximately 500 workmen (and women), besides the technical and manufacturing supervisors. The laundry packing department worked in three eight-hour shifts, seven days a week. The day shift included women soap packers, but most of the heavy-lifting was done by men. I first met and spent some time listening to veteran supervisors, Mathew, Tellis and Zakaria, the three shift foremen who walked me through the various shop floor operations, and within a few days, we got to know each other well. In a couple of weeks' time, I felt well settled, enjoying my new, mid-career, move to manufacturing. It did not take me long to get a good grip of the basics of soap manufacturing.

The soap factory was located on two cavernous floors. On the upper floor was the soap-making department, called the pan room, where pre-heated oil blends were saponified, in large stirred tanks called soap pans, by gradual addition of aqueous caustic soda. The process of 'finishing', or completion, of a vat of soap was more of an art, mastered over the years by the very competent pan room shift supervisors, Sangam, Patel and Tukaram, assisted by experienced pan room workmen. After saponification, the liquid soap was next 'washed' with brine, while still quite hot and the molten 'washed' soap was finally pumped into 'finished' holding tanks. From the holding tanks, liquid soap is pumped to the ground floor and transferred on top of five vertical scraped surfaces, giant spray dryers (Italian-made Mazzonis). The dried soap flakes are constantly scraped while descending into the conical bottom of the Mazzonis, and then extruded through long, chilled water-cooled, spiral scraper/extruders, flowing out as a long bar which is automatically cut into tablets by rotating auto cutters, stamped, wrapped and finally manually packed, into cardboard boxes, and placed on wooden pallets. The loaded pallets are next transferred, by lift trucks, to the storage warehouse.

The laundry packing department, with the five Mazzoni dryers and packing machines, were spread out across a long shop floor. The roof was a long corrugated ceiling. A foot bridge, running across the manufacturing and packing operations, on the shop floor, was used by supervisors and engineers to monitor the continuous operations, and troubleshoot when required. I frequently joined the supervisors to watch the operations, working like clockwork. Any machine stoppages or repairs were immediately attended to by the engineering staff. Each manufacturing line had a weekly service schedule, and at all other times, the lines worked non-stop, 24/7, meeting quality and output targets. The objective was not only to meet, but exceed targets in every shift, seven days a week. Walking amongst the machines, one could feel a sense of pride and ownership amongst the workers, supervisors and engineers, across the well-operated laundry packing shop floor. I soon got into the spirit and rhythm of the laundry packing department and the shift employees. The work environment exuded pride, especially when there were no interruptions, which was easier to sense, rather than describe.

My wood-and-glass, air-conditioned office cabin, next to the shop floor, provided a little privacy and a clear view of the shop floor. The sound and rhythm of the shop floor machinery was somewhat dampened by a plywood ceiling covering the top of my office. In the office, I enjoyed an occasional break to have a cup of tea and sometimes smoke a cigarette. The office also provided some privacy for meetings with my supervisors and engineers, and when necessary, with the union leaders.

Looking back to my move from R&D to manufacturing, although seamless, my role had changed as chalk and cheese. I had taken to manufacturing rather smoothly. During the initial days, walking around the shop floor and getting to gradually know individual workers, and learning the ropes from the supervisors, seemed valuable to me. I enjoyed meeting and talking to people, besides being keen to get to know them as individuals, and occasionally talking about homes and families. I always stayed late after office hours, especially if there was a stoppage for any reason, such as a machine breakdown, shortage of liquid soap feed from the pan room, etc. I would stand along with the shift supervisors and engineers, until full production resumed, before leaving the factory. I frequently spent time with the supervisors over tea, in the employees' canteen and we got to know each other rather well very soon. It helped that I had moved into manufacturing at short notice besides my innate friendliness, when it came to interacting with people. Above all else, the goal that bonded me with the workers and supervisors was the daily pressure to meet or exceed targets—every shift, every day and every week. Narasimham, who was my soap factory engineering colleague, in charge of services to soap packing departments, was very friendly and cooperative. Normally, we met at least once a day for a chat over a cup of tea, in my laundry packing office. A couple of times, every week, I would drive down to the factory, at night after dinner, and just walk through the department, to say hello to the shift supervisor and encourage them, hoping that production would exceed plans. I would chat with them over a cup of tea, before driving back home. Although it was not my intention, word did get around about my frequent, unannounced visits. In the event of breakdowns or stoppage of production, I remained in the factory until normalcy was restored—no matter how long it took. Soon, I got to be known as tough and demanding, but also as a helpful and fair individual. I came to know about this after a while, when my supervisor colleagues shared with me their views as colleagues.

At the time, there were two senior union leaders working in the soap factory, named Babu and Raju. Shortly after I had taken charge of the laundry packing department, both dropped in to meet me and introduce themselves. I invited them to my glass-and-wood office, ordered tea for the three of us and offered them cigarettes. Neither smoked. We could be seen from the shop floor. Between us, the ice was broken during our first meeting. Babu and Raju had apparently come to check me out as the new and rather unusual laundry packing manager, and confirm the gossip going around, about the new manager, with no prior experience or training in manufacturing. During our first meeting, I patiently listened, as they narrated their hold on workers and their heroic past accomplishments as union leaders. Over time, we got to know each other, and their meeting me was no longer a curiosity. All through my short stint in the Bombay factory, I did not encounter any awkwardness, with either the workers or the union leaders. I had started to enjoy the change, but remained nostalgic about my young days in research.

After just a few months in the laundry packing department, I was transferred to the pan room, and designated as the soap making manager. Normally, managers spent at least a couple of years in each department. Soap making was a complex 'art', which could only be mastered, I was informed by supervisor Sangam, after years of experience. Sangam was the senior supervisor of pan room and a devotee of Satya Saibaba. He took a personal interest in me, and with lots of patience, taught me the art of soap making. We became good friends. Although I don't think I ever became an expert 'soap maker'!

Birth of Nivedita and Becoming
a Soap 'Expert'

On 18 September 1970, Connie gave birth to our bonny daughter, in Calcutta. I happened to be in Calcutta on assignment, and was absolutely thrilled to get the first glimpse of our first born. Connie's dad, Mesho, and her mother, Mashi, lived close to the army's Command Hospital, where Mesho also happened to be in command in 1970, when Nivedita was born. Connie returned by air to Bombay, after a couple of months, along with Nivedita, in a baby hand carrier. Baba and I had gone to receive them at the airport. After Connie's flight landed, Baba was so excited that he walked across the tarmac, to greet his first grandchild. This was at a time well before the modernization of airports, choice of airlines and stringent security protocols. I watched from the terminal, Baba with the child carrier and Connie, as they walked to the terminal building. Connie looked very tired, Nivé had cried almost continuously on the flight and was still wailing and Baba with a big grin on his face, carrying his first granddaughter, it all remains etched in my memory.

In 1971, when I had been the pan room manager only for a few months, general factory manager K.P.V. Menon one day asked me to go to the head office to see TT. When I met TT at the head office, he told me that I was to go to Calcutta, to assist HLL's Garden Reach factory, to sort out severe problems in the manufacturing and packing of laundry soap. I was completely taken by surprise on being given such an assignment. I was also a bit intrigued wondering, given my brief exposure to manufacturing, why I was being sent to Calcutta to sort out what sounded like a rather serious manufacturing problem! At the time, I had been in the Bombay factory for less than a year.

The news of my troubleshooting assignment to Calcutta had already spread in the Bombay factory, even before I returned to my office after meeting TT. KPV obviously had prior knowledge. He wished me well and told me confidently that it should not take me more than a month to sort out the Calcutta soap problems and then to return to Bombay. I never thought of asking him how he had come to this conclusion, that I was going to sort out the 'problem' in a month.

The next day I flew to Calcutta, and was driven from the airport, in an office car, to the Grand Hotel. I checked in and then proceeded, right away, to the HLL's Garden Reach factory, which I had not been to before.

The factory general manager, Bertie Pereira, and senior production manager, Susim Datta, had both been in charge for a while. Susim had been transferred from Bombay, and he had been succeeded in Bombay by Gaja Borker.

I was kept waiting for more than an hour before meeting Bertie. I soon realized that both Bertie and Susim were not at all pleased that TT had sent me, as an 'expert' to sort out the Garden Reach 'soap problem', considering my brief period in the Bombay factory!

My meeting with Bertie, after having been kept waiting, was rather cold and formal. He summoned Susim, his deputy, and asked him to take me to the soap factory so that, as he cynically put it, I may 'solve' the problems they were facing. Neither of them seemed at all pleased by my sudden appearance. Both of them were wearing ties and full-sleeved shirts as senior managers, as was the dress code prevailing at the time. I was in my usual half-sleeved shirt with an open collar. The laundry shop floor at Garden Reach was similar to the one in Bombay, although a bit smaller. It had three Mazzoni spray dryers compared to five in Bombay, and six packing lines.

While the shop floor was reasonably clean, there were piles of soap scrap all over the floor and the three Mazzoni spray dryers were shut. Aniruddha Mullick, the laundry packing manager, had a small glass-framed office at one end of the shop floor. Chatterjee, the engineer, and Salim and Maqbool, the shift supervisors, had all gathered to meet me. I had not met any of them before. Datta left me with Mullick and departed. Laundry packing manager Aniruddha Mullick had risen from the ranks, and was very well-regarded and respected. The soap factory engineer, Chatterjee, and the pan room manager, Arun Banerji, were both very experienced as well. The Calcutta manufacturing managers and staff were friendly and very welcoming. My meeting with Mullick and Chatterjee started with them briefing me about the production problems. During our meeting, we had hot cups of sweet tea and Bengali samosas from the factory canteen, which were very tasty. I had not been offered lunch. Our conversation was friendly and the managers made me feel very welcome, compared to my icy reception by Bertie and Susim.

Arun, Mullick and Chatterjee very well understood, as did Bertie and Susim, what the production problem was all about. Soap is ideally manufactured using beef tallow. Since beef tallow import was restricted by the government, the oil mix which HLL was using for soap making was instead made up of palm oil, coconut oil and exotic minor oils such as castor, rice bran, sal, etc. This was the era of severe import restrictions and HLL's R&D lab was working closely with the factories to introduce novel minor oils, as an import substitution measure. The prime consideration was to choose a cost-effective mix of hydrogenated oils, to sustain profitability, a challenge compounded by government price controls. Cost-effective oil-mix policy was guided by the purchasing department and scrutinized by TT's senior colleagues in the head office. The oil mix used for the Calcutta soap production happened to contain a high level of castor oil, which was difficult to hydrogenate. The oils for soap making were processed and hydrogenated at HLL's Shyamnagar factory, which was located about 20 miles from Calcutta city.

Since all these factors were already known, I was bewildered as to what else I could do to solve the Calcutta soap manufacturing difficulties! After spending a couple of days in the soap factory, I went to visit the Shyamnagar factory and meet Anil Chakravarty, the factory manager. Anilda, as he was universally known, subsequently became one of my closest personal friends.

I spent close to a month in Calcutta, mostly at Garden Reach, and eventually the only way the manufacturing problem was resolved was by changing the fat mix to one which was slightly more expensive but process-compatible. No miracle here! During my stay, I made several very good friends in the Garden Reach and Shyamnagar factories. Calcutta, at that time, was going through the final phases of the West Bengal government brutally suppressing the Naxalite movement. One frequently saw dead bodies lying on the roadside. It was all very, very gruesome, and we all travelled in car pools, to and from the factory, in order to feel safer, in numbers.

At the end of one month, I returned to Bombay and moved from the soap factory as the head of the detergent department, in 1972. I, as well as my colleagues, were surprised at the frequency of my transfers. Martin Lobo was my new deputy, in the detergent department. Chairman Rajadhyaksha visited the factory one day, to enquire amongst other things why the detergent unit's utilization was not up to scratch. Prem Chadha was still the detergent manager and I was about to take over from him. The chairman was, basically, a very thoughtful and polite person. He had graduated in chemical engineering from MIT and was recruited in London. He succeeded Prakash Tandon in 1968 as the chairman and retired from HLL in 1973. After retiring, Vasant was appointed as a member of the Planning Commission by the Government of India. He was succeeded by TT as chairman, while David Webb continued as the vice-chairman.

After a year as head of the detergent unit, I was promoted to the next level, as a grade-1 manager, and appointed as head of the development department of HLL. Later that year, I had to again go to Calcutta. In the meantime, Bertie had been succeeded as general manager of Garden Reach by Kachru, a venerable, well-regarded engineer. Susim continued as Kachru's deputy. Garden Reach factory was in turmoil due to severe labour unrest. It was not clear at the time why I was being sent to Calcutta again!

The Garden Reach Workers' Union was in a state of severe agitation, led by an outsider, a militant Congress trade union leader, Laxmi Kanta Bose. Bose was, in turn, being challenged, by an upcoming and extremely reckless young Congress trade union leader, Samir Roy, who was out to grab the leadership of Garden Reach factory. The factory had been brought to a halt by a strike called by Bose, while Samir Roy preached violence.

On my second visit to Calcutta, I once again stayed at the Grand Hotel for the next several weeks, and remained a silent onlooker of the efforts of Ranjan Banerjee, personnel director; Shamdas Gurshahani, director, legal; Kachru, the new general factory manager; assisted by Prakash Ram and Sunil Bose, factory personnel managers, to resolve the labour dispute. There were also non-stop, daily discussions with Laxmi Kanta Bose, in Ranjan Banerjee's suite, to find ways to reach an agreement, and restart operations at Garden Reach. I frankly had no role or title, except to sit and watch the proceedings. After endless negotiations, the dispute was ultimately resolved, and the strike was called off. The Garden Reach factory reopened, Datta was transferred and returned to Bombay and I was appointed as deputy general manager, under Kachru, at the Garden Reach factory.

After a month of my appointment, Connie and our infant daughter, Nivedita, joined me, and for the time being, we stayed at the Grand Hotel in Calcutta. Not long after, we moved into a spacious old company flat, in Jubilee Court on Shakespeare Sarani. Our second daughter, Amrita, was born on 27 September 1974. I used to be always apprehensive of being transferred to Calcutta, but actually, we began to enjoy our new situation. Calcutta turned out to be a very friendly city. The Garden Reach labour problem had been dealt with comprehensively, and once again peace, production and amity had been restored at the factory. But that is a different story by itself.

After a few months, Kachru moved to Jammu, in 1974, to build HLL's new detergent factory. TT had succeeded Rajadhyaksha as the chairman, in 1973, and Herbert Barr was sent by Unilever to succeed TT as HLL's technical director. I succeeded Kachru as the general manager, Calcutta. Anilda moved from the Shyamnagar factory, to take over as senior production manager at Garden Reach. Aniruddha Mullick, the laundry packing manager, was appointed factory manager in Shyamnagar. Everything seemed to move at a fast and furious pace, and in the right direction.

Calcutta: 1973–76

After my brief experience at the University of Kalyani in 1962, I had promised myself that I would never work or live in Calcutta. However, I had to face such an eventuality in 1973. I had just been promoted as the development manager in Bombay, when I was told of my transfer to the Garden Reach factory, in Calcutta. My designation was yet to be announced. In 1973, Kachru, the head of engineering in the Bombay factory, was appointed as the general manager of Calcutta, replacing Bertie Pereira. Bertie and his deputy Datta were transferred back to Bombay, in the middle of a very severe industrial unrest in the Garden Reach factory, in 1973. It also happened to be the period during which the Naxal movement in West Bengal continued to be systematically decimated, by the heavy hand of the Congress government in power, under Chief Minister Siddhartha Shankar Ray. After general elections, trade unions tend to realign themselves with the political party in power in the state. Sudhangsu Ray, the union leader in the Garden Reach factory, had shifted the union's loyalties to the Congress as well. The external trade union leaders, Laxmi Kanta Bose and Samir Roy, were also 'Congressmen'.

After a long and drawn-out strike and endless discussions between HLL and union leader Bose, for days on end, a settlement was finally signed between the Congress union and HLL. The next day, the Garden Reach factory reopened and to everyone's relief, the machines, once again, began to hum. My designation was deputy general manager, reporting to the general manager, Kachru. After a long strike, even after manufacturing recommenced, the work environment and the relations between workers and managers remained strained. Due to the internal trade union rivalry between the new Congress Union and the previous Communist Union, the environment within the factory remained sullen.

I continued to stay at the Grand Hotel temporarily, and formally took charge of my new role the day the factory recommenced operations after the strike. Virtually everyone in Garden Reach factory had met or interacted with me, during my 'troubleshooting' visit in 1971. In early 1974, Connie and Nivedita joined me in Calcutta, and after staying for a few weeks at the Grand Hotel, we moved to a company-allotted flat in Jubilee Court on Harrington Street (Shakespeare Sarani).

In the aftermath of the long years of the socially and economically ruinous Naxalite violence, the overall environment in Calcutta continued to be tense. Threats of kidnapping and senseless killings were reported virtually every day. Nivedita had to be driven to her new school accompanied by a bodyguard, in the car.

Samir Roy, a leader in the Youth Congress and one of the several lumpen troublemakers, captured the leadership of the workers' union at Garden Reach factory, from the ageing Laxmi Kanta Bose, with whom the management had signed the recent agreement. Roy and his fellow cohorts started freely moving around the factory, threatening managers and especially workers belonging to the Communist union. He not only carried a gun but was also escorted in an open jeep, by armed 'bodyguards', driving around the factory, without permission or consent of the management. Widespread workplace and social indiscipline were serious and threatening leftovers from the years of Naxalite violence and lawlessness in West Bengal. Indiscipline had apparently spread amongst employees, even before the long shutdown of the factory. Very soon, after the settlement between management and Laxmi Kanta Bose, and the factory reopened, Kachru was transferred to Jammu, to build the new detergent factory of HLL. Before I had time to settle, I succeeded him as the general manager.

Anil Chakravarty moved from Shyamnagar to succeed me as deputy general manager and Nirmal Sen took charge as factory manager, at Shyamnagar. The day after I took charge as the general manager, Samir Roy sent word that he wished to meet me. I sent my reply conveying that I would meet him, provided he deposited his pistol at the main gate and left his 'bodyguards' outside the main gate of the factory. Samir Roy flatly refused to follow the pre-conditions, at first, so I had the factory gates shut and locked. Very soon, he agreed to deposit his gun at the gate and leave his companions outside the factory. He then once again sought a one-to-one meeting with me. I sent word for him to come to my office. The news of a gun-less, cohort-less, and jeep-less Samir Roy walking to meet me in my office immediately spread all around the factory and even in the neighbouring locality. That incident turned out to be the beginning of the end of Samir Roy. I had not realized that the episode would turn out the way it did. We had a polite meeting over a cup of tea. Roy was keen to find out what sort of person I was.

Our stay, at Jubilee Court, was brief but very enjoyable. Chandi Basu, the Calcutta branch manager of HLL and his wife, Rama, were our next-door neighbours. Our flats were old and spacious. I had first met Chandida in Bombay in 1962, and we had become friends. Within a few months, Chandida, as he was popularly known, was succeeded by Inder Singh. Inder and his wife, Shagufta, became our new friendly neighbours. After our brief stay in Jubilee Court, we moved to another company flat on New Road, Alipore. Our second daughter, Amrita, was born on 26 September 1974, in Calcutta. Our short stay in Calcutta, 1973–75, was eventful and enjoyable. We were saddened when it was time to move back to Bombay. Our time in Calcutta had been very exciting and happy. My apprehension of working in Calcutta was wrong.

Anilda (A.C. Chakravarty, deputy general manager) and I became not only very good friends, but we also made a formidable team. To deal effectively with our wayward union leader Samir Roy, I had to interact closely with the West Bengal government, as well as pull some powerful, local political strings. The union leadership of a violence-prone Samir Roy was soon brought to an end. The factory returned to its former amicable environment, while Samir Roy soon faded away from the scene. Before I returned to Bombay, the manufacturing output, productivity and cordial human relations reached unprecedented heights, in an environment of peace and discipline, which lasted many years. Prakash Ram and Sunil Basu, our HR team, must get most of the credit for the results we achieved. They worked diligently, behind the scenes, to create an excellent and sustainable situation. I learnt a lot about human relations watching and working with Prakash Ram and Sunil Basu.

In addition to Anilda, Prakash Ram and Sunil Basu, there was a group of excellent managers at the Garden Reach factory. Chief Engineer K.K. Nayar, Senior Production Manager Debu Bhattacharya, the team of shop floor and services managers, as well as our internal union leaders, helped transform Garden Reach, from a perennially trouble-prone factory of HLL to one of its most productive and reliable units. It is worth mentioning here that in due course, the Calcutta factory proved to be a major strength, to sustain HLL during one of the most corrosive strikes in Bombay during the 1980s. Sadly, due to prolonged union agitation, the Bombay factory had to be shut down permanently.

In 1975, I had to go to the UK, to attend a Unilever management programme. Connie accompanied me during this trip. I got to know Prof. Ram Charan, the famous management consultant, who was one of the faculties of the management programme I was attending. The day Connie and I returned to Bombay, on 25 June 1975, Emergency was declared in India, by Prime Minister Indira Gandhi. The impact of the Emergency became progressively evident, due to the coercive and draconian measures. Prem Chadha had moved from Ghaziabad to Calcutta, to take charge of Garden Reach during my absence. Prem soon succeeded me, as the general manager of Calcutta, when I moved to Bombay, as the general manager of the Bombay factory, in January 1976.

I must admit that Connie and I were a bit sad to be leaving Calcutta. We had made some good friends in the city; we also enjoyed shopping together, every week, at the well-known Jagu Babu's Bazar. We patronized a particular retail shop, one vegetable vendor and one fishmonger in that market. These became our regular weekly shopping stops. On our last weekly shopping visit to 'Jagu Babu', before returning to Bombay, we thanked and took leave of our regular shopkeeper and fish vendor. Like typically sentimental Bengalis, they refused to accept payment for the goods we had bought on this, our last visit. Each of them insisted that they had earned enough from us and were sad to see us leave. We experienced a depth of genuineness and feeling, typical amongst people of that city, as we had not experienced anywhere else where we had lived, either before or since, and which we were going to miss.

1977–80

In June 1977, Susim Datta and I were appointed to the board of HLL; Datta as director responsible for chemicals and I as the technical director of HLL. Amrita and Nivedita were enrolled in Cathedral School. After returning to Bombay, Connie completed her BEd degree successfully, but decided not to pursue a career in teaching. Life quickly became more busy and hectic, while time seemed to be flying fast. In the era of strict government controls, virtually on everything, our emoluments as board directors were very modest; however, certain permissible perquisites, such as medical expenses from HLL, provided some relief, especially the medical assistance, including those of ageing parents. My time as a director on the board was relatively short. In 1980, I succeeded Thomas as HLL's executive chairman.

The company was already facing serious and growing labour unrest in the Bombay factory. Datta Samant, the most prominent trade union leader at the time, had already forced the closure of Bombay's more than 100-year-old textile industry. It was rumoured at the time that Samant had colluded with some of the mill owners, as the land on which the mills were situated had become more valuable, compared to the textile business. Datta Samant rapidly went on to capture the unions of several other large companies around Bombay. Several companies were rumoured to have buckled and settled with Samant. Companies which could not afford to settle, or would not buckle, shut down their operations in Bombay, permanently. Hundreds of thousands of workers lost their jobs and livelihood, and the Maharashtra government seemed helpless to rein in this marauding trade union leader. Hindustan Lever was a rare exception, to stand up to and confront Datta Samant successfully.

The Emergency imposed by Indira Gandhi in 1975 was lifted, and fresh elections were held in 1977. Mrs Gandhi's Congress party was soundly defeated and the Janata Party, which was cobbled together on a 'common' platform of opposition parties, who had come together under the guidance of Jaiprakash Narayan, won a resounding victory and formed the new government. Morarji Desai was designated as the compromise prime minister of the new Janata Party, with a cabinet composed of candidates belonging to the constituents of the Janata Party, including some sulking prime ministerial aspirants. It was not a propitious start and had been only reluctantly agreed to, by the persuasive efforts of Jaiprakash Narayan. Indira Gandhi lost her own seat from Rae Bareli along with her son Sanjay, who had become a rather reckless, extra-constitutional power centre during the Emergency, and began to be hounded in the courts of law by the new Janata government for the excesses during the Emergency. The Janata government was so single-mindedly and visibly pursuing to punish the Gandhis that the new government's actions began to be seen, by the public, as spiteful acts of revenge. The infighting within the Janata Party itself eventually led to the downfall of its government within two years. At the end of 1979, fresh general elections were held. Indira Gandhi and the Congress party returned to power with a thumping majority, and Mrs Gandhi, once again, took over, as the prime minister of India, in January 1980.

On the home front, Connie in her own silent ways, looked after all our domestic affairs, my parents as well, and Nivedita and Amrita's education, as they grew up, happily. On some days, during the week, we visited my parents, who lived in Worli, and especially on weekends.

In 1978, we had acquired our first black-and-white television, when we lived in Alhambra—TV in India then broadcast news and entertainment by a single state-managed broadcaster, called Doordarshan. Towards the end of 1978, Unilever had announced that TT was to be appointed as executive director on the board of Unilever. This was a first for a non-European and a unique honour and recognition for TT, as well as HLL. TT moved to London in 1979 and joined the Unilever board, while still continuing, in charge of HLL, as its chairman! This was a rather unusual arrangement. All through 1979, TT visited India very frequently. As always, he was very competent, ambitious and highly goal-driven. It was his persistent and relentless efforts which persuaded the Indian government, during Emergency, to lift pernicious price controls on HLL products.

After the easing of price control, HLL was able to recover from the debilitating losses it was suffering. He also persuaded Unilever, in the face of serious doubts on their part, to permit HLL to make a very large investment in its chemicals business. The proposal was to manufacture Sodium tripolyphosphate, a major ingredient used in its detergent products. This investment was essential, to fulfil the draconian FERA (Foreign Exchange Regulation Act) rules and meet 'high technology' goals, which would legally entitle Unilever to retain 51 per cent shareholding in HLL. This exercise, to meet FERA conditions, turned out to be a long-drawn-out affair. Majority shareholding by Unilever was strenuously opposed by many Congress, as well as Communist, politicians and bureaucrats, until the end of 1980. The circumstances which satisfactorily brought the FERA saga to a legitimate closure are touched upon in another episode, described later.

The Herbert Barr Episode

Herbert came to Mumbai in 1973, from Unilever, London, to join the board of HLL, as the technical director, in place of Thomas, who had just succeeded Vasant Rajadhyaksha as the chairman of Hindustan Lever.

Herbert, a New Zealander, had first moved from Unilever, New Zealand, to Unilever Plc, London. He was normally relaxed and had a cheerful disposition. After joining Hindustan Lever, he was surprised by the long office hours, as well as the work culture and austere lifestyle of managers in India.

In 1973, I had just succeeded Kachru as the general manager in Calcutta. Herbert and I got along very well from our very first meeting, and he looked forward to his trips to Calcutta. However, he was always terrified during our road trips to and back from the HLL Shyamnagar factory. In order to overcome his tension over the chaotic road traffic between Calcutta and Shyamnagar, I suggested he may try putting on eyeshades. With eyeshades, Herbert felt relaxed and we carried on our normal conversation during our Shyamnagar trips.

In the winter of 1974, Mrs Barr accompanied Herbert on one of his periodic visits. Anilda (Anil Chakrabarty), my colleague and deputy at the Garden Reach factory, arranged a boat ride along the Ganga for the Barrs, along with us and our spouses. We spent a very enjoyable sunny winter morning, sailing along the Ganga, enjoying a picnic hamper.

The following day, Connie and I had arranged to host a dinner, at our home, for the Barrs, to meet a few of our colleagues and their spouses. Herbert and I were at the Garden Reach factory that morning. Connie had taken Mrs Paddy Barr for some sightseeing and shopping.

Herbert and I, as usual, walked around the factory, visiting the different departments, briefly chatting with the department heads and supervisors. As usual, at around 1 p.m., we joined all the managers for lunch. After lunch, Herbert and I walked down to my office for a relaxed cup of coffee.

While Herbert and I were chatting over coffee, suddenly in mid-sentence, Herbert slowly slumped and rested his head on my desk. I immediately summoned the factory medical officer, who rushed in with his aids, and began checking Herbert's pulse and breathing, and informed me that Herbert had passed away, apparently due to massive heart failure.

The news of Herbert's demise had quickly spread across the factory.

I had just witnessed a stunning and unimaginable tragedy. The factory doctor had already urgently summoned a city cardiac specialist and an ambulance. Both reached the factory promptly.

As expected, the cardiac specialist confirmed the cause of Herbert's sudden and shocking demise.

I had already called and informed Connie that Herbert had suddenly taken ill and asked if she could come to the factory, with Mrs Barr, right away.

In the meantime, I had also called and informed Chairman Thomas of this most tragic event. The factory had come to a standstill, and the workers had gathered in stunned silence on the lawns in front of my office.

Herbert's body was moved to a morgue soon after Connie and Mrs Barr had reached the factory. We also contacted and informed their son in New Zealand. He immediately made arrangements to travel to Calcutta and reach the next day.

The next morning, Aspi Modi, one of HLL's board members, travelled to Calcutta, and we held a prayer meeting, along with all the employees, of the factory, in memory of dear Herbert. The prayer meeting in Herbert's memory was a deeply sad and silent event. Within a very short span of time, Herbert had endeared himself to everyone in HLL, by his warm and outgoing nature. We were going to miss him dearly.

After the prayer meeting, the workers returned to their departments and restarted operations. Mrs Barr and her son decided that Herbert be buried in the old English cemetery of Calcutta. A solemn funeral service was held the following morning, and Herbert was laid to rest.

We were all still in a state of shock, and the impact of the tragedy was yet to be fully absorbed. Arrangements were made for Mrs Barr to return to Bombay and then on to New Zealand, along with their son.

After a few weeks, I received a deeply touching letter from Mrs Barr, along with Herbert's favourite chemistry textbook, which Mrs Barr informed in her letter that Herbert would have very much wished for me to have. It will always be one of my prized possessions.

Herbert Barr's sudden death has left a very deep and lifelong impression on me, which I felt fit to record for posterity.

Mother Teresa:
A Saint in My Lifetime (1973)

In 1974, while I was posted in Calcutta, one morning, I received a phone call from Chairman T. Thomas. He enquired if I had heard of one Mother Teresa. I had not, but told the chairman I would find out and get back to him. Chandi Basu, the Calcutta branch manager, helped me locate Mother Teresa's address. A few days later, Chandida (elder brother in Bengali) and I, went to meet Mother, at the Mother House of the Missionaries of Charity. While we waited to see her, in walked a diminutive and slightly bent elderly lady, in a blue-bordered white sari. This was Mother Teresa of the Missionaries of Charity, in person. We introduced ourselves and explained to her that we worked in HLL and that we had come to learn about her activities, on behalf of our chairman, Mr T. Thomas.

Mother responded enthusiastically and informed us that the ideal way to learn about the activities of the Missionaries of Charity would be, if we were able to spare the time, to spend the day with her, as she went about her work. Basu and I readily agreed and accompanied Mother on her daily rounds. First, we drove to the 'House for the Dying', which is located right next to the famous Kalighat Temple. The enormous place is a hospice for the poor, who had been abandoned on the streets of Calcutta. The House for the Dying was a neat and spotlessly clean cavernous hall. The environment in this hall exuded peace and silence. It is dedicated to the care of a large number of inmates, lying on very clean beds, in completely aseptic surroundings. There were close to a hundred beds, and a number of young doctors and sisters of the Missionary of Charity were busy attending to the seriously ill and some who were nearing death. It was a deeply moving experience for Chandida and me. No one fussed around Mother or us during our visit. We then spent the next few hours going around with Mother and visited some other locations, which were all under the care of the Sisters of the Missionaries of Charity. One of my most stunning and deeply transformative experiences was our visit with Mother Teresa to a corrugated tin-roofed shelter with open sides, occupying a broad sidewalk near Sealdah station. A number of Sisters of the Missionaries of Charity were busily engaged in ministering to a large number of children of different ages. Mother told us that this place was a day-care shelter, for the children of beggars, plying in and around the Sealdah station. There was a group of children in one corner of the shed, attending a study class being conducted by one of the Sisters, at the other end there were groups of children of different ages, being supervised by other Sisters attending to them. In another corner, there were a few children who were ill and they were being cared for by a different group of Sisters. One unusually frail baby amongst this sick group appeared seriously ill. Mother Teresa sat down on the floor and picked up this sick baby on her lap. Then she summoned me to squat next to her and gently placed the sick infant on my lap. At first, I felt very flustered, not quite knowing what I was supposed to do. That was when Mother told me, 'Dr Ganguly, the infant on your lap is dying; please smile, so that she carries your smile as her last mortal memory, along with her, to heaven.' While the child was on my lap, I watched the life of the infant slowly ebbing away, and shortly the baby died on my lap. I was stunned by this experience and completely overwhelmed. I had never before encountered any incident such as this, or have ever since. I was in tears.

After spending the rest of the day with Mother Teresa, going around Calcutta, I returned home. I related to Connie about my encounter with Mother Teresa and the events of the day. My first experience of meeting Mother Teresa has left a lifelong impact on me. Whenever I recall the events of that first day, I always feel a sense of reverence, which has remained deeply rooted in me ever since. Also, since that day, Connie and I have remained committed to our lifelong attachment with the Missionaries of Charity. It began in Calcutta, continued in Bombay. We remained in contact with Mother Teresa until her passing. While we lived in Calcutta, Connie regularly visited the Mother House and spent time assisting Sisters to prepare packets of medicine, meant for the different locations, in and around the city. Mother had set up a large place for taking care of lepers, in Tiljala on the outskirts of Calcutta, as well as a number of other homes, for the poor and destitute. As well as several other locations, in India as well as abroad.

After we moved back to Bombay in January 1976, our interaction with Mother and Missionaries of Charity entered another phase. Mother persuaded Chairman Thomas to provide a space in a central location of Bombay city to set up a shelter and care home for the poor, the abandoned on the roadside and the sick of the city. We located an old and very infrequently used set of warehouses of HLL during our search, which Mother Teresa felt were well suited for what she had in mind. My colleagues in the Bombay factory assisted in excellently sprucing up a couple of warehouses, in 1976. The location in the congested lane called Sankil Street, in central Bombay, was to be named as Asha Daan, and inaugurated by her on 8 January 1977. Mr Thomas, I and a large number of our factory employees and several residents of the locality came for the event. Asha Daan was dedicated to the sick, the deformed and abandoned, including infants and children, who were to be looked after with love and care by a team of Sisters of the Missionaries of Charity. Asha Daan was their new home, in Bombay. We also spruced up a smaller shed, and converted it into a residence for the Sisters of Asha Daan, along with a chapel, for their daily prayers. The place has since expanded and now accommodates over 400 men, women and children, who are sick, deformed and abandoned, but cared for with love and dedication by the Sisters of the Missionaries of Charity, and it is maintained by Hindustan Lever.

I am convinced that our family has been truly blessed, by the prayers of Mother Teresa and our association with her during her lifetime, and ever since by our association with the Missionaries of Charity. This is one of the most important episodes in my lifetime. As a family, we are truly blessed, by the love and prayers, showered on us, by Mother Teresa.

My father passed away on 7 January 1991, and Ma on 13 June 2001. On their death anniversaries every year, a special meal is served to all the inmates of Asha Daan, in my parents' memory. Our association with Asha Daan will continue for as long as we live, and that of HUL, hopefully, forever.

N.B.: While my work on this manuscript was in progress, Connie tragically passed away on 28 October 2019. Our daughters and I plan to mark her remarkable life by arranging a special meal at Asha Daan every year on her birthday as well.

The Final Decade (1980–90)

It may be appropriate to briefly recall that in 1970, I had moved from R&D to manufacturing. In 1973, I was transferred to Calcutta and returned to Bombay in 1976. I joined the board of HLL as the technical director in 1977. Towards the end of 1979, I was informed that I was to attend a management programme, at the Sloan School in MIT, in February 1980. I had not attended any specialized management courses earlier, other than within HLL and Unilever. I quite looked forward to attending the MIT, Sloan School, programme.

On my way to Boston in February 1980, I was requested to stop in London for a couple of days to meet TT, Chairman Sir David Orr, chairman of the Overseas Committee Frazer Sedcole, and a few others in the Unilever House, London. After reaching London on the appointed date, I first met TT. TT was unusually congenial as well as in an uncharacteristic mellow mood. To my utter and complete surprise, TT informed me that he had recommended to Sir David Orr that I should succeed him as the next chairman of HLL. I was stunned by this unexpected news. I suddenly recalled those brief moments, after my PhD oral examinations, when Dr Robert Whitney had shaken my hand and addressed me, for the first time, as Dr Ganguly, in 1961.

After hearing this most unexpected news from TT, and in my rather happy and excited state of mind, I next went to see the Unilever chairman, Sir David Orr. He was always extremely courteous and a very pleasant person. Sir David had served in the British Army, on the Eastern Front, during World War II, and was a recipient of the Victoria Cross. After the war, Sir David Orr had joined Unilever, and was appointed as the vice-chairman of Lever Brothers in India. Connie and I had spent time travelling in India with Sir David and his wife, Phoebe, during Sir David's trip to India in 1979.

As I sat down, across Sir David, in his office, on the sixth floor of Unilever House, the chairman congratulated me, officially conveying my appointment as the next chairman of HLL. Following my meeting with Sir David, I phoned Connie in Bombay, to share the exciting and totally unexpected development. Connie, by nature, was not excitable, but on hearing that I would be the next chairman of HLL, she felt very happy for me. I cannot recall when the official announcement in HLL was going to be made, but for the time being, it remained confidential.

That evening, TT had invited me to his home in Roehampton, for dinner. His wife, Susy, is a wonderful human being and a genuinely caring person. I spent an enjoyable evening with them.

The next day, I travelled from London to Boston, and from the airport to Dedham, a suburb of Boston. Dedham was MIT's off-campus estate, for residential courses. Individual rooms were allocated to each participant for our stay, during the thirteen weeks' duration of the programme. I very much enjoyed attending the lectures and participating in the discussions, on the MIT campus and a few in Dedham. I found the experience novel, intensive and enriching. I got to know two of the faculty members rather well—Professors Arnaldo Hax and Scot Fitzmaurice—and remained in touch with them for a number of years. Participants' spouses were invited to join in the final week of the thirteen-week programme. During that week, exclusive lectures for spouses were a part of the programme. During this last week, the participants and spouses went out in groups around Boston and enjoyed lovely meals in some of the well-known Boston sea food restaurants. All in all, a most enjoyable experience.

After MIT, Connie and I spent a couple of weeks holidaying with our good friends Lee and Nagesh Mhatre, in New Jersey. Officially,

I took over as the chairman at the AGM (annual general meeting) in
June 1980 from TT, although I had moved to the chairman's office
after returning to Bombay in March 1980.

 In Delhi, the Indian National Congress had returned to power,
under Indira Gandhi's premiership, in January 1980. After I had
formally assumed office, as the chairman, TT and I went to Delhi
together, to meet some of the key cabinet ministers. In June 1980,
TT was now responsible for Unilever's chemicals and agricultural
business. He had come to Bombay and we went to visit the new
HLL tripolyphosphate plant in Haldia, West Bengal. During our
trip, we heard the news of Sanjay Gandhi's fatal plane accident.

 The sudden death of Sanjay Gandhi was a very heavy blow to the
prime minister. Not long after the tragedy, Mrs Gandhi persuaded
Rajiv Gandhi to assist her, in place of Sanjay. Rajiv was reluctant
to leave his job as a pilot in Indian Airlines. Subsequently, Rajiv
resigned from Indian Airlines and started working full time in Mrs
Gandhi's office. I had met Rajiv briefly, a few times, during my air
travels and when he was a pilot in Indian Airlines. One of my board
colleagues, Shunu Sen, happened to be one of Rajiv's contemporary
at Doon School. A very close friend of Indira Gandhi, Mrs Pupul
Jayakar arranged my more formal introduction to Rajiv Gandhi.

 Over the next few months, Rajiv and I met frequently, and got
to know each other well. One of the important tasks which was
unfinished, was HLL's long-drawn-out FERA case regarding Unilever's
majority shareholding in HLL. TT had pursued the FERA issue
relentlessly during his time as the chairman of HLL. There was a
deeply entrenched opposition to Unilever's majority shareholding in
HLL, especially amongst the middle echelons of civil servants, a couple
of cabinet ministers, as well as the Reserve Bank of India, to prevent
Unilever from holding 51 per cent shareholding in HLL, in spite of
HLL having fulfilled all the FERA requirements to do so legally. One
former finance minister is supposed to have made a damaging 'file
noting' that Unilever should not be permitted majority shareholding
in HLL, under any circumstances. This comment was not only

legally incorrect, but damaging as well. During my early months as chairman, I frequently went to meet the then finance minister, Pranab Mukherjee, regarding HLL's FERA status. He seemed to be persuaded about the legitimacy of our case. One of his key officials, Dr Nitish Sengupta, was even more than convinced about HLL's legal case, for Unilever to hold 51 per cent shares in HLL.

However, the attitude amongst some of the junior finance ministry officials, against multinationals, was deeply ingrained. It was during this difficult phase that I met Rajiv Gandhi, to apprise him of some detail about HLL's FERA case, as well as the travails that the company had been subjected to for over five years. He patiently listened about the untiring efforts of my predecessor and Suman Sinha, then the head of HLL's Delhi office and his staff, as well as the relentless efforts of Mathew Panikar, HLL's director of finance, with the RBI, in Bombay. Eventually, the decision to permit Unilever to retain majority shareholding in HLL was cleared by the government, in December 1980. The final decision was entirely based on HLL legitimately fulfilling all the FERA rules of the Government of India, and without seeking any favour. The day HLL was officially informed that Unilever had been allowed to hold majority shareholding in HLL, having fulfilled all the conditions under FERA, was indeed a red-letter day. TT had worked hard and relentlessly on this issue during his chairmanship.

HLL's efforts finally bore fruit, and I had the privilege of running the last mile. The key lesson of the FERA episode is that, in India, even after fulfilling all the legal requirements of a particular issue, Herculean efforts were necessary, to persevere, in the face of insurmountable, unfair reasons of the government in power. The unanticipated break, in December 1980, eventually led to the resolution of HLL's FERA case by our tirelessly defending the legal justification and interacting with people willing to listen, at the highest level, in the government.

By 1987, I was already the longest-serving chairman of Hindustan Lever. I worked long hours because my work was exciting, challenging. HLL could not have delivered excellent and consistent high performance, but for the dedication, commitment and grit of the HLL employees, the members of the board, and the quality of our managers. The company's history of recruiting from amongst the country's best talent, HLL's uncompromising commitment to meritocracy, transparent fairness, caring for all its employees and absolute intolerance of dishonesty are widely known and admired. The unfortunate history of the Bombay factory was as much due to the cussedness of union leaders as also the unintended consequence of the practice of employing temporary labourers, seasonally. The annual AGM speech by the chairman of HLL focused on contemporary business issues, opportunities and challenges faced by the private sector, and especially multinational companies, in India. The HLL AGM speech remains an iconic yearly statement, which successive chairmen have kept up, since Prakash Tandon. Prakash Tandon was the first Indian chairman of HLL, a person of great vision, wisdom and leadership. He was succeeded by luminaries like Vasant Rajadhyaksha and T. Thomas.

During 1980–90, I was actively involved with the science and technology institutions of the Government of India. I was introduced to Mrs Pupul Jayakar by her niece Shyama and her husband, Nihal Kaviratne. Nihal was one of my valued colleagues in HLL, and remains a close friend. Mrs Jayakar was known as the doyen of Indian arts and crafts, as well as a friend of Indira Gandhi. Prof. Nurul Hasan, minister of science and technology, and Pupul Jayakar were instrumental in my getting to know Indira Gandhi. I had only briefly met the prime minister earlier, and Rajiv may have also briefed the PM on the travails of HLL's FERA case.

Mrs Gandhi presided over the Society of CSIR (Council of Scientific and Industrial Research), the apex science body of the country. I was appointed as a member of this apex body in 1982, the only non-government member. The other members were two senior government officials and two cabinet ministers. Prof. Nurul Hasan had earlier inducted me as a member of the governing council of the

CSIR (1981–90). As the chairman of HLL, I had gradually established strong, professional acquaintance with certain senior bureaucrats in Delhi. I found the time I had to spend in Delhi, interacting with the government, usually long-drawn-out but productive. The work of previous HLL chairmen, in Delhi, starting from Prakash Tandon, followed by Vasant Rajadhyaksha and T. Thomas, before me, had already established certain useful precedents.

As the biggest multinational company in India, at the time, HLL chairmen and the company's dedicated team, in Delhi, kept in close touch, on the constantly shifting views and attitudes of the Government of India regarding multinationals, and ensuring that the government was kept abreast about HLL's business operations. For example, during the post-Independence years, the government's attitude towards multinational companies used to be very unfavourable. For several years, HLL had remained hemmed in by restrictive government licensing policies, price controls, shortage of foreign exchange and dependence on raw material imports. To top it all, the government's classifying consumer products as a 'non-priority' sector created more hurdles. Even HLL, having the requisite licences and permissions, for its manufacturing capacity, the company was almost continuously subjected to unending and time-consuming scrutiny, in its head office as well as manufacturing units.

India's foreign investment priority was restricted to 'High Technology'. The term 'High Technology' used to be prone to subjective interpretation, under FERA. HLL faced obstacles on numerous fronts. Better sense began to slowly dawn, during the decade of 1980. But India's economic policies and growth were still restrictive. In 1991 India was virtually forced to change its economic policies, due to a precarious foreign exchange shortage, high debt and the stark reality of what the country faced. The 'reforms' of 1991, were not the outcome of an evolutionary or a well-planned process, but had become compelling. Mrs Gandhi had signalled the need for change. Narasimha Rao and Dr Manmohan Singh made it happen.

During the decade of 1980–90, HLL had to also deal with deteriorating industrial relations in its largest manufacturing unit, its Bombay factory. The factory contributed 60 per cent of the company's revenues. The workers had switched their allegiance from their long-standing leftist, but sensible, union leader Madan Phadnis to Dr Datta Samant.

Datta Samant made his presence felt in Bombay, after capturing the unions in the textile industry. He was reported to be totally uncompromising in negotiations with mill owners. Prolonged strikes eventually led to the closure of almost all the textile mills in Mumbai, rendering hundreds of thousands of textile workers unemployed. But after virtually all the textile mills had shut down, Samant turned his attention to, and started capturing, the unions of a large number of other companies in Bombay and its surrounding suburbs. His success was attributed to a combination of violence and some companies rumoured to be 'buying peace'. As a consequence, Samant soon emerged as a political force in Maharashtra. Samant went on to win in a general election, and became a member of Parliament. In this rapidly changing scenario, Prem Chadha, HLL's technical director at the time, and I started exploring possible alternatives, as the Bombay factory continued to face more and frequent work stoppages and disruptions. Primarily, we crafted a strategy and a plan, to speedily and significantly reduce HLL's overdependence on the Bombay factory. The basic idea was to rapidly disperse manufacturing capacity, by acquiring/building a number of modern and manageable-sized manufacturing units, at other locations. In pursuit of this strategy, we were helped by a new government policy to generate more employment, in 'backward' regions, in the country.

HLL's strategic plan was implemented, over the next four years, and in due course, HLL's overdependence on its Bombay factory was very significantly reduced.

Some years later, after I had moved to London, I accidently ran into Datta Samant, as he was emerging from a Cartier shop, on Sloan

Street. He was carrying, in his hand, an expensive-looking, gift-wrapped package, and unsuccessfully tried to avoid me, but could not. He seemed to have done rather well.

During the time when HLL's Bombay factory was facing severe labour problems and trade union militancy, the hugely supportive role played by Calcutta's Garden Reach factory became invaluable. The Calcutta union leaders and workers displayed unprecedented commitment and significantly increased output. HLL's Garden Reach factory, headed by Anil Chakraborty, general manager, his management team, the workers and trade union leaders, displayed commitment and whole-hearted support, by significantly increasing levels of output, in every shift, over several months. As a consequence, the Garden Reach factory became a source of critical support while the Bombay factory was on prolonged strike. HLL's Calcutta performance was hailed by the Communist chief minister of West Bengal, Jyoti Basu, in one of his public speeches at an industry conference. Basu proudly and repeatedly referred to the example of HLL in Calcutta, the productivity of its workers and harmonious work environment, as an example of the changing scenario of West Bengal and its attraction for investors!

Another challenge in the 1980s was when HLL's detergents business faced a serious competitive challenge to its market leadership in the detergent sector and its well-known brands Surf and Rin. The popularity of a low-cost and manually mixed and cheap detergent brand, Nirma, and its rapid capture of market share were unprecedented. Nirma's market success was soon copied by the launch of a number of low-cost, regional brands, which flooded retail outlets across north India, and eventually spread to the rest of the country. Nirma also heavily advertised its brand and started flooding the retail trade and shelf space across India. Nirma and similar low-cost copycat brands started eating into HLL's market share and leadership. Although at HLL we had initially underestimated the competitive threat of cheap brands, this impact on HLL's detergent volume growth and market share became quite evident and we were forced to acknowledge the seriousness of the threat to HLL's detergent products and its market leadership.

In response, HLL set up a dedicated team, exclusively tasked to create a low-cost but 'quality brand', on a war footing. Not long thereafter, the task force innovated and launched a new brand, Wheel. The combination of a cost-competitive brand, of assured HLL quality, and a brilliant marketing strategy for Wheel, soon made its prominent presence felt and rapidly captured significant market share. The late Prof. C.K. Prahlad, the renowned management guru, described low-cost products such as Nirma, Wheel, etc., as fulfilling the demands of Indian consumers at the 'bottom of the pyramid'. Prahlad missed the fact that 'low cost' need not mean 'poor quality'. HLL's dedicated team for the new business model, the rapid and successful launch and marketing of Wheel, eventually dominated the 'bottom of the pyramid', not only in India, but also in some other Unilever companies in developing countries, much before Prahlad coined the term.

In 1980, Ranjan Banerjee, HLL's vice-chairman, and Jagdish Chopra, marketing director, retired from the board. Finance director Charles Miller-Smith became HLL's vice-chairman.

Also in 1980, Chris Jemmett replaced TT, as a member of the Unilever overseas committee for India. Before the change TT and I had agreed to appoint Gerry Alcock, a senior Unilever marketing specialist, as vice-chairman, to succeed Charles Miller-Smith. Gerry was a competent marketing manager, but turned out to be quite a maverick, and was sent back. Mike Flemming, Unilever chairman in Thailand, was then appointed to replace Gerry as vice-chairman of HLL.

By the time I was invited to join the Unilever board in 1990, TT had already retired. Chris Jemmett had also joined the Unilever board. He and his wife, Kate, remain our good personal friends. Although Chris tended to be pompous, in his initial interactions with HLL he took my feedback to moderate his ways, graciously. Chris is basically a decent person. In 1985, Chris handed over responsibility for India to Patrick Egan. Patrick and his wife, Tessa, were also extremely friendly and a warm couple. Patrick has since, unfortunately, passed away, but Connie remained in touch with Tessa.

My relationship and friendship with Patrick was possibly one of my closest amongst my contemporaries in Unilever. Chris and Patrick were great supporters of the India business in Unilever. Patrick's father had worked in India during 1930–40, and Patrick had spent part of his impressionable young years in Lahore, and spoke Urdu reasonably well. His affection for India was genuine and strong.

Following the retirement of Ranjan Banerjee and Jagdish Chopra, and with Charles Miller Smith returning to the UK, we inducted new directors on the board. Prem Chadha was appointed technical director—we had joined HLL as trainees on the same day in 1962 and were very close personal friends; Shunu Sen, an outstanding marketing leader, as the director for detergents; Govind Menon, director, R&D, and Suman Sinha joined the board at about the same time. Following the retirement of Shamdas Gurshani, M.K. Sharma succeeded him as head of HLL's legal and secretarial functions—one of the most, if not the most, critical positions in the company. Mathew Panikar, head, finance, Susim Datta, in charge of detergents, and Bipin Shah, chairman of Lipton & Brook Bond, were already on the HLL board. As I look back, I was indeed fortunate to have had a formidable team of colleagues during the decade of my chairmanship.

Prem Chadha had earned his well-deserved reputation as HLL's successful technical director. Besides being responsible for manufacturing, he was very successful in dealing with trade unions, and managing the consequences of the rise of Datta Samant. Prem led the execution of the strategy to drastically reduce and eventually completely do away with HLL's dependence on the Bombay factory. In 1985, Prem went to Japan, as technical director of Nippon Lever.

As I look back to the decade of 1980–90, HLL (not yet HUL) was, at the time, the largest multinational in India, and well known

in the public domain for its products. However, the real strength of
the company was its people. The process of recruiting and developing
talent and career growth, through well-structured career plans, based
upon leadership qualities and meritocracy, remain the core strength
of the company. One of the distinctive traits of potential leaders is
their natural trait to identify amongst subordinates, future leaders and
nurture them, rather than being preoccupied with one's own future!

The other major strengths of HLL were its core of outstanding
managers in its HR department. Stalwarts like Rindani, Prakash
Ram, Sunil Basu, Tarun Sheth, R.D. Relan, Umrao Bahadur and their
successors, were a huge asset. Their colleagues in the legal department,
such as Chandy Basu and M.K. Sharma, were at the formidable core
of the company. To face the threat of low-cost washing powders, the
Wheel team was led by Sanjay Khosla and Naren Nanda—under
Detergent Director Shunu Sen, they earned well-deserved fame for
capturing the 'bottom of the pyramid'. Amongst the rising stars of the
time were Gopalakrishnan, Keki Dadiseth, Nihal Kaviratne, Anirudh
Lahiri, C.V. Narasimhan, Debu Bhattacharya, R. Ramananthan,
R.R. Nair and Gurdeep Singh. While Anil Chakravarty was the pillar
of strength in manufacturing, Suman Sinha's successful leadership,
supported by his team in Delhi, was noteworthy for their perseverance
in successfully dealing with complex problems. Kalbag in R&D used
to be recognized as the pre-eminent chemical engineer in India.
There were several other emerging leaders amongst the upcoming
generation, pushing HLL towards expanding horizons. My apologies
to those whom I have missed.

People will always remain the core strength of the company.
HLL's branch managers and powerful sales force ensured the
company's dominance of markets across the country, and last but not
the least, HLL's shop floor workers and supervisors in the factories.
HLL's legendary stockists and customer-facing retailers, innumerable
retail outlets in cities, towns, villages and hamlets across India are
the partners in the core of HLL's success. They all operate like
clockwork, reaching across to millions of consumers, all over India.

On a personal note, without Meher Gyara, Arnaz Bhiwandiwala and Phiroza David, the silent but dedicated team in the chairman's office, my own tasks could not have been as seamless.

The spread of TV in India, during the 1980s, changed advertising. Traditionally, newspapers and cinema hoardings, in cities and towns, had dominated the media. In villages, roadside walls were prominent and served as hoardings. The age of digital has dramatically transformed the way we work. For example, the association of Lux with leading Bollywood film stars has survived in India, although the medium has changed. HUL has kept growing dramatically, still a high-performing enterprise, of dedicated employees, and a new generation of digital savvy owners and operators of wholesale and retail trade, to successfully challenge mushrooming online business competition, changing tastes and demands of the Indian consumers. To repeat a well-known adage, 'change is the only constant', which best defines the company.

During the 1980s, the HLL board was primarily made up of full-time directors and had only one non-executive director. In 1980, Vaghul, the executive chairman of ICICI, joined the board as the non-executive director. The evolution of public limited company boards in India followed the modernization of the company law department, especially after the 'Cadbury Report on Corporate Governance' in the 1990s. Most publicly quoted company boards now have more independent directors, as well as statutory board committees on audit, governance and compensation.

In early 1980, we moved our residence from Alhambra to nearby Goldcroft, on Warden Road. Goldcroft is a spacious duplex flat, where TT and his family had stayed, before he moved to the UK. We enjoyed our daughters, Nivedita and Amrita, growing up, under the watchful and loving care of Connie. On average, I spent about twelve hours most days at work, when in Bombay. I toured frequently, to different parts of the country, on market visits or to various factories. In 1980, I had to visit Delhi, nearly fifty times, by Indian Airlines, which was the only domestic airlines at the time and flights were frequently delayed. The saving grace was the HLL guest house in Delhi's India International Centre, which Prakash Tandon had wisely leased while it was being built. In most remote factory locations and metropolitan cities, HLL maintained comfortable guest houses, the cost saving compared to staying in hotels was not insignificant, while the comforts were always even better. As they were growing, our children's birthdays were joyful events as well as our brief family holidays, mostly in India, which was something we looked forward to, every year. During the week, we went across to see my parents, in Worli, in the evenings. One day, my mother asked me, out of curiosity, what my office was like. So, one Saturday morning, I took Ma and Baba to see my office in HLL House. I took them around on a brief walk, around the fifth floor. Kurup, who looked after the guest flat on the seventh floor, served us tea. I introduced my parents to Meher and Arnaz. The office gossip was that some of my colleagues may have felt somewhat compelled to come to the office on Saturdays. Looking back, long hours and Saturday mornings in the office used to be somewhat of an Indian habit.

Long hours at the workplace were considered by some Unilever colleagues abroad as a third-world management practice. It was said that in the third world, as people did not have hobbies, they did not know what to do with weekends. Not strictly true! But we did enjoy our weekends while living in Holland and England, during Connie's and my secondment in 1969–70.

Every year, HLL had a number of Unilever visitors. Visits by one of the Unilever chairmen or board members were not that frequent. Patrick Egan came to India at least a couple of times a year. If accompanied by spouse, Connie and I accompanied them to one of our units outside Bombay, and sometimes, on a brief holiday. These were welcome breaks, but meant a lot of preparatory work for my colleagues.

In Delhi, my meetings with senior Indian civil servants, or a cabinet minister, were related to important corporate issues concerning the company. Suman Sinha and our team in Delhi were exceptionally helpful, to fix the meetings. Suman's successor Bharat Mahey carried the torch very effectively. Over time, I came to know Pranab Mukherjee, then finance minister, and Narayan Dutt Tiwari (NDT), minister of industry and commerce, well. In the 1970s, due to the strict licensing regime and the pernicious FERA regulations, TT had established rapport with Sheikh Abdullah, then chief minister (CM) of Jammu and Kashmir (J&K), and T.A. Pai, commerce minister, amongst others, in Delhi. TT persuaded them, and HLL got permission to build a new detergent factory in Jammu. The proposed factory in Jammu, and a couple of small packing units at Pampore and Ganderbal, in Kashmir, were meant to create at least some jobs, hence the permission to invest. In 1981, Kamal Nath, a young Congress member of the Lok Sabha, helped HLL obtain permissions to set up a detergent factory in Chhindwara, which used to be his constituency in Madhya Pradesh, and subsequently, to create more jobs and disperse industry from urban cities. Narayan Dutt Tiwari, helped set up a factory in Uttar Pradesh and another in Maharashtra. HLL also acquired a loss-making detergent unit in Mohali, Punjab, and successfully turned it around. All these new units were key to HLL's dispersal strategy, away from its overdependence on Bombay.

Amongst most of the senior civil servants HLL had strong support, due to our persistent efforts and professional reputation. Some of the supportive civil servants of the time were Dr Nitish Sengupta, Nandu Singh, Abid Hussain as well as Cabinet Secretaries Pratap Kaul and D.V. Kapoor. In Prime Minister Rajiv Gandhi's office, Gopi Arora was a good friend.

HLL also maintained regular contacts with the British high commission in Delhi. As an important subsidiary of Unilever in India, we were invited to various important events, such as the visit of Queen Elizabeth to India, etc.

Prime Minister Margaret Thatcher visited Bombay, as part of her visit to India, in 1984. I happened to be the president of the Bombay Chamber of Commerce and Industry. The Chamber hosted a lunch in her honour, she was accompanied by Denis Thatcher and a few senior British officials. It was one of the major events of Bombay Chamber that year. During lunch, Mrs Thatcher raised the issue of corruption in India. Mrs Thatcher wondered how HLL handled the problems. I remember telling her that HLL never paid, even a rupee, to run its successful business in India. Subsequently, when Margaret Thatcher delivered a post-lunch speech, she made a point of mentioning our brief conversation about corruption, and repeated it during her subsequent press conference.

Return to Europe

I moved to London in March 1990, to join the Unilever board as executive director, responsible for R&D, engineering, safety and a number of related activities, succeeding Sir Geofrey Allen. Connie, Nivedita and Amrita joined me a couple of months later. Prior to moving, Nivedita had to complete her second year at St Xavier's college in Bombay, and Connie had also arranged for Amrita to successfully complete her 'O' levels, in Bombay. Mrs Dorothy Miller Smith, Charles's wife and a good friend since their time in HLL, was extremely helpful, for Connie to familiarize with our new surroundings, and Amrita to join the Francis Holland School, situated close to our flat, near Sloane Square. Nivedita joined University College, in London, to complete her graduation. Amrita successfully completed her 'A' levels, and subsequently graduated from University College, London, as well.

After graduating, Nivedita moved to Glasgow University, to pursue doctoral research in genetics. In spite of being scholastically very bright, she lost interest in her PhD programme, working under her adviser, who was a well-known geneticist. Nivé and I had a heart-to-heart chat about her loss of interest. I encouraged her to pursue whichever subject she wished to, going forward. Nivedita then moved to Oxford University, to study intellectual property law. After graduating, Amrita joined Sussex University, and completed requirements for her master's degree in psychology.

Our home for the next seven years was a large, well-appointed and very well furnished serviced apartment, with a garage in the basement, next to Sloane Square station, on Holbine Place. My office car was a Ford, and for our personal use we acquired the newly launched Toyota model, the Lexus. Lexus was the best automobile I had ever driven. Our company chauffeur, Bill Collier, was good at his job, but somehow gave the impression of being a touch dodgy! Sadly, a few years later, he had to be asked to leave, by Unilever's administrative department, following some unsavoury incident, according to the police.

Unilever looked after our stay very well. We had been already close friends with the Jemmets and the Egans, and soon got friendly with my other colleagues, in Unilever and their spouses, besides our old friends in the UK. The weather in London is frequently cold and wet. Connie and I carried memories, from 1970, of the winter smog and the coal miners' strike. The weather seemed to have improved, or at least that was our impression of the first summer. Connie and I enjoyed long walks, from our flat, to Hyde Park, in the evenings and on weekends. We frequently went to see plays, and in the summer, we looked forward to attending operas at Glyndebourne, and other seasonal social activities.

I had started my career in the HLL's R&D department in 1962, before moving on to manufacturing in 1970, and general management. As a Unilever board member responsible for R&D I seemed to have come full circle!

My colleagues on the Unilever board were very friendly and helpful. Not surprisingly, R&D was considered as a 'cost' centre of amorphous value by my board colleagues who were in charge of different business groups. The Plc chairman, Sir Michael Angus, was a person of formidable gravitas, although a very kind and considerate individual. At my very start as a Unilever board member, I had an interesting, private conversation with Vice-Chairman Ronnie Archer, at his initiative. Ronnie was the third member of the Unilever special committee, the other two being the Plc and NV chairmen. I thought hard about whether I should, at all, recall my conversation with Ronnie Archer, but then I decided to skim over it, considering it was sensitive, and the individuals were no longer alive.

Ronnie Archer used to be the vice-chairman of HLL, in the early 1960s, and lived a few years in Bombay, along with his wife, Catherine. He had succeeded Jim Davies with whom I had an encounter, in 1962, which I have referred to elsewhere in the book.

In 1990, soon after I joined the Unilever board and moved to London, Ronnie invited me to spend a weekend at his home, in the countryside. After work, one Friday afternoon, Ronnie and I travelled by train from Waterloo station, and were picked up by Catherine, his wife, at a station, whose name I am no longer able to recall, and driven to their home. Most board members lived in the countryside, in homes with beautiful gardens and surroundings, in picturesque English villages. They preferred to get away from the city at the end of the day. Most of them travelled by train to and back from work, during the week. I spent an enjoyable Friday evening dinner with Catherine and Ronnie, at their home, recalling their time in Bombay. On Saturday morning, after breakfast, Ronnie said that we should have a one-to-one chat. The gist of what Ronnie wanted to tell me came as a complete surprise. He ambled on, about what he wanted to talk about, which was something I was already aware of. Ronnie was basically trying to tell me about some unseemly episode in HLL. Ronnie then advised me, if I had already heard or were to hear any whispering about the 'India Episode', in the corridors of Unilever House, I should ignore these. Ronnie had tried to be frank, but subtle. I was well aware what Ronnie was trying to convey.

I appreciated his very kind and honest effort, but knew that it was water under the bridge. The rest of that weekend with Catherine and Ronnie was most enjoyable, especially with the sunny weather. I had carried with me a box of chocolates, as a gift. After our Saturday lunch, Ronnie consumed most of the chocolates from the large box while chatting with me. At the time of my joining the Unilever board, Ronnie's health was already failing and he was to retire soon. Not long after retiring from Unilever, Ronnie passed away.

My secretary in London, Barbara, her assistant Liz Jones, and Ray Moran, the very competent head of commercial and administration, in the research division, assisted me with their dependable and excellent service and support, throughout my tenure on the Unilever board.

Soon after I joined the Unilever board in 1990, it was time for the annual budget discussions. As the principal service provider to the product groups, Ray and I had to meet each of the directors responsible, along with his commercial head, to discuss the group's annual business plans, and the annual estimates, for R&D and related services. My first budget meeting was with one of the product group directors, whom I had known while he was chairman of Unilever, Thailand.

During the budget meeting, right at the start, my board colleague informed me that he was seriously thinking of discontinuing funding R&D, as it had not been of any value to his product group, for the last few years. As the new R&D chief, I patiently listened to his monologue. I also noticed that Ray, who had been working in R&D for a reasonably long time, seemed taken aback by the director's opening statement. Before moving to Unilever as a board member, I was heading one of Unilever's largest and valued subsidiaries, as the chairman of HLL. I was also well aware of the critical views of the Unilever business heads, who were unhappy about the impact of R&D on their profit centre. I had heard stories from my predecessor, who had been appointed to the post from academia. I was not entirely taken by surprise by my board colleague's opening salvo.

After he had finished speaking, I did not respond immediately, but waited briefly and then to the utter surprise of Ray, and the director and his colleagues, I started collecting my papers, to signal that as far as I was concerned, the annual budget meeting, for the day, was over. I then explained to the director and his commercial manager that I needed time to estimate the cost of shutting down the R&D facilities, dedicated to the group's business, along with the cost of retrenching the scientists and support staff who worked on the projects, funded by the business. I would only then schedule our next meeting, with a revised budget, for discontinuing the product group's R&D activities. This revised plan would consist of annual estimates of shutting down costs the particular business would have to bear.

Word of my first annual budget meeting and discussions rapidly spread in the corridors of Unilever House. In a prompt about-face, my board colleague immediately requested another meeting, to more specifically explain the instance and history which he was trying to convey earlier (very English!). Apparently, he was very unhappy regarding the cost effectiveness and value of R&D, to his business group. It gave me the opportunity to explain that R&D would work on projects and priorities funded by a business group, only if the customer needs were clearly defined. I also explained to my colleague that R&D was neither qualified to suggest nor should it try to guess, the business needs and its customer priorities. Therefore, as soon as the business group provided us with the information, Ray Moran and I would meet them, with a revised budget proposal, specifically addressing business priorities, for the annual plan. I concluded by reminding that R&D was neither qualified nor competent to guess what a particular business may need, to drive its growth and market share.

The news of the R&D discussion with the business group director spread rapidly. Once the suggested process of preparing the annual plan was agreed upon, my colleague Ray Moran was delighted with the outcome and the way forward. I was glad to have clarified, at least to an extent, R&D's role and accountability in Unilever. Unilever's R&D was dispersed, with laboratories across the UK, France, Germany, USA, India and, later, China, in 1996. Challenging costs and value of R&D by each of Unilever's businesses had to be the base. I was absolutely firm that henceforth, R&D would only work on problems which were defined by each Product Group, in terms of markets and competition, and which would reflect in terms of R&D projects, timetable and costs, to be mutually agreed. Ten per cent of the budget was allocated for 'basic' science programmes, of Unilever laboratories as well as at universities, of long-term business relevance and potential benefits.

The R&D management committee had as its members the heads of each of the laboratories, the coordinator of the basic research programmes, besides the heads of engineering, patents, safety, environment, etc. Unilever research was well known, and had strong links with many of the European and American academic institutions. The management committee met once a month to review the status of the major business-sponsored R&D programmes. Status of goals, targets and accountability were the key measures.

I visited each of the Unilever R&D units in the UK, Netherlands and US, once a month, to review the progress of the important projects, and to interact with various groups of scientists and engineers. I also visited the R&D centre in India, for review, once a year. Ray and I formally met the special committee, to present the consolidated annual budget, highlights. We also met the special committee once a quarter, to review the status of important business-related issues.

Compared to my role in HLL, as the chairman, during the previous ten years, my role in Unilever was different. I had to ensure that R&D was entirely driven by business goals and priorities.

The 1990s happened to be a sort of tipping point for R&D, across many industrial sectors. The role of R&D, in various industries, had become more challenging and costly. The cost of discovering and marketing a new and successful drug in the 1990s had grown to astronomical levels. In the service sector, IBM closely integrated its R&D with the front end of its business, in order to compete with more innovative and agile emerging digital competitors. In Unilever, we had to transform R&D to deliver business priorities, market challenges and opportunities.

I was invited to be a member of the Advisory Board of Research Councils (ABRC), the apex body of the UK government, to discuss, review and allocate funds to National Research Councils. The research councils, in turn, funded R&D programmes in the UK universities. The ABRC also advised the UK government, on the effectiveness of R&D funding.

I was also a member of the fourth (1994–96) 'Framework Committee' for R&D funding, of the European Union, which met periodically, in Brussels. The committee was tasked to review funding of programmes, across disciplines for EU member countries. This 'Framework' exercise provided an interesting glimpse of the sheer complexity of the EUs budgetary exercise.

When we lived in London, Connie and I were invited 'to tea' at 10 Downing Street, by Prime Minister John Major. We were introduced to some of the other invitees. It was a very interesting and enjoyable evening. The other was an invitation to the Buckingham Palace, by the queen. I also served on two committees related to industry for the UK government. I think these culminated in a CBE, in 2006. Some years later, I happened to meet former prime minister John Major, at a small dinner in Delhi. He recalled meeting me at 10 Downing Street, when he was PM, and told me during dinner that my services in the UK were greatly valued. I guess, he would have been briefed regarding the background of the guests, for him to even recall!

I met Prime Minister Indira Gandhi, Rajiv Gandhi and some cabinet ministers during the 1980s. Once, in the course of a small buffet dinner, hosted by Mrs Gandhi at her home, for members of the CSIR governing council, there were a few other invitees as well. During the buffet, we were to help ourselves, from a vegetarian spread. Mrs Gandhi was sitting, with her plate in hand, on a cement step, close to the dining table, and suggested that I sit alongside her. She seemed quite interested, enquiring about my family, which school Nivedita and Amrita, our daughters, went to in Bombay, the weight of their school bags, as well as about Connie and our life as a family, in Bombay. I recall the evening being pleasant, polite and informal. I seem to have monopolized a fair bit of Mrs Gandhi's time, so when we rose, to replenish our plates, Narayan Dutt Tiwari drifted towards me. He was, at the time, one of Indiraji's senior-most cabinet ministers. Over time, we came to know each other well. As Mrs Gandhi started going around, meeting the other guests, Mr Tiwari pulled me to a side and whispered, 'I don't wish to know what you and the prime minister were talking about, but I would advise you, never share whatever you may have talked about with anyone else either. Everyone at the dinner is curious and very keen to know what you and the prime minister were talking about.'

His parting words of advice were, 'this is Delhi'. Those were words of wisdom, from Narayan Duttji, which I will always remember. During that decade of the 1980–90, NDT, as he was fondly called, was extremely helpful in enabling HLL to disperse manufacturing facilities across different locations in India, which I have already referred to, in the context of our problems in Bombay. This dispersal of industries coincided with the governments policy to generate more employment, in what were called the 'backward' regions of India.

I recall some significant events during the prime ministership of Rajiv Gandhi (1985–90). His drive to computerize the administration, speed up decisions and reduce corruption was ridiculed by the opposition, as well as many amongst India's hidebound bureaucracy. There were almost organized efforts against computerization, to overcome Delhi's legendary bureaucratic delays. I was a witness to some of the means to create hurdles. Indian bureaucracy continues to be the principal hurdle to reforms, even to this day, and in spite of regime change.

The assassination of Mrs Gandhi, in 1983, by one of her own Sikh bodyguards, was one of the three most traumatic events in my life time. The aftermath of the prime minister's assassination led to violence and riots, in and around Delhi, and several innocent victims, belonging to the Sikh community, were killed. The Delhi riots were rapidly brought under control. After Rajiv Gandhi became prime minister, the hurdles to reform, by some of Rajiv Gandhi's own cabinet ministers and bureaucrats, succeeded in slowing down efforts to modernize India's economy and hold ministers and civil servants accountable. In 1989, Rajiv Gandhi was politically betrayed by some of his own cabinet colleagues, and the so-called 'Bofors scandal'. The economic crisis in 1991 forced the first major 'Reforms', during the prime ministership of Narasimha Rao, and implemented under

Dr Manmohan Singh. While computerization and automation have slightly improved, the iron grip of administrators and bureaucracy remains one of the important hurdles in India's economic growth and dynamism.

Towards the end of the year 1990, general elections were announced in India. One late evening, in November 1990, I received a phone call, at our London residence, from Pranab Mukherjee. He said he had a message for me, from Rajiv Gandhi. Mr Gandhi wished to nominate me as the Congress candidate for Lok Sabha from a North Calcutta constituency. This missive, from Rajiv Gandhi, was totally out of the blue. While I was still on the phone, speaking to Pranab Babu, Rajiv Gandhi's message started sinking in. I politely explained to Pranab Mukherjee that not only I had no experience in politics, but even more frankly, I had absolutely no desire or any inclination whatsoever to enter politics.

Pranab Babu then explained to me that I was being allotted a 'safe' seat, and in which even a 'lamp post', on a Congress ticket, would win in North Calcutta. I had to once more explain that I had no desire, whatsoever, to join politics, under any circumstances. Pranab then cautioned me that the next call I was going to receive would be from Mr Gandhi himself. This news worried me very much. Not long after I had finished speaking with Pranab Babu, I received a call from Rajiv Gandhi's office. I was now in a panic. To my great relief, it was Mr Gandhi's senior aide, Gopi Arora, who was a good friend of mine. Gopi tried to explain, and impress upon me, the keenness of Rajiv Gandhi to talk to me. Gopi had just called to connect me to Mr Gandhi. I pleaded with Gopi and tried to impress upon him the reasons I did not wish to speak to Rajiv Gandhi. I was afraid that Mr Gandhi's persuasive request may compel me to agree. Gopi was very wise, and he must have felt the depth of my apprehension. He agreed to convey my position to Mr Gandhi, as best he could, hopefully, without causing offence. Connie and I were hugely relieved, by the end of our most unusual and trying evening.

During the following weeks, the Indian general election campaign gathered momentum. I spoke to Rajiv Gandhi a few times; he sounded confident of the Congress party returning to power. The very last time I spoke to Rajiv Gandhi was ten days before he was assassinated, when he had told me that he would like to see me in Delhi, soon after the elections were over, and that he would let me know the date, shortly.

Rajiv Gandhi was assassinated on 21 May 1991, during the Congress election campaign, at Sriperumbudur, in Tamil Nadu. The dastardly act was plotted and carried out by a group of Sri Lankan Tamil extremists, belonging to the LTTE. Under the pretext of garlanding Rajiv, a woman terrorist detonated a concealed explosive device. Rajiv Gandhi as well as several others who were crowding around him were blown to smithereens. When I heard the shocking news of RG's assassination, I happened to be home in London and shed tears of anguish, deep shock and extreme grief. Recalling the incident, even while I write this account, emotions weigh heavily on me.

My tenure on the Unilever board was exciting and enjoyable. I undertook frequent trips across the UK, Holland, as well as other Unilever companies across Europe, as my responsibilities required. I also visited the US, once a month. My secretary, Barbara Lawton, was very competent, polite and hard-working. She especially made sure that all my travel documents, visas, etc., were up to date. One of the welcome features of living and working abroad was the sanctity of the weekends, which Connie and I learnt to enjoy.

Over time, the transformation of R&D towards a modern and effective 'Business Driven' objective was welcomed by all my colleagues, but took much longer than I would have liked. Cees Okkerse, my 1969 Dutch boss, in Vlaardingen, was now in charge of basic and exploratory research, towards which 10 per cent of the annual R&D budget was allocated. The head of engineering, Toon Edelman, another Dutch senior manager, retired after three years. I had known both Cees and Toon since 1969. Cees and his wife, Gre, were our very good and old friends. I had known most of my other colleagues, the heads of various units, who were members of the management committee of the division. Our efforts to make R&D relevant for business, progressed smoothly, but gradually. To transform a long-entrenched culture was a big challenge. Ray Moran, head of finance and General Administration, in the division, was of great help and support to drive well-defined business objectives. Ray, who was, in a manner of speaking, the 'Custodian' of the annual budget coordinated the management committee's priorities, of Unilever businesses.

Patrick Egan, executive director and member of the Overseas Committee and to whom I used to report, as chairman of HLL, was still on the board, when I joined in 1990, prior to his retirement. Connie and I met Patrick and his wife, Tessa, frequently. Patrick passed away a few years after his retirement.

It is more than twenty years since I retired from Unilever in1997; I fondly remember my time on the board, while Connie and I remained in touch with our friends in the UK and Europe. Sir Michael Angus had introduced me to Lord Colin Marshall, chairman of British Airways; subsequently, Lord Marshall invited me to join the BA board as a non-executive, independent director (1996–2005). Mike Angus, after retiring as chairman of Unilever, became the chairman of the Leverhulme Trust (LHT). The Leverhulme Trust had been set up by the first Lord Leverhulme, donating a large number of his Unilever Plc shares, which yielded a handsome annual income for the Trust, as Unilever dividends. The board of trustees and the director of the LHT are responsible for the disbursement of the annual income, to education, research, the fine arts and training of 'tradesmen', principally in the UK. After I retired from Unilever, I was invited to join as a trustee in 2000 and served until 2016.

During our stay in London, Connie and I made quite a few new friends, outside Unilever. Over time, Robin and Sherna Chatterjee became very close to us. The Chatterjees and we visited each other frequently, and together, enjoyed many holidays. Robin gallantly and resolutely battled cancer for over five years, but sadly passed away in 2016.

Amongst the many attractions of London are its numerous museums, art galleries, theatres and plays, virtually round the year. Glyndebourne performances were special summer attractions, every year. We looked forward to attending the black-tie evenings, of the Glyndebourne performances, and the fine dining, in the intermission. We invited some of our friends to join us, at Glyndebourne, every season.

We remained in touch with many of our former English and Dutch colleagues and their families, as well as some others, working for Unilever, in Japan, Africa, US and South America, and of course, India. We remain in close touch, with Iain and Katie Anderson, as well as Chris and Kate Jemmett, and catch up during our annual trips to London, or when they visit Mumbai occasionally. The Jemmetts and Andersons also came to Delhi, especially to see us, when I was a member of the Rajya Sabha.

Nagesh was one of my very close friends, since our Illinois student days. Nagesh settled down in the US. He and his wife, Lee, built a beautiful home, in Los Altos, in Silicon Valley. We met frequently in Mumbai, London and Los Altos. Lee and Nagesh, Connie and I enjoyed a very nice holiday in Napa Valley, the Mecca of American wine, we also visited Russia together and went on a driving holiday, across Scotland. Our holiday in Scotland was made even more enjoyable, as I loved to drive my favourite car, the Lexus. Connie had planned out our Scottish holiday destinations, with the help of my Scottish colleague and our dear friend, Iain Anderson. It was probably one of our more memorable breaks in the UK. With advancing years, Nagesh's health became fragile. He sadly passed away in 2016. We meet up with Lee occasionally.

It was also during our stay in London that Connie and Amrita had a wonderful holiday, visiting the historic sites in Jordan. Our family holiday in Umbria, in Italy, with Robin and Sherna, was probably one of the most memorable. Amrita, Nivedita and Minnie, my cousin, separately toured across Italy and then met up with us, at a farm house we had rented in Umbria, for the week. John and Meher had also come with us. Memories of that beautiful summer in Italy will always linger. Of all our holidays, the ones to Italy were the best.

Towards the end of our stay in London, we were told that our flat in Tarnbrook Court was available, if we wished to acquire it. While the idea and price seemed reasonable and attractive, we sensibly concluded that it was too large a premises to be used as a holiday home. Since Connie and I had decided not to settle down in the UK, it did not make sense to acquire a large flat. Connie, however, wisely, and sensibly, felt that we should try and acquire a smaller place nearby, since one or both our daughters might decide to continue to live in the UK. Besides, I anyway had to visit London, after we moved to Mumbai, at least once a month, to attend BA board meetings, and once a quarter, for the Leverhulme Trust meetings. Acquiring a 'pied-a-terre' made good sense. Connie's wisdom prevailed, and in 1996, we acquired a one-bedroom flat, in Chelsea Green, close to Sloan Avenue and Kings Road. The Unilever administrative department helped us in formally acquiring and refurbishing our new flat. At the time, Nivedita was away, studying at Oxford, and Amrita had joined Sussex University, for her postgraduation.

In 1994, following the retirement of Chairman Sir Michael Angus, Mike Perry succeeded him. In 1995, Floris Maljers and Mike Perry informed me, and some of my other colleagues, Okko Muler, Iain Anderson and Charles Muller Smith, that our main offices were to be relocated from Blackfriars to the Dutch head office, in Rotterdam. I informed Maljers and Perry that my domestic circumstances necessitated my family to continue to reside in London. Since, in any event, all Unilever directors already had offices both in Rotterdam as well as in the London head offices. Barbara continued to work in my London office. Unilever NV provided me with a fully furnished flat, in a thirty-three-storey building across the quadrangle from the new Unilever NV head office, in Rotterdam. While Oko, Iain and Charles moved their residence, I started to stay in my flat in Rotterdam for part of the week. The arrangement worked out satisfactorily.

My Dutch secretary, Artie Lois, was a wonderful and caring individual. Artie and Barbara effectively coordinated all my meetings, appointments, as well as my tours. During lunch, in Rotterdam, I usually had a sandwich and buttermilk, in my sixteenth-floor office, or occasionally went down to the lunch room, for a 'hot' meal, as the Dutch call it. My apartment was airy and very well furnished. Connie and Mr Kooij (who had assisted our move to Schiedam in 1969 as well), arranged the necessities, in my Rotterdam apartment, for my weekly stay. My Dutch office was tastefully furnished, with modern Dutch furniture. I also bought a second B&O music system, the other one being in London.

I started living and attending office in Rotterdam, two to three days every week, and lived on my own. The rest of the week and weekends, I spent in London. Over time, with my weekly travel schedule, I became a familiar face at the London City and Rotterdam airports.

Connie, and sometimes Amrita and/or Nivedita, would come to Rotterdam on weekends, and we drove around, to visit different parts of Holland. We soon settled down, to the London–Rotterdam schedule, which worked well. My colleagues, Okko, Iain and Charles, moved their spouses and acquired homes. Oko in Rotterdam and Charles and Iain in Wassenar. We settled down well after the change, because and above all else, Unilever is a very caring and generous company, in spite of being a touch abstemious, which had well stood the test of time and generations.

Connie, Amrita and I finally returned home to Mumbai at the end of 1997, and settled down in a flat, in a building named Pemino, on Altamount Road. Thus began the next chapter of our lives.

A Start in China

Unilever's manufacturing unit and business in China had been taken over by the state in 1949. In 1995, we began to explore ways to set up a modest Unilever R&D presence in Shanghai. After undertaking a survey, we identified a suitable laboratory space, on the premises of the Chinese Institute of Organic Chemistry, in Shanghai, which was available on lease. We followed up with a team of my senior colleagues, from URL Port Sunlight, led by Dr Fred Chang, as our interlocutor and facilitator.

On our team's follow-up visit to Shanghai, I was invited to meet the mayor of Shanghai, who is the head of the Shanghai 'State'. I met the mayor and his officials. The mayor was very welcoming and said he was ready to assist in our effort to set up Unilever's first R&D unit in Shanghai.

The Shanghai Unilever Research Centre was subsequently set up in the Chinese Institute of Organic Chemistry. During this period, I visited Shanghai frequently to review progress and update the mayor. In less than a year, the Unilever research centre at the Chinese Institute of Organic Chemistry was formally inaugurated by Unilever chairman Maurice Tabaksblat and the mayor of Shanghai. After the inauguration, the mayor bestowed upon me, the honorary membership of the Shanghai Academy of Sciences. Over the years, Unilever and URL presence in China has grown, as a part of Unilever Research, Worldwide.

After I retired in 1997, I had no reason to visit China any more. However, I did go to Beijing in 2010, as a member of an Indian government delegation. The visit was a brief one, with a packed busy schedule. On the penultimate day, our delegation was invited to yet another formal dinner. The venue for the dinner was one of the number of beautiful bungalows in the inner sanctum, on the rear of Tiananmen Square. Members of our delegation were lined up to be individually welcomed by our host. He first shook hands, spoke briefly with our leader and presented a gift, and moved to the next person, with a gift for every member, until he reached where I was standing in the line. He looked at the list and said to me that he had met only 'one Ganguly', and would I be the same person? Before I could reply, he suddenly embraced me in a bear hug.

I was flabbergasted, until he reminded me that he happened to be the former mayor of Shanghai, and now a member of the Central Committee of the CPC. The banquet seemed to be an endless succession of dishes, each chased by a shot of Mao Tai. By now, after many banquets, we had experienced how cautious one had to be, of the endless toasts. The dinner lasted until midnight, when our leader and members profusely thanked our host and began taking his leave. As we started slowly departing, we suddenly heard our host's loud voice, 'Ganguly, stay.' We were all a bit taken aback. Our delegation then departed, without me, as I had been asked to stay back.

The dinner was cleared out, fresh glasses of Mao Tai and bottles appeared. The former mayor of Shanghai poured shots of fresh drinks and for the next two hours, related, almost in a monotone, how he had rebuilt Shanghai, by moving the residents of whole areas at a time to a new township built for this purpose some distance away from the city. It was an amazing story. He did seem proud while describing, but shared regret, having caused enormous hardship, in the lives of millions of people. As the Mao Tai began to take effect, he had to pause frequently, before continuing his narrative. I remained very quiet, listening to him, and started wondering what the purpose of this narrative was all about! It was a stunning and unimaginable story. Just before 2 a.m., he held my hand and, surrounded by his caretakers, walked me to the car, which was waiting to take me back to our hotel.

We promised each other that we would meet again, knowing it may be highly unlikely.

It was past 2 a.m. by the time I reached our hotel. The head of our delegation and a couple of my fellow delegates were pacing the lobby; they were worried about what could have happened to me!

We all heaved a sigh of relief, and went to sleep for a few hours, before our fairly early flight to return to Delhi. Our delegation was very well looked after during our visit. While we were waiting in the VIP lounge at the airport to board our flight, my fellow delegates were naturally curious to know why I had been requested to stay back. The former mayor of Shanghai had not specifically told me that his narrative was confidential. Considering the subject of the conversation, and in China, I decided to remain discreet about the details, until now. Even in this account, the details of what seemed to be an unimaginable and gargantuan enterprise and its impact on the residents of Shanghai, could only have been undertaken by China.

Jakobus Maximilian Sekhar Hubert Maria Raitz von Frentz, AKA Max

Our older daughter Nivé and Christian met in Oxford, in 1995, where they were both postgraduate students. They fell in love and got married in February 2000. Max was born on 15 May 2002 in Brussels, a full five weeks ahead of his due date, causing a great deal of consternation as Nivé took ill, but soon recovered, in an excellent hospital. Since Max was born premature, he had to spend a few days in an incubator, and emerged healthy, to the mighty relief of the whole family. For Max's delivery, originally Nivé and Christian were to travel to London. Connie was at home in London, awaiting their arrival, while I was in Amsterdam, for a board meeting. Nivé had suddenly felt ill, and had gone to see a doctor in Brussels, where they were living. She was diagnosed to be suffering a bout of eclampsia, and had to be rushed into the emergency ward of a maternity hospital, and Max had to be prematurely delivered by caesarean procedure. To everyone's great relief, mother and son came through very well, Max was kept in an incubator, being five weeks premature. Connie and I rushed to Brussels to be with them and meet our first grandson.

It was fastest to travel by Euro Rail. Chris came and picked us from Brussels Midi Station and lost our way to the nursing home. He passed on the road map to me to help guide him, which confused matters further. Although it is the capital city of Europe, the roads and directions were somewhat confusing. The year 2002 was just before the age of satnav. I guess they expected cars to have one of those really helpful electronic map readers, in which you feed in your starting point and your destination. The rest is provided by a road map screen and voice over. It was fairly late in the evening by the time we reached the nursing home and found a parking place. Nivé looked a bit wan, but happy. We were pleased to see her. Soon, Chris and I went to have a first glimpse of Max, in the incubation room. One had to enter through air-locked double doors, into a room where there were, I guess, a dozen babies in small, transparent, temperature-controlled, incubator boxes. A couple of nurses were scurrying around and everything looked very businesslike. Max's incubator was fairly close to the entrance, and I could see a tiny face, head covered with a cap, and his vital functions were being continuously monitored and recorded, with the help of sensors. Even in the dim light, I could see his face clearly with traces of postnatal tissue which all newborns carry, during the first few days after birth. Nivé had the stuff all over her when she was born thirty years earlier, as a full-term infant. Memories of Nivé's birth in Calcutta came rushing back.

It was getting late so we departed and returned the next morning. Nivé looked rested and happy. She had a good breakfast. Chris and I trooped back to the incubator room to bring Max to his mother, for a spot of breast-feeding. Chris and I had to wear face masks, as before. One of the nurses lifted Max out of his incubator crib and handed him over to Chris, who carried him comfortably, as we went back to Nivés room. Max was in the very early phase of breast-feeding and Nivé announced that he was doing OK. It was my turn to hold Max in my lap. Once I got him in the crook of my forearm, it seemed quite easy, although Connie was very nervous until Chris and I took Max back to his incubator.

Brussels is famous for its cuisine. Some claim that better French food is served in Brussels than in France. I cannot judge, although I have always enjoyed eating out in Brussels as much as I have done in Paris, over the years.

It happened to be Chris's birthday. We presented him with a pair of old-fashioned, gold cufflinks, dating back to 1895. Chris has good taste in clothes, shoes, ties and accoutrements, etc. He liked the gift.

We left Nivé to rest for a bit, and walked to a bistro, where we had booked a table for lunch. The food, pâté, fish, salad were all excellent, washed down with a bottle of 1999 Pouilly Fumé. Connie, Chris and I enjoyed the lunch. Nivé would have loved to be at the lunch. When we returned, Nivé was trying to eat her hospital lunch of mashed vegetables, soup and bread—all very nutritious and strength-giving, but hardly haute cuisine.

On our way back to London, on the Euro Rail again, back to Waterloo, discerning what it felt like to be grandparents. Max is now studying at the University College, London, his mother's alma mater.

We have watched with joy and excitement, for the past few months, the slow and steady growth of infant Max. I am not sure Max recognizes anybody other than his mother yet. They have returned to Brussels after spending time with us in London. Connie and I also returned to our home in Mumbai. Amrita had returned with us in 1997.

In 2001, Amrita decided she wished to marry her young Sikh friend Jess. They too would move to their new home down the road from us, and begin their new life. It has been an eventful journey from Bangladesh to Bombay, America, London, Rotterdam and Brussels, and many other places in between. We look forward to the future, with the same sense of anticipation, as we have ever since Connie and I were married in 1967. Wish life were that simple!

Part IV

Remaining Engaged

After formally retiring from the board of Unilever Plc and NV in 1997, I remained an independent non-executive director on the board of British Airways (BA), until 2006. In India, I took charge as a non-executive chairman of the Indian subsidiary of ICI (India) Plc. ICI Plc had appointed me while I was still in London. ICI's chairman's office in Mumbai was spacious and well-appointed, with Amy Bharda as my private secretary. Even after I exited ICI (India), after a few years, Amy continued to work for me over the next twenty years. She worked with me as a special assistant, for the longest period. Amy is an outstanding professional. We moved to the new office, I as the non-executive chairman of First Source Solution, an IT offshore service provider, promoted by ICICI Bank. I was also an independent board member, on the boards of ICICI Bank and subsequently, the Reserve Bank of India, Mahindra and Mahindra, Dr Reddy's Laboratory and Wipro, and after a few years, I became the non-executive chairman of the Anandabazar Patrika (ABP) Group. I continued to serve as a trustee of the Leverhulme Trust in London, for close to ten years. I was also nominated as a member of the Prime Minister's Advisory Council on Trade and Industry, the India–USA Business Council, and the National Knowledge Commission, by Prime Minister Dr Manmohan Singh. Subsequently, the Government of India also set up an investment commission, chaired by Ratan Tata, with Deepak Parekh and me as members.

Thus, for twenty years, since retiring from full-time work as a director at Unilever Plc and NV, I remained professionally active, with sufficient time to spare, for annual holidays with Connie. We used to visit the UK every year, and some years, more than once, and I was glad to have more time to play golf. I have briefly described, in separate sections, my six years as a nominated member of the Rajya Sabha (2009–15) and nine years (1999–2009) on the board of the Reserve Bank of India.

After we came back to live in Mumbai, Connie convinced me that I should have a separate and independent office space of my own, which was very wise. In my life's biggest tragic setback, Connie passed away in October 2019. We had been married for fifty-three years. I am unsuccessfully grappling with the aftermath and the uncertainties of life without Connie. Amy and her husband had to stay in Australia for long periods for a permanent visa. Her only daughter and her family have settled in Australia. Dhanashree, who replaced Amy, started assisting me after Amy went to Australia, and in the COVID lockdown, working from her home office.

In 1998, a good friend Narayan Vaghul and I started a private venture, offering consulting services, following the India launch of my book *Business Driven R&D; Managing Knowledge to Create Wealth*. After an initial burst of demand for our professional advisory service, we discovered that even in the late 1990s, R&D was of very limited or even of no interest to Indian private sector businesses, barring a few rare exceptions. R&D had always been desultory in India's public sector industries, as monopolies. While the primary preoccupation of Indian promoters and the Indian state was to keep out foreign investors, and competition, in the garb of 'self-reliance'. Not much has changed even as I relate this story. Subsequently, Vaghul and I established India's first knowledge park, in Hyderabad. The objective was to provide modern laboratory modules and services to budding innovators. The venture was sponsored by ICICI Bank, and enabled with the lease of land, on the outskirts of Hyderabad, by the enthusiastic chief minister of the undivided Andhra Pradesh,

Chandra Babu Naidu. It was the first institution of its kind in India, and is now prominent amongst its global peers as a very successful and modern centre for R&D and innovation start-ups. As for the technology consultancy service which we had started, Vaghul and I transferred the company to our three young colleagues. Sadly, investment in R&D and innovation remain buzzwords across Indian industry. However, India's venture capital funded success, as well as the explosion of digital services companies, are transforming India's old industrial scenario.

Sadly, innovation and R&D in India are not much different, compared to when I started my professional career in 1962. In spite of India's history of restrictive economic politics, India is now an emerging economy. Since 2020, the waves of the COVID pandemic are both socially and economically one of the biggest setbacks for a large section of the Indian population.

I have always been optimistic throughout my past and still live in the hope for the proverbial glimmer of light at the end of the tunnel. When I was young and full of confidence and optimism about the future of India, I lit my lamp of an imagined future, which most young people do. Over the years, the glow has become, sadly, feeble and weak. Every generation lights its own lamp. Succeeding generations continue to live in hope, and in search of that glimmer, of a better future.

Reserve Bank of India

I was invited to join the board of the Reserve Bank of India (RBI) in the year 2000. Dr Bimal Jalan had been appointed governor of the RBI, by Inder Gujral, then the prime minister of India. Dr Jalan, and subsequently, Dr Venugopal Reddy, enjoyed a comparatively greater degree of autonomy within the ambit of the RBI Act, in close and frequent interactions between the finance minister, the prime minister and the governor. The precise definition of 'RBI's autonomy' remains somewhat ethereal. Following my nomination to the Rajya Sabha in 2009, I had to step down from the board of the RBI. During my nine years on the board, I learnt a great deal about Indian banking in general, some major international central banks and global regulatory agencies.

From its inception, in 1935, RBI's mandate was well defined. Its spheres of authority and accountability are wisely balanced, with its autonomy in operations. In that context, the more recent episodes, between the Government of India and the RBI, are unfortunate.

After stepping down from the board of the RBI in 2009, I felt persuaded to record some of my key learnings and experiences at the RBI. My objective is to try to briefly describe, in layman's terms, the critical role of RBI in the management of India's economic health and financial well-being.

Following my appointment to the board of the RBI, by the Government of India, in the year 2000, I stepped down as a non-executive director from the board of ICICI Bank. I left the ICICI Bank board with a tinge of sadness. I had enjoyed, and learnt a good deal, about banks in India on the ICICI Board. One of my fellow directors on the board of ICICI, Narayan Murthy had to also step down, prior to joining the RBI Board, at the same time as I did.

One of the longest, if not the longest, serving non-executive directors of RBI was Yezdi Malegam, the well-known and much respected chartered accountant. Mr Malegam's presence hugely enriched the regulatory and audit role of the RBI board. RBI's 'independent directors' were strangely nomenclatured as 'Non-Official Directors', under the BRA (Banking Regulations Act). The title is an example of what may have been inherited from the British, and the RBI Act of 1935, drafted by a Royal Commission, which had recommended the creation of a Central Bank with the specific mandate to 'separate the control of currency and credit from the Government and to augment Banking facility throughout the country'.

The RBI board is chaired by a Government of India-appointed governor and three full-time deputy governors. The first woman deputy governor, K.J. Udeshi, had been appointed just before I joined the RBI board. Dr Y.V. Reddy, deputy governor, succeeded Bimal Jalan as the governor when Dr Jalan was nominated to the Rajya Sabha in 2003. The senior-most ranks of managers of the bank were designated as directors, although they were not members of the board. All the senior staff of the RBI, with whom I had interacted, were, without exception, very professionally competent. As a matter of fact, the management cadre of the RBI, as well as other ranks, were professionally competent and committed as well. In brief, I believe the RBI is one of India's pre-eminent national institutions of the Government of India.

Dr Y.V. Reddy was followed by Dr Duvuri Subbarao, while I was still on the RBI board. Dr Subbarao was succeeded by Dr Raghuram Rajan, followed by Dr Urjit Patel. Dr Urjit Patel resigned before his term was over and was succeeded by Shakti Kanta Das, at the time of drafting this chapter.

I especially wish to briefly mention the stellar role of the RBI in anticipating and being prepared for India to face the global financial crisis of 2008. India's economic policies and modest progress of reforms had made the economy very fragile. In 1991, India finally implemented long-pending fiscal and economic 'reforms'. For the first time, a traditionally inward-looking Indian economy introduced drastic policy changes, to loosen the stranglehold of historic shibboleths. Fortunately, the 'reforms' enabled India to be more or less shielded from the Asian financial meltdown, during the mid-1990s. India's ability to weather the post-2007–08 global economic crises was also, to a very significant measure, due to RBIs early warnings and advice.

Following the 2008 crisis, RBI, along with other major international banks and regulatory bodies, played an active if somewhat understated role, in the establishment of the G20. Former RBI governor Venu Reddy's latest book, *Advice and Dissent: My Life in Policy Making*, provides a detailed description of that period.

While on the RBI board, I was appointed as a member of RBI's Technical Committee on Monetary Policy, an advisory group constituted to deliberate on the state of the Indian economy. The technical committee's deliberations and gist of its advice reflected the status of market-related issues. RBI held formal weekly board meetings, on Wednesday, in Mumbai. These meetings deliberated the key dynamics and undercurrents of the Indian economy, as well as major monetary and banking issues.

Board of Financial Supervision

As a member of the board, I was also one of the members of the Board of Financial Supervision (BFS). In its quarterly meetings, the BFS reviewed the RBI's annual inspection reports of different public as well as private sector banks in India. The financial inspection reports reflected the quality and status of oversight and control exercised by the boards of individual banks. The diligence with which the BFS recommendations were being implemented by the majority of the public, as well as the private sector and foreign banks in India, indicated the need to improve management and oversight. In this respect, public sector banks needed even more diligence. Overall, the management and board of most banks in India needed to significantly raise standards of governance and accountability.

Governance of banks operating in India, in general, was inadequate. The DBS crisis and the collapse of the Madhavpura Mercantile Cooperative Bank, in Gujarat, were timely wake-up calls, about unsatisfactory governance and management oversight. Madhavpura was only the tip of the iceberg. The Banking Regulations Act, to some extent, also seemed to be responsible for the history of the poor state of governance, especially in the cooperative and many public sector banks.

Governor Reddy constituted a 'consultative group of directors of banks' to review and report on governance in banks, and nominated me, on behalf of the RBI board, to chair the group. Our brief was 'to review and recommend measures to improve the quality of governance in banks and financial institutions operating in India, as well as to recommend measures to match global best practices'.

The consultative group, as a part of its deliberations, held formal discussions with a number of chairpersons of public as well as private sector banks, and with some of the leading experts on governance in the financial sector.

Following deliberations, our group submitted its final report of recommendations to modernize and upgrade governance practices in banks, for consideration and adoption by the statutory boards of banks conducting business in India. The Government of India approved the recommendations of the group. The recommendations were mandatory for all the private sector banks. Implementation in public sector banks, however, had to await amendments to the BR Act. The large number of financial institutions in the cooperative sector, even after the Madhavpura debacle, remained outside supervisory preview.

After a few years, another report, on board governance in banks, was published by the Dr P.J. Nayak Committee. The committee, once again, underscored the alarming state of governance in banks, especially in the public sector banks. The recent enactment of the Indian bankruptcy laws has revealed the extent of the crisis of accumulated non-performing assets (NPAs) in the books of public sector banks, as well as the large-scale defaults, malfeasance and frauds, and the variable state of supervisory and fiduciary management in Indian banks.

These confirm the serious deficiencies regarding the quality of assessment and the history of borrowing entities, as well as accountability of lenders. The cost of periodic recapitalization of banks may be practically unavoidable, but the poor compliance of banks, regarding prompt corrective actions, is unfortunate, and costly.

In the absence of strict fiduciary accountability of the board of directors, of virtually all banks, and questionable technical competence as well as vigilance and dependability of statutory auditors, performance of banks in India is unlikely to improve significantly in a foreseeable time frame.

During my tenure as an independent director on the board of ICICI Bank, I happened to chair the board's investment committee. For evaluation of projects solely funded by the bank, the fiduciary process was clearly laid down, and follow-up of progress was compulsory. In fact, depending on the size and complexity of a project proposal, scrutiny and advice by sector experts must be mandatory. This is how most international banks are supposed to operate. India's large and growing number of NPAs reflects the state of commercial banking in our country.

A critical factor is also the variable quality of the annual statutory audit. Yezdi Malegam, chairman, and I, as members of the RBI's board audit subcommittee, raised serious concerns regarding the shortcomings and variable quality of audit reports, especially of bank branches spread across the country. Hopefully, things may have improved over time!

India's financial sector is growing rapidly. Digital banking is facilitating access to customers, customer numbers have grown and services have also improved across India. The growth of NBFCs adds to the regulatory challenges. Operations such as demonetization, GST-SGST, digitization, demand a different order of supervision and oversight. Investments for continuous learning for skills are critical in every bank and NBFC. However, audit has been, and remains, a challenge.

The SME Sector

It is well known that in India, the small and medium scale enterprises (SMEs) generate more jobs and wealth, compared to the more visible large manufacturing and services sectors. Access to bank credit remains a major hurdle for MSMEs (micro, small and medium enterprises), not dissimilar to the agriculture sector in India. This, in spite of the fact that a dedicated bank, Small Industries Development Bank of India (SIDBI), was established fairly early. The RBI has, from time to time, set up working groups, to assess the state of the SSIs' (small-scale industries) access to lenders. I chaired a working group in 2004. Our working group first reviewed the status of the recommendations of the previous Kapoor Committee, on the same subject. That review had concluded that although some progress had been made to improve access of the SSI sector seeking bank loans, the overall fulfilment was significantly short of demand.

Our working groups study revealed the need to promote credit rating for the SMEs, in order to improve access to NBFCs (non-banking finance institutions or companies) and real-time monitoring by SIDBI. Our working group recommended resources marked for SMEs to be significantly raised, supported by access to professional credit rating. Our working group also suggested to annually publish official data, on the progress of ease of doing business and access to credit by the SMEs. The urgency, to enable SMEs to rapidly grow across India, and data on the sector's contribution to exports and employment generation, must be publicized in the public domain.

Looking back to my time on the RBI board (2000–09), while improvements seemed to be slow compared to what might be desirable, impressive progress continued on various fronts. Progress of digitization was spreading across bank operations, which will be the only means to modernize banking in India and raise performance to international best practice.

I will conclude this section, with only a brief account about CAFRAL (Centre of Advanced Financial Research and Learning). The centre was launched by Prime Minister Dr Manmohan Singh, on 18 March 2006. The operations of CAFRAL commenced under a governing council chaired by Dr D. Subbarao, the governor of Reserve Bank of India. I continued as a member of the governing council until 2017. Dr Subbarao was succeeded by Governor Dr Raghuram Rajan, as the chairman of CAFRAL. The goal of CAFRAL, 'to pursue cutting-edge research, training and education in the fields of banking, securities and insurance,' achieved significant progress and prominence, under former deputy governor Usha Thorat, the first director of CAFRAL, which soon became part of its international peer group.

My time and experience on the RBI board was professionally satisfying. It was a valuable learning experience as well, getting to understand at least some of the intricacies of its wide-ranging responsibilities and challenges. RBI's impact on the Indian economy has always been and remains critical. The close involvement and interactions of the governor and deputy governors with their peers in key international regulatory institutions and other central banks, are also of immense value. The balance between autonomy and accountability of the RBI vis-à-vis the Government of India, is a finely nuanced process, which normally operates seamlessly, outside the media and public glare. Successive governors of the RBI and finance ministers of India must have dealt with issues of autonomy and accountability, with wisdom and foresight.

After nine years on the board, as well as some sub-committees of the board, and working groups, the one aspect I admired, above all, was the uniformly high quality and calibre of professional managers in the RBI and the central bank's HR policies and practices. Succession and career-planning of the managers were planned and executed in ways which are comparable to the best. Issues raised by staff unions were handled with wisdom, foresight and fairness. It made me wonder sometimes as to how the consistently high quality and commitment of the RBI employees, at various levels, could be so different from many other government departments and institutions, with whom I had interacted over the years.

Location of RBI's headquarters, away from Delhi and in the heart of Bombay's business district, probably serves as the ideal interface between the state and a large section of India's private sector. Besides professional HR practices and RBI's policy on meritocracy, in development of people and careers, there is one other factor worth mentioning. The secondment of many of RBI's senior managers, to international regulatory as well as other banking institutions, has a positive impact on the outlook and attitude of managers.

Notwithstanding frequent, and presumably unavoidable, interventions from the banking division of the finance ministry, the quality of professional management in the RBI has remained consistent. Be that as it may, the RBI is a unique role model in India, of professionalism, in a state institution. I have since wondered how transformational it could have been if some of the other departments, dealing with trade and commerce, had greater presence in Mumbai's business district!

My time in the RBI will remain an important landmark of my professional career!

Rajya Sabha

In the summer of 2009, Connie and I were in London on one of our annual visits. One morning, we received a phone call that the Congress president wished to speak to me. I wasn't home, so her office said that they would call back later. When I was able to speak, I was informed that it was proposed to nominate me to the Rajya Sabha (RS).

I had avoided being drawn into politics all my life, because I neither had the inclination nor wished to get involved. In the past, I had been requested to join the Congress party, consider ambassadorship to a major Western nation (1985), become a member of the Planning Commission, contest a general election (1991). Nomination to the Rajya Sabha seemed comparably benign. I was wrong. An unexciting six-year term (2009–15) in the RS confirmed my lifelong belief not to join politics.

The President of India officially nominates a candidate for the RS, on the recommendation of the prime minister. There are twelve seats in the RS for 'nominated members'. A vacancy takes place every time a member completes a six-year term, in the upper house. In November 2009, H.K. Dua, a well-known journalist, and I took oath on the same day and had seats next to each other, in the 'Upper House'. The swearing-in ceremony for the occasion was solemn, and the welcome by fellow members was warm.

Members of the Lok Sabha (LS) and RS are provided residential accommodation, a monthly allowance, personal secretarial support, etc. I was allotted a good address and a broken-down bungalow in the Lutyens's area. It was soon repaired and nicely restored, by the Public Works Department.

All through my term (2009–15), I planned and recorded brief notes, of some key events of the deliberations. Subsequently, going through my notes, I tried to recall some of the events. Normally, in a calendar year, Parliament meets in three sessions, the Budget Session, the Monsoon Session and the Winter Session. The Budget Session commences in February. The President of India addresses a joint session of the LS and the RS, in the Central Hall of the Parliament. The address by the President highlights the government's achievements during the previous year, and the key programmes and plans for the ensuing year.

The President's address is simultaneously broadcast, publicly, and sets the scene for the Budget Session. During the Budget Session, the nation's annual Budget, or the Finance Bill, is presented in the LS, by the finance minister. In the weeks following, the Finance Bill is discussed and debated in the LS as well as the RS, even though the RS does not have any statutory role in approving or otherwise, on matters classified as 'Money Bill'. However, the important issues raised by members during the RS debate are replied to by the finance minister, in the RS. The only exception is in the event of a Constitutional Amendment, introduced by the RS. The Railway Budget used to be presented by the railway minister and discussed separately, until the Railway Budget was merged with the Finance Bill, in 2014.

Since 2010 was my first full year as a nominated member of the RS, I will try and narrate the formal events in the RS for that year, and as a framework for the following five years, highlight a few exceptional events.

2010: 'The Role of the Opposition Is to Oppose'

One particular practice which remains uppermost in my mind is the very infrequent and the two-minute time limit, for nominated members to intervene in debates and discussions of any topic on the 'floor' of the House. This was, we were informed, a technicality due to which each nominated member is considered to be independent, and not a part of any political party. In any debate, political parties were allocated time according to the number of their sitting members, and the party in turn usually assigned one or two amongst its members to speak on the party's behalf, on a subject being discussed. In contrast, if a nominated member wishes to participate in a debate, he/she is allocated a maximum of two minutes to have the floor. This technicality is applied almost mindlessly, by whoever happened to be chairing a particular motion.

The original objective of India's founding fathers was to nominate a few members to the Upper House, from amongst academics, artists, scholars as well as persons of eminence, in different professions, so that they may provide a broader perspective on issues, beyond politics and the 'party line'. That's one of the reasons, probably, why the Rajya Sabha is known as the 'House of Elders'! The rest of the members are politicians elected by the members of state assemblies. During debates, each party submits the name of one or two of its members, to speak on behalf of the party on a particular issue. Therefore, the speakers have all the time to elaborate on their party line.

As nominated members in the RS, all of us felt that to restrict only one or at the most two members to speak during any debate, and each for only two minutes, was not only inadequate but also unfair. The time restriction on nominated members defeats the purpose of what might have been the original idea for their presence in the Upper House or the House of Elders.

Even during other interventions, such as the 'Zero Hour' or the 'Question Hour', nominated members were not supposed to intervene, while political members normally did both to draw the attention of the chair, to allow them to register their view for the record. We, the nominated members, felt unhappy about the state of affairs, and as a group, sought an appointment with the chairman of the RS, the vice-president of India, Dr Hamid Ansari, in order to convey our unhappiness as well as to suggest some mitigation.

The chairman of the RS invited all the nominated members and met us over a cup of tea. We had already submitted our proposal, which, in summary, was that, since there were twelve of us, if the chairman agreed to consider the nominated members as a 'group', the maximum time allocable for debate would add up to twenty-four minutes. At his discretion, the chairman could allocate five or ten minutes, not necessarily the full twenty-four, to the nominated members' group. The nominated members, in turn, could select one or at the most two, from amongst the twelve, to participate and present our views, in the debate, on an issue, appropriately. To our disappointment, Chairman Ansari, whom I had personally known, over several years, and held in high esteem, felt that it would not be appropriate to even explore our request and seek official advice since the procedures had been well-thought-out and enshrined. We listened to his response, but would have expected him to at least explore our request, instead of expressing helplessness!

The purpose of nominating citizens of eminence, from outside the political sphere, over time, had become ornaments of silence! I felt that if those, who are sounded out about being nominated to the RS were to be aware of what awaited them, many may have, politely, declined the honour. Much later I realized the wisdom of Dr Ansari. In politics, as in other worldly matters, change is the only constant!

I must, however, conclude, by sharing a glimpse of an unexpected, and somewhat amusing, outcome. Following the disappointing outcome of our meeting with the chairman, we decided that the two minutes' time allocated to one or two of us, who wished to speak on an issue or a bill, during a debate, must prepare and put on record a few of the most critical points. From then on, I kept practising how to make the best use of the two minutes, whenever I had important points to be recorded. Before my RS term ended, I earned the moniker and got known as 'Two Minute Ganguly'. I also made sure that if I wished some of my important views to be on record of a particular deliberation, I also submitted brief notes of intervention, for the record of the RS proceedings.

The title of this section was an observation made by the late Arun Jaitley, who was the leader of the opposition (LOP), in 2010. It best captured the frequent chaotic scenes of disruptions of the proceedings of the RS. During my very first week in the Rajya Sabha, I was bewildered by the very frequent disruptions of the House, by groups of members jumping on their feet and raising loud voices of dissent, on some issue, which was mostly not clear. The chair was then frequently forced to adjourn the proceedings of the House, for varying lengths of time, from ten minutes to longer periods. Nearly all the members would then troop out of the RS and pour into the Central Hall of Parliament, talking in groups and drinking endless cups of coffee, or sharing snacks while gossiping with journalists or former members, in the Central Hall. I wondered sometimes, seeing some former members, virtually every day, in the Central Hall, when Parliament was in session, what was it they enjoyed about coming to the Central Hall.

The frequent adjournments of the RS were confusing during my early weeks, and I had asked Mr Jaitley if there was any method in what I felt was mindlessness! The LOP, whom I knew reasonably well, replied that 'the role of the opposition is to oppose'. He also reminded me that I had strayed into 'the citadel of Indian politics,

which is best avoided by a professional like me!' The snacks in the
Central Hall, and in the members' dining room, were always of very
good quality and inexpensive, which members enjoy, as their rightful
due and possibly as a compensation!

Members of the Rajya Sabha and Lok Sabha are nominated
on different standing and select committees of Parliament. I was
nominated to two standing committees of Parliament, one on
water resources and the other the COPLOT (Committee for Papers
to be Laid on the Table) of the Rajya Sabha. I was also one of the
members in two select committees of the finance ministry and
second, the home ministry. The standing committees' agenda was
usually on contemporary and very relevant issues. Secretaries and
additional secretaries of the ministries, and the subordinate staff
of the committees, made detailed presentations on major agenda
items for the standing committee, and the discussions between the
minister and members were very worthwhile. On the other hand,
water being a 'state subject', and on the concurrent list of the Central
government, the impact and outcomes from deliberations, of the
standing committee, were far less interesting. The important items in
the select committee agenda, such as river linking projects, building
of dams, etc., seemed to be forever delayed, mostly because of
interstate disputes. One of the serious problems is the rapid depletion
of groundwater, across large parts of our country. Rapid depletion
of groundwater is exacerbated by the availability of free power for
the agricultural sector, growth of population and erratic rainfall. The
select committee faced endless delays of annual reports of most major
projects and incomplete audited accounts, which had accumulated
over many years. Members of the standing committee were eager to
visit some of the project sites, to better understand the reasons for the
prolonged delays. How far such visits made any difference, I failed to
understand. During my six years in the RS, I did not join even one
tour, within India or abroad.

More than once, I tried to unsuccessfully raise the issue of the
Chinese plan to divert Himalayan melt, with potentially adverse

to extremely adverse effect on the Brahmaputra and its tributaries. I had even sent a note to Prime Minister Dr Manmohan Singh about this threat. Recently, the issue of the Chinese diverting the Tibetan melt was once again reported in the Indian media. The usual response of China, that it was conscious of India's concerns, sounded as hollow as usual. The source of the Brahmaputra, and the Chinese strategy, needs much more public discussion in India, and aggressively raised in the international fora.

The home and the finance consultative committee meetings usually started with a presentation by the secretary of the ministry on one of the current and important topics, followed by fairly detailed discussions led by the minister and the members of the select committee, from the LS and the RS. In finance, topics included economic growth, banking as well as issues of critical importance. The agenda of the consultative committee of the home ministry usually included insurgency in Kashmir, and parts of the North-east, the growing Naxal menace, but above all, the long-overdue need to modernize India's police and paramilitary forces. These committee meetings were extensive deliberation on the agenda topics, and especially of the realities and challenges.

The select committee deliberations were usually nonpartisan and objective. However, partisan views were not entirely avoidable.

During my early days in the Rajya Sabha, my friend, the late Murli Deora, a veteran Congress politician from Mumbai and a cabinet minister in the then United Progressive Alliance (UPA) government, was of immense help and support to me. He ensured that I was allotted a decent residential accommodation, at No. 10 Dr Rajendra Prasad Road, as well as in other matters. I found that all the Rajya Sabha staff, without exception, were very polite and helpful. But as a nominated member, even though one is extended all the courtesies, I soon realized that, since I did not belong to any political party or group, I had sufficient time to listen to all the political chatter and whispered exchanges, in the corridors of Parliament and the Central Hall. Such exposures were quite a revelation.

According to parliamentary rules, a nominated member is also free to align with a political party within the first six months of entering the RS. Once a nominated member declares his/her intention to align with a particular party, the member has to move to a seat in that section of the House which the party is occupying. During my tenure, Mani Shankar Iyer, a veteran Congressman, joined the RS, as a nominated member, and almost immediately moved to the Congress benches. In contrast, Prof. Bhalchandra Mungeker, a former vice-chancellor of Bombay University, apparently had political ambitions, so after being nominated, he joined the ruling party and moved to the Congress benches in the RS.

There was once a rather minor but 'juvenile' episode, concerning my seat number in the Rajya Sabha. My RS seat happened to be number 100. Derek O'Brien of the TMC requested me to exchange my seat with the one allocated to the cricketer Sachin Tendulkar, who had been nominated to the RS in 2013. I advised Derek, privately, not to pursue this silly issue. Newly nominated members Tendulkar and Bollywood actress Rekha were rarely seen in the RS, not more than a couple of days during the year. It was sad that certain nominated members eroded the original objective of their presence.

In 2010, the first part of the Budget Session, and the motion of thanks, to the President of India, the Rajya Sabha was frequently disrupted on a variety of issues, such as rise in prices, inflation, corruption, etc., etc. After several days of frequent disruptions of the proceedings and adjournments, a few serious debates, however, did take place. I recall having briefly intervened, during the discussions, on the President's speech. To my utter ignorance and some regret, my intervention was taken on record as my maiden speech. I was unaware of the concept of the maiden speech. A new member is entitled to speak on any subject of the member's choice, during his/ her first delivery, without any time limit. Had I been aware of this tradition, I could have prepared and delivered my maiden speech at an appropriate opportunity, and which I had lost, due to my brief intervention. In retrospect, I have no regrets whatsoever. During my six-year term, in spite of the time restrictions, I was called upon, or decided, to intervene frequently, on issues which I wished to comment upon, on topics such as economics, education, R&D, agriculture, etc.; subjects on which I was able to intervene sensibly.

Arun Jaitley (LOP), Sharad Pawar (minister of food and agriculture), Ghulam Nabhi Azad (leader of the House), Sitaram Yechuri (CPM) were amongst the handful of excellent speakers. Some members rambled on endlessly, usually exceeding their allotted time, and had to be repeatedly requested by the chair to take their seat.

In every session, a number of bills were listed in the agenda, to be taken up for discussion. In March 2010, in a debate on the bill for reservation (33 per cent) of seats for women, I recall that the speakers were frequently disrupted and some of the MPs had rushed into the well of the House, forcing frequent adjournments. With all the shouting, it was difficult to understand the issues which provoked the protest. One was left wondering whether it was for or against the reservation of seats for women! This was the only occasion, during my six-year tenure, that the chairman, Hamid Ansari, expelled some senior RJD (Rashtriya Janata Dal) and SP (Samajwadi Party) members, for the rest of the Budget Session.

The annual Budget Session is spread over two sittings, with a break of a few weeks in between. Besides the vote of thanks for the President's address, the major items in 2010 were the Railway Budget and then the Finance Bill. As already mentioned, while the RS does not vote on 'money bills', important issues in the budget are thoroughly debated in the Upper House, and officially communicated to the LS. The RS debate on the Finance Bill is supposed to convey appropriate checks and balances regarding the annual budget.

RS deliberations, debates and observations have played a critical role in the final outcome of every annual budget.

During 2009–15, I was told by some of the members, who had been members of the RS for several terms, that the frequency of disruptions and adjournments, forced by members of the opposition, had apparently increased significantly. It was obvious that being out of power for prolonged periods built frustration in politicians occupying the opposition benches, and this was possibly one of the reasons for the frequent outbursts and disruptions. A probable way to get media and constituency attention! Frequently, when meaningful debates did take place, it was indeed amazing how the quality of discussion would rise in eloquence, wisdom and foresight.

I wondered, as did many of my fellow members, whether live TV coverage of the proceedings of the House may be encouraging, at least some of the speakers, to address their constituencies rather than the topic under discussion. It was not unusual for speakers to turn around and address the press gallery, at the rear of the House, hoping to grab a headline the next day or even the same evening. Anxiety to remain visible and active was very important.

In my early days in the RS, I saw hordes of TV and press reporters, and their cameramen, rushing to catch the attention of MPs when we were emerging from the Parliament building. Several members were keen to give a sound bite, or even rambling long statements. Visibility was eagerly sought. I became curious, watching hordes of TV cameras, every day, rushing towards especially prominent MPs, for sound bites. I asked one of my acquaintances in the media, What was the usual outcome of this daily media frenzy? My acquaintance, privately revealed that the media tried to be discriminating. Sometimes, neither the microphones nor the cameras were actually recording an interview. But what the prominent leaders said during these interviews, for which the TV channels competed, was mainly 'Breaking News'.

After the Budget Session, the Parliament reconvenes for the Monsoon Session. I had attended a two-day orientation programme for new members in 2010. All the lectures, as well as speakers, were very informative. One of the more exciting announcements during the orientation programme was that Parliament would soon move to paperless communication. This was going to be revolutionary. Members are inundated, every day, with papers and reading material. By the time I completed my term, in 2015, the 'paperless' objective was still a work-in-progress. In the meantime, each MP was given an iPad, with an individual email ID. Members continued to be inundated with papers when my term came to an end, in 2015.

Dr Hamid Ansari, vice-president of India and chairman of the Rajya Sabha, while delivering his talk, at the familiarization programme, lamented that parliamentary debates, of late, were failing to raise the hopes and aspirations of the Indian people. While the parliamentary committees seemed to generally function well and effectively, he said, these were not sufficient, by themselves, and much remained to be done!

The secretary of the ministry of statistics and programme implementation, spoke on the very important topic of the Member of Parliament Local Area Development (MPLAD) fund, and the procedure to effectively utilize these funds allocated to each MP, to construct, build and provide durable community assets in the MP's own constituencies. Nominated members were, however, permitted to support projects across India, as they considered appropriate. For example, the MPLAD projects which I supported with my MPLAD funds during my term were one of the most satisfying memories of my tenure as a nominated MP. After my term ended, I published two booklets, describing each of the projects which I had supported, in various states across India, under the MPLAD Scheme. On the whole the MP orientation programme was extremely worthwhile for first-time MPs.

One of the highlights of the Monsoon Session is the progress, or the lack of, the annual rainfall. Over the years, the variability in the pattern of onset, delay and erratic progress of the monsoon, in India, has increased. The scarcity of access to potable water and dropping levels of groundwater, in several parts of the country, are serious problems. Climate change had not yet become the issue it has since!

Sadly, in India, the annual spoilage of food grains, vegetables, fruits, pulses and virtually every agricultural produce is one of the highest in the world. The economic distress in the farming communities has also grown. The frequent incidents of suicides by indebted farmers is a grim national reality. The problems in India's farming sector have always been endlessly discussed, without much progress. Although India has built an impressive buffer stock of grains, the annual losses due to insufficient storage, enclosed storage capacity, inefficiency and monopoly, of the Food Corporation of India, are tragic. The procurement, storage and sale of fruits and vegetables, in India, are also subject to the near monopoly of the APMC (Agriculture Produce Marketing Cooperative), in each state. In the absence of sufficient modern storage, and due to seasonal glut and distribution inefficiency, up to 40 per cent output of fruits and vegetables are wasted annually in India. The distress becomes stark when the annual monsoon rains are either delayed or fail in parts of the country.

The final session of the year is the Winter Session, during the months of November and December. The House adjourns sine die before Christmas. During the 2010 winter session, there was a big hue and cry following the Comptroller and Auditor General of India's (CAG's) critical report on the 2G spectrum auction. Telecom Minister A. Raja, of the Dravida Munnetra Kazhagam (DMK), a coalition partner of the UPA2, had to resign. The critical CAG report was going to remain a hot topic for a while!

In other developments that year, the telephone tapping and the Radia tapes scandal also burst into the public domain. One Neera Radia headed a well-known private advisory and liaison service business in Delhi. She served a list of well-known private sector clients. Ms Radia apparently had extensive contacts across various ministries of the government. Following the exposure of the telephone tapping, the Rajya Sabha proceedings were disrupted even more frequently than usual. Not much business was transacted.

Parliamentary Legislative Research Services (PRS)

It is worth briefly describing this unique and independent private institution, which was set up as an NGO by one Dr Madhavan. PRS held weekly workshops on key issues, for members of Parliament when the House was in session, and seminars addressed by experts, on important bills and other issues being debated in Parliament. All MPs were free to attend these sessions and quite a few did so, regularly. PRS had also launched similar programmes in a few states. PRS introduced a novel 'research assistants' programme, to assist interested MPs in their parliamentary tasks. This programme attracted a number of bright and fresh graduates, from all over India, every year. From amongst the applicants, 30–40 are chosen as research assistants by PRS, every year.

Incidentally, another valuable source of information is the Parliament Library, which provides MPs, on request, the previous six months' press clippings on any topic of contemporary interest. PRS frequently also issued research papers on major national issues. Most MPs are aware of PRS's activities, as a source of information on contemporary topics. The staff of PRS is easily accessible to MPs and a reliable resource for information and assistance. I have acknowledged separately the contribution of the PRS fellows who were assigned to me, and who also helped to evaluate the MPLADS proposals which I explored to support or sponsor, as well as helped in the periodic follow-up of the progress of each MPLAD project sponsored.

During my tenure in the Rajya Sabha, I was fortunate to be assigned two PRS fellows as research assistants, during consecutive years. Under the supervision of my special assistant, the PRS fellows quickly gained familiarity with the processes and priorities of my work schedule and tasks, as an MP. The research assistants were diligent and thorough in the tasks assigned to them. Their support was valuable.

During 2009–15, the number of days Parliament worked in each calendar year kept dwindling. In the 1950s and 1960s, Parliament used to meet 125 or more days in a year. This gradually reduced to seventy days or less in a year. Calculated after taking into account adjournments, etc., the net hours devoted to debate and pass legislation have kept on reducing. Consequently, the number of bills approved, without discussion, deliberation or even voting, has grown.

In retrospect, during my six-year term in the Rajya Sabha (RS), the image I had in mind of this august institution and my experience turned out to be different. The RS still provides certain checks and balances, regarding legislations and bills, which, naturally, depends on the mix of MPs belonging to different parties during a period. The late Arun Jaitley once told me, quite pithily, that 'the role of the opposition is to oppose'! Such opposition is sometimes constructive, but more often devoid of logic.

Considering the collection of my personal experience, I am fortunate that I had the exposure, but disappointed in my expectations, at the end of my tenure. In my brief farewell speech, I thanked my fellow members, for their unfailing kindness and courtesies, and expressed hope that nominated members in the future may be able to add better value during their tenure. My most rewarding experience was supporting a large number of very deserving projects, under the MPLAD programme, in different parts of India.

My exposure to a wider spectrum of Indian politics reinforced my long-held belief that I was unsuited for it as a profession.

Encounters and Episodes

A close friend of mine suggested during the course of one of our occasional conversations that I should consider writing about some of my more memorable encounters, which sort of stand out.

I thought over the suggestion and felt it may be an interesting exercise, but I would have to be mindful of the people linked with the different episodes and any sensitivities! Above all, the narrative is subjective in the sense that these were my personal experiences!

Early Encounters

Going Astray: Other than in fiction, I have not come across personal narratives of the adventures and misadventures of ordinary people. I have already narrated a couple of episodes from when I was about ten or eleven years of age. I was just not interested in either my studies or my school. The high school I attended was not amongst Mumbai's top, or even middling grade, institutions. The only well-known alumnus, I learnt, was the late Nani Palkhiwala. As an aside, during childhood, my sister and I were taught to read and write Bengali at home, by the unrelenting efforts of our mother. In school, I consistently ranked in the bottom quartile of my class. How I eventually made it through school, and joined college, is the first fork of my post-failure past. Throughout my school years, my father kept engaging a succession of private tutors, but not one of them succeeded in kindling my interest. However, my father never chided me, but my mother did, for my utter indifference and poor performance in school. I have earlier narrated a couple of my misadventures, when I had decided to walk away once from home after getting a spanking from my mother, after she was informed by our domestic help, who had escorted me back from school through heavy rain, that I had dropped my report card into a roadside drain. In spite of my warning him not to tell my mother my misdeed, he did so promptly, as soon as we reached home. I felt deeply humiliated by Ma's spanking, and decided to walk out of home. The second episode is my absence, without permission, from school, which I have described earlier.

The Tipping Point: I reached my life's first tipping point when I was past fifteen, but not yet sixteen years old. After high school, I got admitted to Jai Hind College, the only college at the time which would admit me, with my less than modest SSC supplementary results, and also because my sister was already studying in the college.

What triggered the tipping point, I have not been able to quite pinpoint! But starting from my first year in college, my scholastic interest and performance, even if I modestly say so, became suddenly exceptional. The principal triggers were our teachers. Jai Hind was derisively nicknamed as a 'Sindhi College'; it was set up by a group of educationists who had emigrated from the province of Sind in Pakistan, as refugees, after Partition, in 1947. The zeal, commitment and scholastic antecedents of these pioneers were the hidden secrets. In my third year in college, I was among six students selected for additional and rigorous coaching of our subjects and repeating laboratory work after college hours. This special coaching was given by senior faculty members. I and another batch mate were top rankers in the university that year. Later on, I wondered that if I had done better in school and joined one of the well-known and venerable colleges of Bombay University, would I have missed this tipping point!

Comprehension and Brevity: During my postgraduate years in the USA, the exposures and experiences slowly started to shape the way

I think, work and communicate. During my early college years in India, the quality of the examinees' answers were assessed, for accuracy but strangely also by unusually lengthy narratives of answers. In my first 'surprise' test in the US, I knew that I had done well. The next day when our answer papers were returned to us, I was shocked to have scored a zero, out of 100. I felt crestfallen and very disturbed. At the end of the class, as we were dispersing, I was asked by the professor to stay back. He was aware that I had just arrived from India, with an excellent scholastic record and I must have appeared totally crestfallen. The professor, that day, gave me the best advice on brevity I had heard. He said that my answers were correct, for both the questions in the test, however, the answers could have been written in two brief paragraphs. I had instead filled up two pages and rambled on unnecessarily. He advised me to let this experience be a lesson. He said, 'You are now in America. Brevity signifies clarity and comprehension.'

The second episode, during my early days as a student in America is also worth recalling. My PhD professor, Dr Robert McLaughlin Whitney, was a well-known physical chemistry scholar. I had just started work on my MS research project for my thesis, alongside the prescribed courses. I was required to successfully complete both, to be qualified to proceed for my PhD.

My MS research work required reproducing a published analytical test, for application in my research work. It seemed fairly straight-forward, and actually, it was. I failed to reproduce the published test, in spite of repeating several times.

After several days, one morning, Bob told me, 'Ashok, when you are able to reproduce the analytical test correctly, please phone me right away, no matter, whatever the time may be.' One early morning, at around 2 a.m. I suddenly stumbled upon the mistake I had been repeating. I phoned Bob, at his home, at around 3 a.m., to convey the good news. Bob arrived at the laboratory soon after, looking very fresh. We sat down at my work desk, and Bob went through my latest experiments, shook my hand and presented me with a carton of Kent cigarettes (this was before the discovery of the connection between smoking and cancer). Bob then explained to me that by detecting my own mistake, I had learnt my first lesson, about the pursuit of enquiry.

Another episode was after about three years in America. On a lovely sunny spring evening, Bob and I were walking back home from our department. We took a shortcut across a neighbourhood church yard, when Bob suddenly stopped and wondered if I was aware of the significance of the spot we were walking through. It happened to be a shortcut at the rear of the church, the graveyard. Bob suddenly stopped and told me, 'Ashok, you must remember, everyone who thought that they were indispensable, rests here.' Indeed, a simple, but profound human frailty.

On another occasion, Bob and I attended a lecture on the campus, by a well-known American astronomer. The subject was black holes. The lecture on this very complex topic was delivered with stunning clarity. After the talk ended, Bob and I were walking back together. Bob wondered if I had enjoyed the lecture. I said that I had never before heard a lecture on a subject about which I knew nothing explained so simply and clearly. That, Bob told me, was the proof of the speaker's own understanding of the subject; no matter how complex any topic may be, if a speaker is able to clearly explain a very complex topic, in simple terms, to a lay audience, that is the difference between one who knows his subject and someone who does not.

Take Care of Your Money: Following my secondment to Unilever R&D in 1969 and 1970, Connie and I lived for a year in Holland and then in London. In London, there was an unusual episode, soon after we had moved there in 1970. On my first day, in the head office, I was scheduled to meet someone in the personnel department. I had not met him before. The first thing he told me, when we met, entirely unsolicited, was that I should be careful with my expenses while in London. He went on to add that apparently people from 'my part of the world', was the term he used, tended to get 'carried away', while in London. I immediately stood up, and told him that while he was 'wasting' his life at his threadbare desk, I wanted him to know, that I had already lived in many parts of the world, and that, in future, as far as I was concerned, he should mind his own business, and walked out of his room. The next day, he sought an appointment to see the research director, to complain about the previous day's episode, and was apparently told by the director, instead, to apologize to me for his unsolicited rudeness.

Sustaining a Tradition: Multinationals running businesses in India were considered as the relics of the British Raj. Ideally, they were expected to pack up and leave, or, if at all they continued their business in India, they would have to do so under the watchful glare and scrutiny of the Indian government. It was known that the company's first Indian chairman, in response, was supposed to have decided that in order to respond to any 'shadows and doubts', it was important to appraise the government regarding HLL's operations in India, and in order for the company to ensure this, to respond to all the queries of the government as promptly as possible. On the advice of a very senior civil servant of the government, Unilever had diluted its holdings, in its Indian subsidiaries, by offering shares, in the company, to the Indian public. The local shareholding turned out to be only a temporary palliative. Draconian legislations such as the MRTP (Monopoly and Restrictive Trade Practices) Act and FERA (Foreign Exchange Regulation Act, subsequently the FEMA), alongside new departments, such as the DGTD (Directorate General of Technical Development), were instruments to not only discourage foreigners from investing in India, but also to keep a close watch and restrict multinational businesses from operating in India.

While 'commanding heights' of the Indian economy were to be the exclusive domain of state enterprises, large and locally owned, private companies, continued to thrive as monopolies, some of them, not beyond covert practices, to gain unfair advantage. Under these circumstances, the only option for a company like HLL was to try and build objective rapport, and professional contacts, with the appropriate civil servants, and frequently with the ministers of the government as well. The sole objective was to build mutual understanding and trust.

I must mention HLL's former chairman Prakash Tandon, who had developed very clear professional boundaries of such relationships. Contacts and relationships with the government have continued to be nurtured by successive generations. After retiring, Prakash Tandon and subsequently his successor, Vasant Rajadhyaksha, joined important state institutions in Delhi, as professional managers, and the government started to appreciate the value of professional management, in certain activities of the state. I recall this process is best described as, 'The government's national policies and attitudes are extremely critical for managers of business to understand, in relation to their commercial activities, and it is equally important for the government to be aware of the importance of professional expertise, in India's economic growth and employment generation.'

Interactions with Delhi continued to be strengthened by chairman T. Thomas, firstly to convince the government of the ruinous price controls during Emergency, while it took time to take measures, by the company, which would entitle Unilever to retain majority shareholding in HLL, by fulfilling the conditions under FERA. The activities of our professionally managed company must be visible in the public domain, which has been ensured by the succeeding generations of managers.

West Bengal: I have described, elsewhere, the details of the labour troubles in HLL's Calcutta factory and the rise of militant, politically involved trade union leaders, in the 1970s. I and Sunil Bose, the factory personnel manager, had to interact with one minister, Pradip Bhattacharya, in charge of 'Closed and Sick Industries' (a very appropriate title, at the time). He was apparently the 'minister' at the time, looking after the Congress party's trade union wing. We had sought an appointment to meet him, during the height of our labour troubles. I had met him once before, along with Dr Ranjan Banerjee, during a previous strike, when the minister had been not only unhelpful, but had also behaved rudely. Therefore, before my second meeting, I had apprised a senior cabinet minister of the lawlessness and violence of the gun-toting Samir Roy and his cohorts. We were ushered into Minister Bhattacharya's office in Writers' Building. Without looking up, he waved his wrist, for us to sit down, alongside union leader Samir Roy and his cohorts, who were already in the minister's chamber before we arrived.

A thuggish young man sitting in the chair next to me turned to me and introduced himself as 'Shanta of College Street', as he also gestured his role, by raising both his hands, and shooting phantom revolvers in the air. Without looking up from his files, Minister Pradip Bhattacharya listened to our brief submission. He summoned his secretary and asked himself to be connected to HLL's chairman in Bombay. As soon as the minister was connected to Chairman Thomas, although we could not hear, TT apparently told him that only I was authorized to discuss with the minister all matters on West Bengal, and terminated the call, without waiting for a reply. My acquaintance, the senior cabinet minister's phone call came soon after the minister had been rebuffed by TT. Bhattacharya handed me his receiver. The cabinet minister, whom I had briefed earlier, told me, 'Don't worry, Ashok, I have told Bhattacharya to sort out all the issues today, as well as rein in Samir Roy.' I handed back the phone to Bhattacharya. I don't know what transpired in their brief exchange. After Bhattacharya put down the phone, the minister's demeanour suddenly softened. Very politely, he told me that he was grateful for my visit and that he would sort out all the issues with Samir Roy right away. He walked Bose and me down the corridor, to see us off, and we knew right away that we had won the battle.

Almost forty years later, I once again came face to face with the same Pradip Bhattacharya, in 2012, in the RS which he had just joined, as a Congress member. He acted as if I was a long-lost 'elder brother' and in a typical Indian gesture, bent down to convey respect, with a broad smile of familiarity on his face. I suddenly recalled his arrogant ways, as a young minister for sick and closed industries, in

Siddhartha Shankar Ray's Congress government in West Bengal. I wished Bhattacharya well, before I went on my way.

Jyoti Basu: When I was posted in Calcutta, I came to know two well-known individuals. One was the revered Mother Teresa and the other, the Communist chief minister of West Bengal, Jyoti Basu. I have written in a separate chapter about Mother Teresa, and our family's lifelong association with the Missionaries of Charity. I made a courtesy call on the chief minister after taking charge of HLL's Calcutta operations in 1973. From our very first meeting itself, the vibes felt good. I received frequent messages, to meet with the chief minister, mainly to discuss ways to attract investments, and employment, in West Bengal. I had suggested to the chief minister that he may wish to consider setting up a small and informal advisory group of local business chiefs, to interact with him and suggest ways to make things happen on the ground. The chief minister thought it was a good idea, but sadly, it remained on paper. I can only speculate that he may have informally sounded out the party and his cabinet colleagues, most of whom had spent their lifetime shutting down industries in West Bengal. The large numbers of educated youth from West Bengal kept moving to other Indian cities and towns, in search of employment or pursued higher studies and settled abroad.

In due course, I got to know Jyoti Basu quite well and we also met socially. In his periodic address to industry chambers, he routinely mentioned the excellent cooperation between the HLL unions and management, and the fact that HLL factories in West Bengal had the highest productivity, compared to its other units, in the rest of India. I remained in contact with Chief Minister Jyoti Basu through the 1980s, and even after I moved to London, in 1990, especially during his annual visits to London. Jyoti Basu was considered to be one of the best chief ministers in India, but sadly, not much changed in the state of West Bengal.

I clearly recall the time when a coalition government was being put together in Delhi. The consensus choice for the prime ministership, apparently, was Jyoti Basu. Sadly, the Communist Party of India (Marxist) did not agree to Jyoti Basu becoming the prime minister of India.

<u>Maharashtra</u>: The company's head office and its largest units were in and around Bombay. Over the years, the company had established excellent rapport with senior bureaucrats, as well as successive chief ministers of Maharashtra. HLL's head of legal and secretarial function, Chandrapal Mahimker, had a very important role, to keep in touch with the appropriate officials in the state. My reasonably fluent Marathi, since my childhood, was always helpful in meetings with the state chief ministers. I warmly recall my frequent meetings with Chief Minister Vasant Dada Patil and my interesting encounters with Abdul Rahman Antulay. Over the years, Sharad Pawar and I became, and remain, good friends. It may sound repetitive, but it is worth reiterating, that HLL never sought favours but was known to always seek justice and fairness, in all its dealings with the state, also in Delhi. When appropriate, the intervention and intermediation of state chief ministers, or Delhi, became necessary. Unfortunately, during the period of militancy of Datta Samant, while the then chief minister of Maharashtra wanted to rein in Samant, he was unable to do so effectively.

On another occasion, HLL was put in a very awkward situation, during the chief ministership of Abdul Rahman Antulay. In the 1980s, Antulay had set up a trust, in the name of Prime Minister Indira Gandhi. Antulay started collecting funds for the trust, from a number of industries in Maharashtra. When the chief minister had approached Hindustan Lever, he was politely explained our policy. In retaliation, HLL started to face mild regulatory irritants. It was during this period that the British deputy high commissioner hosted a reception in honour of the visiting British prime minister Margaret Thatcher. Connie and I were amongst the invitees. During the evening, we had momentarily moved away from the crowd, and Antulay, ambled across, to where Connie and I were standing. I introduced Connie to him. He right away started to tell

Connie, whom he was meeting for the first time, how unhelpful I was, not supporting the foundation he was setting up in honour of the prime minister. Connie, of course, knew nothing of what Antulay was talking about, and listened to him politely. To get Antulay off the company's back, I was soon forced to seek help, through the principal secretary to the prime minister. The very next day, the irritants suddenly stopped, while my interactions remained cordial.

The Delhi Years: HLL's 'Delhi office', as distinct from the company's Delhi branch, used to be manned by a handful of professionally dedicated, and highly committed, group, reporting to Suman Sinha, who was subsequently succeeded by Bharat Mahey. The 'Delhi office' was responsible for all matters concerning HLL and the Government of India. The term 'follow up' acquired a whole new meaning in this context. The 'usual method' was uncompromisingly abjured by HLL, and this was widely known. So how did matters concerning the company move forward towards whatever was going to be the final outcome. Besides detailed briefing of officials, starting at the clerical level and then progressively moving upwards, P.M. (Priya Mohan Suman) Sinha and Bharat Mahey, and on some matters, the chairman of HLL, had to intervene, in order to expedite matters, up to the secretary of the ministry concerned.

Nihal Kaviratne, one of my colleagues, and his wife, Shyama, had introduced me to one of Shyama's aunts, Pupul Jayakar, who lived in Delhi and used to be the acknowledged authority in all matters concerning the arts and crafts in India. She also happened to be close to Prime Minister Indira Gandhi. It was through Mrs Jayakar that I came to know Professor Nurul Hasan, the minister for science and technology. Minister Hasan had requested me to join the board of the CSIR, as a member. Sanjay Gandhi died in a plane accident in June 1980. He was in charge of Mrs Gandhi's personal office. His older brother, Rajiv Gandhi, who was a pilot in Indian Airlines, was persuaded by the prime minister to leave his job and assist in her personal office, which he reluctantly did.

I had briefly met Rajiv Gandhi (RG) as a passenger, while he was one of the pilots of our plane on my flights to visit HLL's new detergent factory in Jammu, via Chandigarh. During the stopover in Chandigarh, passengers travelling onwards and the crew were in those days permitted to deplane on the tarmac, sip hot coffee bought by passengers in plastic cups from a vendor. On my second trip on this route, RG and I had exchanged greetings and introduced ourselves over a brief conversation. On a couple of my subsequent trips, we had chatted briefly.

By the time I became chairman of the company, all the FERA conditions for Unilever to retain 51 per cent shareholding in HLL had been fulfilled, during my predecessor T. Thomas's chairmanship (1973–80). But the formal permission had not been cleared, apparently, because of a negative noting on our 'FERA file'. After I took over from TT, I had become aware of this critical piece of information. Mathew Panicker, Hindustan Lever board member and chief financial officer, had also been constantly chasing the concerned officer in the Reserve Bank of India (RBI), the nodal body for FERA, in Bombay. But the RBI officer had refused to disclose the reason for the interminable delay. I sought an appointment to meet the new finance minister, Pranab Mukherjee.

During my meeting with Finance Minister Mukherjee, he was, as usual, unfailingly polite and cordial. He had been fully briefed by Nitish Sengupta, senior civil servant in the finance ministry, regarding HLL's FERA case, and he was aware of our predicament.

I did not try to meet Rajiv Gandhi after he had moved to the prime minister's personal office. One of my HLL board colleagues, Siddharth (Shunu) Sen, was a contemporary of RG at the Doon School. At my request, Shunu had met and briefed RG about me, as well as HLL's long-drawn-out FERA saga. Subsequently, I sought an appointment with RG and met him in the prime minister's private office. He was warm and welcoming, recalling our Chandigarh encounter. We had a general discussion about the economy and a few other national issues. I did not raise the topic of HLL and FERA, but Rajiv Gandhi suggested that we should meet periodically, which he felt might be mutually beneficial!

I had first met Indira Gandhi at a CSIR event, in September 1980. It was at a gathering of scientists and technologists, both from the public as well as the private sector, at a Vigyan Bhavan event. Dr S. Varadarajan, HLL's former research director, had resigned from HLL in 1974 and in 1975, he had been appointed as the chairman of Indian Petrochemicals Ltd, a public sector undertaking, in Baroda (now Vadodara). Subsequently, he had been transferred to Delhi, as the secretary of the department of science and technology. During the CSIR event, in Vigyan Bhavan, Mrs Gandhi moved around, meeting the invitees. I had not met her in person previously, when shortly, I noticed her moving towards the spot where I was standing. At that exact moment, Dr Varadarajan rushed forward and tried to introduce me to the PM, I think to tell her that he had recruited me in the R&D department of Hindustan Lever. Mrs Gandhi, with only a hint of a smile, while not looking at Dr Vardarajan, said that if he did not mind, she wished to speak to me. It was a clear signal for Varadarajan to quickly move away. The prime minister told me that she had heard of me, I guess from Mrs Jayakar and maybe RG as well, whom I had met only the week before. After a few minutes, it became clear that indeed, that was how she had heard. After exchanging brief pleasantries, Mrs Gandhi moved on to meet another group of invitees. It was a very brief and pleasant exchange and her gentle rebuff to Dr Varadarajan was quite politely executed.

After a couple of weeks, I received a message from RG asking if we could meet once again. In my second meeting, RG informed me that the government had cleared HLL's FERA case and had instructed the RBI to convey the government's decision to HLL. It was indeed a momentous piece of news.

After my meeting with Rajiv Gandhi, I returned to our guest house, at the India International Centre (IIC), along with Suman Sinha and Bharat Mahey, and their colleagues, all of us feeling extremely relieved and in an unusually jubilant mood. I conveyed the good news to Mathew Paniker (CFO), in Bombay, who immediately got in touch with the RBI. The relentless chase by our unsung heroes of HLL's Delhi office, led by my predecessor Thomas, had finally succeeded.

I put a call through, to the chairman of the overseas committee, and TT, in London, to convey the good news about Unilever's majority shareholding had been officially communicated to HLL.

However, I must hasten to add that HLL's travails in Delhi were far from over. In 1980, I had to go more than fifty times to Delhi, by Indian Airlines, and flights were frequently delayed.

The company continued to be subjected to what at times felt like unending scrutiny, by either the ministry of industry and commerce, or one of the other departments of the Government of India. Suspicions of multinationals, although moderated, continued. In a market of perennial shortages of virtually all goods and services, the draconian Monopolies and Restrictive Trade Practices Act (MRTP) resulted in endless inspections of all HLL's business activities. Ranging from almost endless scrutiny of licences, production capacities, to virtually all the activities. We sometimes wondered who could have thought out such mindless, and interminable, waste of time and effort! I had once sought an appointment to meet the secretary of industries, to seek his advice regarding ways to explore if there was any way to mitigate the endless inspections by the DGTD.

I went to meet him in his office, on the appointed date and time. He kept me waiting for more than half an hour, before I was summoned into his office. The secretary was preoccupied reading some file, which he continued to do without the slightest acknowledgement of my appearance, while I remained standing in front of his desk. After a while, he looked up to me and uttered a single word, 'So!' I reminded him that I had sought a meeting with him, and had been waiting for the last half hour. He again looked at me and gestured, with a nod of his head, to take one of the three chairs across from his desk, and once again, returned to reading the file. After several more minutes, he shut the file, put it away and looked across at me in silence. I briefly explained the purpose of my visit and handed over a one-page summary of what I had said. The secretary suddenly raised his voice, and made a rude remark, without responding to my query. I stood up, ready to leave. I was put off by his rude behaviour. The secretary told me that he had not finished saying what he wished to say and continued his harangue. In brief, he told me, there wasn't anything he wished to do to ease the situation. Our meeting ended abruptly, and before I walked out, he again picked up the file, which he had been reading earlier. I remember him as the rudest civil servant I had ever encountered during that decade. His predecessor, Sharad Marathe, in contrast, was always very patient and polite. The secretary was succeeded by Mrs Otima Bordia, who was exceptionally bright but had a haughty demeanour and was polite without being helpful. Abid Hussein, secretary of trade and commerce, in contrast, was polite and helpful. Abid Hussein had been co-opted into the bureaucracy, from his previous job as a civil servant, in the service of the Nizam of Hyderabad.

Almost all the secretaries to the Government of India, were usually courteous and polite, in their official dealings. Over time, some of them became good friends. Secretaries Gopi Arora and Montek Singh Ahluwalia, from the office of the prime minister, became very good friends. The fact that Hindustan Lever is a professionally managed company was widely known, and even more so when Prakash Tandon, after he retired from HLL, was appointed as the chairman of the State Trading Corporation in 1973 in Delhi, while Vasant Rajadhyaksha, after retiring, shifted to Delhi after his appointment as a member of the Planning Commission. TT continued to interact closely and widened contacts in the government. His efforts to persuade the government to ease draconian price control and subsequently to meet the FERA requirements, for Unilever to retain majority shareholding in HLL, were not only widely lauded, but bore fruit as I have described earlier.

In 1982, I was invited as a member to an apex committee of the government, the Society of CSIR, chaired by the prime minister, Indira Gandhi. The other members, at the time, were Narain Dutt

Tiwari, Vasant Sathe, Prof. M.G.K. Menon and Dr Ramalingaswamy. The committee met once a year to discuss progress and advances in science, technology, medicine, and the status of important national initiatives in R&D and innovation.

Following my first meeting, the committee was invited for a meal, at the prime minister's residence, later that evening. At the first dinner, which I attended, besides the CSIR Society members, there were a few other invitees as well. It was a vegetarian buffet. At the dinner, we helped ourselves, and Mrs Gandhi sat down on a cement step with her meal and invited me to sit alongside her. She seemed keen to know about my family, our daughters' school, the weight of the books they had to carry to school, etc. She seemed genuinely interested to know about my wife and children. After a while, when we stood up for a second helping, I drifted towards a side, aware that I had already spent a fair bit of time with the prime minister and felt that she may wish to talk to some of the other guests. I was suddenly pulled to one side, by Minister Narain Dutt Tiwari (NDT), whom I knew reasonably well. Incidentally, it was Minister Tiwari who eventually initiated the unshackling of the licence permit raj, by permitting large corporations to invest in what was defined as 'backward' areas of India, to generate and disperse employment opportunities. When we were standing closely, Mr Tiwari whispered that he was not interested to know what my conversation with the PM was all about, but even more importantly that I must never share a single word of the conversation, with anyone else either. The term he used was 'let it remain private'. While I had heard some stories of political intrigues in Delhi, this was my first-hand exposure to 'secretiveness'!

While we are on the topic of NDT, as he was popularly called, he once sent me a message, that he was coming to Mumbai, and wished to meet me 'privately', on an important issue, and unusually requested that I kindly see him, alone. Our meeting was scheduled to take place in Sahyadri, the Maharashtra government's state guest house, on Malabar Hill. I had an unstated policy, that whenever I met any politician, or a cabinet minister, other than the prime minister,

I would always have my colleague Suman Sinha accompany me. So in spite of NDT's request, that he wished to meet me alone, Suman and I reached Sahyadri at the appointed time, on that Friday afternoon, to meet NDT. The minister walked in shortly. The first words he uttered were, 'Oh you have brought M. Sinha with you, as usual.' The room where we met was quite large; NDT requested me to walk with him, towards the farthest window in the large room overlooking the sea, where he spoke briefly to me. He then invited Sinha and me to a cup of tea, during which NDT was at his gracious best, which was his normal disposition.

As we were getting ready to take his leave, NDT asked me if he could invite himself for breakfast to my home the next morning! I promptly agreed, and offered to come and collect him the next morning at 9 a.m. NDT, however, insisted that he would come on his own. On our way out, Sinha and I felt that maybe NDT was not going to give up his objective that easily, as it may have seemed. I decided it would be rude to invite Suman to be present as well, the next day, for breakfast, at our home, along with NDT. The next morning, NDT arrived at our residence, promptly, at 9 a.m. For the next one hour, which he spent with my family, he mostly chatted with my wife and daughters, and enjoyed the hot Bengali samosas and jalebees. The issue of the previous evening was not touched upon, at all. My interactions with NDT over the next decade were always friendly and cordial. The government policy for incentivizing dispersal of industries from metropolitan areas, by giving tax concessions, etc., became the core of HLL's strategy, for dispersal of manufacturing capacity, and reduce dependence on the company's largest Bombay factory. The government's new policy was very timely, especially to deal with the militant trade unionism.

Our trips to meet NDT in Delhi used to be frequent, on matters concerning HLL. On one such visit, NDT happened to be very tied up with some urgent meetings, which had suddenly come up, and requested if we could wait, in his antechamber. It turned out to be a well-appointed air-conditioned room, but without a single window. To cut a long episode short, we were stuck in that room for close to three hours, with no way to escape, other than to walk across NDT's office. By the time we were called to meet NDT, both Suman and I had wilted and after a brief exchange of pleasantries, took NDT's leave. He was as cordial as ever and walked us to the door; we were relieved that he had not enquired what we had come to see him about!

Amongst our frequent meetings with NDT, I especially recall one which is worth narrating. Frans Van den Hoven, the Dutch co-chairman of Unilever, was due to retire. He and his wife, Coxy, were visiting HLL and India, as part of his farewell tour. Connie and I accompanied them during the visit to India. The episode is about Calcutta. At the Delhi airport, we boarded the Indian Airlines bus, for the short ride to the aircraft, where it was parked. NDT happened to be on the same flight and also in the same bus. NDT greeted me and Connie, and in turn, I introduced him to Frans and Coxy. We took off from Delhi on time, for a change. I and Frans were engaged in conversation, the fasten seat belt sign had just been turned off. NDT came to where we were seated and requested if I could move for a short time, to his seat, as he, NDT, wished to spend a brief moment talking with the chairman of Unilever. I readily moved to his seat and NDT settled down in mine. For the next half hour or so, Frans and NDT seemed engrossed in conversation.

Afterwards, NDT and I returned to our own seats. Frans seemed pleased with whatever NDT and he had chatted about. Frans also complimented me, regarding the time and effort it must have taken to arrange this sudden 'encounter' with a senior cabinet minister in the Government of India! I looked at Frans, and told him that NDT's presence on the same flight as ours was entirely a coincidence, but Frans, who had a great sense of humour, was not convinced about the 'accidental encounter', which he thought I must have meticulously planned. By the way, Frans also told me, putting on his smile, how NDT had showered praise on HLL, and especially me. This incident turned out to be ridiculous, as far as I was concerned. At that time, I was not quite familiar with Frans's legendary sense of humour.

Our brief visit to Kolkata included a day trip to Haldia and HLL's new chemicals factory. On the way back from Haldia, Frans pointed to one of the several roadside barbers, with customers hunkered opposite the barber, on a piece of brick, a very familiar sight in Bengal. Frans asked me if this was something traditional, and also enquired what the customer seemed to be sitting upon. I explained that what we were seeing was the common man's roadside barber shop, locally called the 'Italian Salon'. Frans was naturally curious. 'Why Italian?' I explained that the piece of brick on which the client had to squat hunched is called 'Ita' in Hindi, and 'Eet' in Bengali, hence the name Italian. Frans completely cracked up and could not stop guffawing. He spread this story not only across Unilever, but also amongst his Dutch friends in Holland. After our return from Haldia, for a change, we had a free evening, and Connie and I felt that Coxy and Frans would want to rest, and put up their feet in their suite, after a fairly long day's Haldia visit. When we entered the hotel lobby, Frans asked me what we were doing that evening; I enquired whether Coxy and he may wish to relax. Frans immediately enquired if we could visit a nightclub, 'to shake a leg', as he put it.

That evening, we booked and took them to a restaurant called 'Trincas'. It was well known for its band ensemble those days. Both Frans and Coxy soon began gracefully dancing the cha cha cha. Connie and I had never stepped on a dance floor, we got up to give them company and we sort of stumbled along, trying to follow the rhythm. At dinner, we were very well looked after, by the manager. Frans asked the manager if the special service was because I was a frequent visitor. The manager mumbled something, and of course, I had been to Trincas only once before, with Kachru, my former boss in Calcutta. Frans had a very good memory, and repeated the NDT encounter, dinner at Trincas and Calcutta 'Italian Salons', when we met, once a year, at the annual Unilever retired directors' gatherings.

I received news that Frans passed away at the age of ninety-seven.
RIP. I will always, happily, recall Frans and Coxy's visit to India.

During 1980–84, I met Rajiv Gandhi frequently and discussed
a broad range of issues. After the shocking assassination of Prime
Minister Indira Gandhi, Rajiv Gandhi succeeded his mother. General
elections were soon held, and Rajiv Gandhi and the Congress party
came to power, with a record 'majority' of seats, in the 1985 Lok Sabha.

We left for London in 1990, but remained in touch with
Mr Gandhi up to ten days before the day he was assassinated by
a Liberation Tigers of Tamil Eelam (LTTE) suicide bomber in
Sriperumbudur. In 1985, I had been appointed as one of the members
of the Science Advisory Committee to the Prime Minister (SAC-PM).
Prof. C.N.R. Rao was the chairman of SAC-PM. The SAC meetings
were usually held in Delhi, and frequently with interactive sessions
with the prime minister. In one of SAC-PM's early meetings, Dr S.
Varadarajan, the secretary of the DST, was requested by the prime
minister for a brief presentation on the leading-edge R&D advances
in India. I was assigned to brief Dr SV, and to especially emphasize that
he had a half-hour slot in the agenda at the next SAC meeting with the
prime minister. When I met SV to brief him, I faced a most unusual
outburst from SV, who said the PM was ignorant of science and
'needed to be educated', and that the half-hour limit was inadequate.
I tried to persuade him that whatever he planned, could he kindly
stick to the allotted time!

On the scheduled date and time, while the SAC-PM was
assembling in the conference room of the PMO, SV arrived carrying
seven carousels of slides. This was a sign of impending trouble. Soon
the prime minister walked in, greeted everyone, looked at the agenda
and settled down to listen to Dr Varadarajan. Seeing the pile of
carousels, the PM looked at me, and I informed him in everyone's
hearing, that I had briefed Dr Varadarajan of his half-hour time slot.
The PM politely (PM was always unfailingly polite) requested SV
to kindly make his presentation. SV, who normally had a mumbling
and murmuring way of speaking, began his presentation by saying

that to do justice to the subject, he would need at least two hours. At which point, the PM got up and left the meeting, without a word. This SAC-PM meeting was over before it had even begun. The agenda for the afternoon meeting was to last for sixty minutes, and of which Dr Varadarajan had been allotted thirty minutes. The PM had a busy agenda every day, well into late night. As soon as the prime minister got up and left, Varadarajan repeated what he had told me earlier, to the other members of the SAC-PM, regarding the PM's unfamiliarity with science. The chairman of SAC-PM and members of the SAC-PM were aware of Varadarajan's polite disposition, but also his scholastic arrogance. I don't know if he ever met the prime minister after that day.

Moving on, I once received an early morning phone call from Arun Singh. He told me that the party was facing a sort of crisis in the RS, from one of their own elderly MPs. He had been agitating for a while about the adulteration of hydrogenated vegetable oil called 'Vanaspati' with cheap beef tallow, in the retail trade. Loose Vanaspati was widely sold through retail outlets across India, as the poor man's 'Ghee'. HLL had its own and well-known brand Dalda, sold only in sealed tins, of half- and one-kilogram weight. Cheap tallow, mixed with unbranded hydrogenated vegetable oil, was apparently being sold in Bihar and Uttar Pradesh. The MP, a Brahmin, had demanded an immediate ban on the manufacture and sale of all hydrogenated vegetable oil in India. If the ban was not announced on that day itself, he threatened that he would go on indefinite 'hunger strike', on the floor of the RS. It had become an extremely emotional issue and would certainly arouse public sentiments.

Adulteration of 'vegetable ghee' with beef tallow had become a very serious menace, and the state governments were actively engaged in putting a stop to it. Arun Singh informed me that the prime minister wondered if I had any advice which could help in persuading the MP not to start his hunger strike, as he had threatened. I told Arun I would need time to explore, as I did not know of any obvious response. After some time, I called Arun Singh back, and told him to get hold of the MP's aide and find out if his boss took vitamin supplements, and if he did, to explain to him about, the material used to produce the capsules in which the vitamins were delivered. Soon, Arun Singh informed me that the threat of indefinite fast had ended without a ripple. It was just a piece of good luck.

As I have mentioned earlier, Gopi Arora, senior adviser to PM Rajiv Gandhi and I had become good friends. Whenever I visited Delhi, Gopi and I would meet in our guest house, at the India International Centre. Gopi was also frequently accompanied by his young colleague in the PMO, Montek Singh Ahluwalia, the well-known economist. My colleague Suman Sinha would also join us at the guest house in the evenings. Such informal evening get-togethers were enjoyable and relaxing, and we spent time discussing domestic politics as well as international developments. One afternoon, Gopi called me and dropped by our guest house for what he had told me was a 'private chat'. Apparently, he had been tasked to ascertain if I would favourably consider moving from industry and join the Congress party. I was seriously taken aback and explained to Gopi of my personal and professional commitments and responsibilities, and therefore the proposition was out of the question. Gopi spent a long time trying to persuade me, in his usual gentle way. I eventually convinced him, to kindly convey to whomever he was speaking to me on behalf of, that above all else I had really no interest whatsoever in getting into politics as a profession. Gopi was, as usual, most gracious, in the face of my rather firm response. Our conversation on this topic was over and we moved on.

Some weeks after this unusual episode, Gopi wanted to meet me once again in private. I guessed that he was conveying messages on behalf of the prime minister. This time, the message was, if I would consider taking a leave of absence from the company, to be appointed India's ambassador to a major capital city in the West. I must admit, I did feel, momentarily, flattered. Although I knew that to seek a break from work, even temporarily, would not be at all appropriate.

These two episodes bothered me, and I tried to avoid visiting Delhi for a few weeks. This was not easy because HLL's problems and priorities were almost endless, and many of these required my presence in Delhi. However, I did agree to become chairman of the board of governors of IIT Kanpur. The board met once a quarter, and for any urgent problems, the director came over to see me at our guest house in Delhi.

In 1991, Indian general elections were announced. I had moved to London in 1990. One evening, in November 1990, I received a phone call, at our residence, and was informed that Pranab Mukherjee wished to speak to me. He told me that Rajiv Gandhi wanted me to be the Congress candidate for Parliament, from a particular North Calcutta constituency. I told Pranab Babu that I did not have the faintest idea of what he was talking about, and the suggestion for me to be a candidate in India's general elections was not only ridiculous, it was completely out of the question. I added that I had no interest in politics. He tried to be persuasive and allay my unstated reservations for the next several minutes. I told Pranab frankly, to kindly thank Mr Gandhi, and that I was just not interested. Before ending the call, Pranab was kind enough to tell me to be ready to receive the next phone call from Mr Gandhi. Connie and I were bewildered by this sudden, unexpected and unwelcome development.

I soon realized that there may have been some discussion with a well-known editor-in-chief of a most popular Calcutta Bengali newspaper as well. I was absolutely resolute that I was never going to join politics. Soon enough, there was a second call from Delhi. To my great relief, Gopi Arora was at the other end. I told Gopi how happy I was to hear his voice and pleaded with him to convince Rajiv Gandhi that I was absolutely sure that I would be more useful to the country as a professional manager, and not as a politician. Gopi tried hard to convey how keen RG was for me to enter electoral politics, until I once more persuaded Gopi of my absolute reluctance in our long conversation! Gopi very kindly took on the task, to convey to RG my pleading. I heaved a deep sigh of gratitude, and thanked Gopi most sincerely. During the election campaign in India, I continued to remain in touch with RG, until his dastardly assassination, in Sriperumbudur, at the hands of the LTTE. It was one of the darkest moments of my life.

I discontinued all my contacts with Delhi, until our return to India in 1997, with one strange episode. In 1996, one of the wealthiest Bombay businessmen sent a well-known newspaper reporter, whom I knew well, to see me in London. The reporter flew down to London, the next day, to convey a message that a seat was being kept for me in Parliament, after I returned to India, following retirement. Connie and I were both highly offended by the proposition. I took the gentleman out to dinner, later in the evening, and wished him a safe journey back to Bombay. I must admit I was surprised at the audacity of the Bombay tycoon! There were a few other episodes with the businessman which I'd better skip.

In the 2006 general election, the UPA 1 government was formed and Dr Manmohan Singh assumed the office of the prime minister of India. A few days later, I got a call on my mobile phone. The caller told me that the prime minister wished to speak to me. I was on the golf course, so I told the caller that I was tied up, and would be free in an hour's time. After the game was over, I returned home and I told Connie about the unusual telephone call. Almost on the hour, the same individual from the PMO called back. I was put through to the prime minister. I conveyed my congratulations and good wishes to the PM. He then told me that he had decided to appoint me as a member of the Planning Commission. Since I had had time to anticipate what Dr Singh might speak to me about, I had correctly guessed that it may be some sort of role in the new government. At this stage in my life, and given my aversion to politics, it was the last thing I wanted to get involved in. So I politely requested Prime Minister Singh if I could call him back.

The PM readily agreed, but added that I would have to do so in the next half an hour, as the press note of the announcement was ready for release. As I put down the receiver, I was in the grip of panic. Connie agreed with me, that I should politely but firmly decline. I called back within ten minutes and was put through once more to Dr Singh. I apologized and told Dr Singh that a serious family matter absolutely required my presence in Mumbai. The PM was insistent that I must seriously reconsider, and get back to him in the next one hour positively. I have always had a very deep respect for Dr Manmohan Singh and found myself, not for the first time, in an extremely awkward predicament. However, my resolve to not be either in politics or in government, remained as resolute as ever. I called back the PMO and conveyed to Dr Singh my deep and sincere regrets.

The PM was gracious and to my great relief, told me that he would need my participation in the future, in other matters of state. Later on, I joined the prime minister's council on trade and industry, as well as the India–USA business council, besides other government committees, all of which did not require me to be a part of the government. I was in the delegation with the prime minister on his first visit to the USA. During the visit, our delegation was introduced to US President George W. Bush, and subsequently, attended the meeting of the India–USA business council. This was the trip during which the India–US nuclear agreement was signed.

Another meeting of the India–USA business council was held during the next visit of Prime Minister Dr Singh, to the USA, when Barack Obama was the President. As during the previous trip, we went to the White House, and were introduced to President Obama. When it was my turn to be introduced to President Obama, Dr Singh, in his own way, mentioned a list of things I had accomplished professionally, in the course of my career. As President Obama shook my hand, he asked me with his characteristic smile, 'How did you get to do all the things Dr Singh just described?' I pointed at my full head of grey hair and replied, 'Mr President, primarily through a journey which turned my hair grey!' President Obama had a hearty laugh and then moved along, still glancing towards me, murmuring, 'I will remember that.' It was one of those 'once in a lifetime' memorable exchanges and encounters.

While I was reasonably active in retirement, one day I received a phone call from P. Chidambaram (PC), the finance minister in Dr Singh's cabinet. Although I knew PC, his phone call to me was unusual. PC told me that the government had decided to set up an 'Investment Commission', to advise on ways and means to expedite major projects and foreign investments, and improve the 'ease of doing business' in India. Could I suggest a few names for the government to consider for the proposed commission? I rattled out a few names amongst the contemporary and prominent Indian business leaders. PC thanked me and concluded our brief telephone call. The next morning, PC once more phoned to inform me that a press announcement was ready to be released about the Government of India's proposal to set up an Investment Commission with Ratan Tata as the chairman, and Deepak Parekh and Ashok Ganguly as members. Before I could react, or utter a word, his call came to an abrupt end. I did not have even the slightest hint when PC had called the previous day. Anyhow, I felt it might be worthwhile to be part of this effort. Ratan, Deepak and I met every week for detailed discussions, as the Investment Commission, and also followed up with a series of interactive discussions, with the relevant ministers and civil servants. Periodically, we also met Mr Chidambaram in Delhi, to report on the status of our task. Our final report of recommendations, we handed to the prime minister, and it was received well.

I will conclude this section with one more episode during the 1980s. Pratap Kaul happened to be the cabinet secretary at the time. We had got to know each other well, to the extent that whenever I happened to be in Delhi, I would try and meet the cabinet secretary, frequently, during lunch break. I still recall fondly, sharing his tasty homemade paratha and aloo sabzi. During one such lunch meeting, Pratap asked me, out of the blue: 'Ashok, how much longer will you continue selling soap?' I had promptly responded saying, 'Pratap, as

long as you have a bath every morning, I will continue to sell soap.'
We both had a hearty laugh, and we both knew what the aside was
all about. Delhi had its lighter moments. Soon, our exchange got
around the Delhi grapevine and gossip circuit. I was glad it did.

Finally, and not very long ago, on a couple of occasions, a former
foreign service bureaucrat, and a long-standing friend of mine, came
to see me in Bombay and enquire if I was, now that I had retired,
prepared to be persuaded to move to Delhi! My friend indicated that
although he was privately talking to me, he was doing so on behalf of
the government. I once again, politely, made it abundantly clear that
I remained, as before, resolutely uninterested. My lifelong belief was
that I am neither cut out nor interested to join politics. My belief was
eventually reinforced by my experience, as a nominated member of
the Rajya Sabha.

I have never met a politician who did not believe that major
economic reforms in India were overdue. I will also always remember
a former senior civil servant, and a very good friend of mine, who
once told me, in another context, that the 'Dharma' of the service is
to loyally serve the government in power, but then went on to add,
that is, without compromising the duty to protect the interests of
the nation. I did not, however, enquire how this obvious dichotomy
worked in practice!

London 1990–97: As I have already narrated, as a Unilever
director, I had offices in Unilever's London head office, as well as
in the Rotterdam head office. I divided my time, during the week,
between the two cities. I had also been invited to join some UK
government committees, besides being appointed as a member of
the UK government's apex advisory board for research councils.
I was also in the fourth framework committee for R&D funding, of
the European Commission, in Brussels. Unilever R&D sponsored
major research projects of relevance to the business, in leading UK,
European and American Universities. As a result, I got to know some
senior academics rather well.

I also chaired the committee of experts, on the Unilever Council for Safety & Environment. As a consequence, I came in contact with the specialist community, in the UK and in the EU. Even after I retired from Unilever, my academic links, especially in the UK, continued, as one of the trustees of the Leverhulme Trust.

I recall an invitation, for Connie and me, to tea, at 10 Downing Street, from Prime Minister John Major. At the evening reception, there were a few other couples, some of whom we had met before. The PM and Mrs Major were warm and welcoming hosts, and it turned out to be a very pleasant, social occasion. Sometime later, Connie and I were also invited to tea at Buckingham Palace. The person most excited about this invitation was our chauffeur Bill, who spread the news through the Unilever drivers' grapevine.

As per the schedule in the invitation, we reached Buckingham Palace on the appointed day and time, and climbed up the main steps, in the palace and were shown to the room, where a few of the other invitees for the evening had already gathered. In a short while, the queen arrived, and was introduced to each of us couples. Besides the queen, there were the Duke of Edinburgh, a cousin of his, besides several courtiers, in train, following the queen.

While meeting the invitees, the queen spent a few minutes with each of the couples. She talked to Connie and me, asking about our family and exchanged pleasantries. I expect that she must have been well briefed already, about all the guests for the evening. The English invitation to tea is usually a sumptuous affair; the Royal Tea was even more so. Connie and I went around exchanging brief words with some of the other royals present and a few of the fellow invitees. The tea went on for over an hour, after which we were whispered to by one of the courtiers that we could seek our leave from her Royal Highness, who bade us goodbye and left from the reception, along with those who had followed her. It was a memorable evening. We never got to know how we happened to be on the list of invitees.

In 1996, Sir Michael Angus introduced me to Lord Colin Marshall, the chairman of British Airways (BA). Not long afterwards, I was invited to join the BA board as an independent director. I served three terms on the BA Board, from 1996 until 2005. There were several memorable episodes, during the time, of which I have selected two. The first one was being invited by the commander on one of my Concorde flights to New York, during takeoff. The takeoff of the Concorde was even more extraordinary, compared to flying as a passenger. The other episode was the inauguration of the London Eye, which BA had partly funded. The chairman of BA and the members of the board joined the mayor of London, the guest of honour, as we raised a toast, in a pod, as the giant wheel, the London Eye, started on its inaugural round. The view of the city on a sunny morning was not only spectacular, but memorable as well.

In 2006, the British high commissioner sent me a letter, requesting my concurrence, to be conferred upon the title of CBE, in the queen's honours list.

Since I had been conferred the Padma Bhushan in 1988, by the President of India, I felt it would be only proper to seek the advice of the Government of India, before agreeing. The response I received was positive.

The official ceremony was held in Mumbai and was hosted by the British high commissioner. Prince Edward, on behalf of the queen, handed over one OBE, one MBE and my CBE.

The event was attended by Connie and our daughter Amrita, as well the family and friends of the two other recipients.

It was some years later, during former UK prime minister John Major's visit to Delhi, along with fellow board members of a well-known American investment bank, when I was invited to a dinner in Mr Major's honour, by the bank's India representative. At dinner, I was seated across from John Major. After we took our seats and guests were being introduced by the host, Mr Major interrupted to say, 'Of course, I know Ashok, we met in London, when he was on the board of Unilever.' As is usual, he would have been briefed about the dinner guests earlier in the evening. In passing he mentioned that he was glad that I had been duly recognized, for all the 'good work' I had done, for the UK government, when he was the prime minister. I wondered what he was referring to, until the penny dropped later, if it could be the CBE!

Like the Padma Bhushan in 1988, the CBE in 2006, the conferment of the Padma Vibhushan in 2009, was also a complete surprise. I have often wondered what awards and recognitions mean, other than a momentary uplift of spirits, but one can never trace to whatever one may have done, to deserve an award!

I should also mention that in 1996, the mayor of Shanghai bestowed upon me the title of 'Honorary Professor–Chinese Academy of Science', which also remained a mystery.

Encounters and episodes are a reality of life. They are mostly unanticipated and create mixed feelings. But the events do remain embedded in one's mind.

Memories of Travels

The COVID lockdown, in March 2020, was the first time in my life I was not able to travel by road, rail or air. At the start 2021, or COVID year two, the likelihood of travelling, still seems remote. I have, now, all the time on my hand. At the beginning, being forced to be homebound seemed a short-term restriction, which soon turned out to be open-ended. I had enough time to remember events of my lifetime.

However, I have no recollection of my first journey, at the age of approximately three months, when Ma brought me, by train, to Bombay from Patna, where I was born.

Ever since, I travelled with Didi and Ma by train on our annual holidays to Patna and Benares, and remember these annual trips, from the time I was three or four years old. Our train journeys were even more exciting when Baba accompanied us.

My first air travel was to the USA, to pursue my higher studies, at the age of twenty. Those days, air travel used to be marketed as glamorous, and even after it had become more accessible. My air travels peaked, from 1990 onwards when I was working and we lived in London, as well as subsequently.

I was once travelling on a British Airways (BA) flight, from Bombay to London, and as I entered the cabin, I found my seat was the one next to Mr J.R.D. Tata, the father of Indian civil aviation, and the famous Maharaja Service, of glamour and comfort. This great, and one of India's only global brands, sadly eroded after the company was nationalized.

On that particular BA flight (most international flights took off or landed in India at odd hours of the night) I handed my jacket over to the hostess and started getting ready to settle down for the overnight flight. I planned to sleep for a few hours, for a busy day, in London. Once the flight took off, I pushed back my seat, pulled up the duvet, put on eyeshades and tried to go to sleep. Jeh (as JRD was popularly called) was wide awake, busy chatting with the cabin crew. I had dozed off, when suddenly, I was shaken awake by Jeh and admonished for not enjoying the aperitif, chatting with the pretty crew members and getting ready for supper. I, of course, could not tell him that I was keen to sleep, and we spent the next hour talking, sipping wine and nibbling bits of the supper. By this time the lights were dimmed; I was wide awake, but glad that Jeh had woken me up.

One of my most traumatic air travel experiences was a flight from Bombay to Calcutta, in April 1967. I was going to Calcutta, to get married. Around April, every year, there are frequent, pre-monsoon stormy weather patterns, along eastern India. I was on an Air India flight and happened to be sitting next to K.P.V. Menon, who was then the newly appointed general manager of the company's factory in Bombay. I had been introduced to KPV earlier, during his introductory visit to the factory. KPV had a very friendly and disarming demeanour. After we took off, we chatted amiably, until the 'fasten seat belt' sign had come on, the plane must have been passing by a nor'wester. Suddenly, all hell broke loose. It felt as if the plane had gone out of control. Several of the overhead baggage doors suddenly flung open, and pieces of luggage were thrown out, while many of my fellow passengers, a number of them, women and children, were crying loudly, out of fear and distress. The passengers had, of course, fastened their seat belts. To be honest, KPV and I were worried as well, experiencing the severe conditions. It felt as if our plane was out of control and its heaving, a signal of some calamity and possibly, even a crash!

The sound of the jet engine's unusual straining added to the fears of the passengers. The disturbance may not have lasted more than

2–3 minutes, but felt like ages, for the pilots to take the plane out of the eye of the nor'wester. Once the plane had steadied, there was a palpable feeling of relief, while the commander's voice came over the tannoy, apologizing for their silence, and then announcing that our flight had been diverted to Delhi. The captain also added that such incidents were not infrequent at this time of the year. Until we landed in Delhi, there was pin-drop silence amongst the passengers. After we landed in Delhi, we were informed that our flight would once again take off for Calcutta, in two hours' time, and that dinner had been arranged at the airport restaurant.

K.P.V. Menon and I soon made our way to the bar, at the terminal. We had not exchanged a word since the traumatic experience on the flight. KPV ordered for us two large whiskies. We loaded our drink with ice cubes, and took large gulps, to steady our nerves. The first words KPV uttered were that whoever I was going to marry, had already brought me good luck. After this encounter, KPV and I became very close and good friends. Whenever we recounted our experience, it seemed to acquire an aura of a life-and-death episode.

Our flight from Delhi to Calcutta landed in the early hours of the morning. KPV and I had skipped dinner, but we were in a happy and jolly mood.

A few days after Connie and my wedding, my parents, Connie and I returned to Bombay by train. Even though the journey took thirty-six hours, those days, trains were a joy to travel on, in comfort and leisure. The AC coupes were very luxurious, comfortable, and the passengers were well looked after. The meals by the railway caterers were impeccable and looked forward to. The meals used to be provided by caterers such as Brandon or Spencer, and the taste of the railway chicken curry is part of my memories of train travel, in better times.

As a couple, Connie and I seemed destined to travel around the world, about which, of course, we had no premonition.

On Christmas eve of 1968, we flew to Amsterdam via Frankfurt, on an Air India flight. We enjoyed a surprise Xmas party on the flight, and each of the passengers received a gift to mark the event. Our arrival at Frankfurt had been delayed due to bad weather, and we had missed our connecting KLM flight to Amsterdam. Air India arranged a meal at Frankfurt airport, and as non-vegetarians, we chose a meal of steak and fritz (fried potato). Our steak, unfortunately, had been cooked rare, and a bit of blood was oozing out, as we started to eat. Since that experience, Connie did not touch another steak.

On the next KLM flight, we reached Amsterdam very late. Connie and I frequently remembered the year 1969, when we lived in Holland, working, and on weekends or holidays, driving to different places in the Netherlands and Europe.

We lived in Calcutta during 1973–75, and enjoyed a few driving holidays, across West Bengal. Our daughters Nivedita and Amrita were both born in Calcutta.

We came back to Bombay in 1976, and lived there until 1990. Every year, we used to take brief family vacations, visiting interesting and historic places, tiger reserves, etc., across India. In 1986, we went on our family holiday to Japan.

From 1973, I was entitled to first-class air travel. My first trip in 1973 was a visit to Unilever's Indonesian subsidiary, in Jakarta, on work, along with one of the directors of our company. I was looking forward to my maiden first-class air travel, on a Singapore Airlines flight. When we boarded the flight, we were ushered to the rear of the plane. The director's wife was accompanying him. As we were squeezing into our seats, the director informed me that he had taken the liberty of converting our two first-class tickets, to include a short holiday for him and his wife. I was disappointed but did not show it. There was another event, in 1986. Dr Arunachalam, the then director of DRDO (Defence Research and Development Organisation), Sam Pitroda, who had spearheaded the spread of landline telephones across India, and I, as a member of the Science Advisory Committee to the Prime Minister (SAC-PM), were invited by Russian President Mikhail Gorbachev, to visit Moscow, following our presentations to him, on science and technology in India, at Prime Minister Rajiv

Gandhi's residence. I must admit that although I had already visited Moscow a few times, I was quite looking forward to the experience, as a guest of the government.

We were booked on an Aeroflot flight, from Delhi to Moscow. When we ascended the steps, the stewardess who welcomed us informed us that seating was free. The plane seemed overfull. It took about ten minutes for the crew to locate three seats for us in the front cabin of the aircraft and help us to settle down. It was a disappointing start to upper-class travel.

The overnight flight was uneventful till we landed in Moscow, and all the passengers were requested to remain in their seats. Three Russian officials entered the plane, and came to where we were seated and informed us that they had come to welcome us to Moscow. Plus ça change. The six of us soon deplaned and each of us and our escort had been allotted separate limousines, in which we drove off from the tarmac. The car and our escorts were assigned for the duration of our stay in Moscow.

We were very well looked after by our hosts and treated as VIPs for the next three days. The daily official programmes were quite packed and very interesting. Evening dinners and social events seemed over-the-top and our return trip to Delhi was luxurious in comparison to the trip from Delhi.

In 2005, I was part of a government delegation visiting China to mark the twentieth year of Rajiv Gandhi's visit to the country. The meetings and programmes for our delegation had been very well organized by the state. We travelled from Delhi to Beijing, by Ethiopian Airlines. I had not heard of Ethiopian Airlines before and I was haunted by memories of my journey, from Delhi to Moscow by Aeroflot, in 1986. Ethiopian Airlines, to my pleasant surprise, was excellent, for their service and hospitality. Our return journey from Beijing, by China Air, in comparison, sadly, was uncomfortable and surprisingly shabby.

I travelled frequently within the UK, either by train or road. I also visited the US for a day or two every month. At the time, the morning Concord flights to New York made it possible to reach New York by mid-morning, work during the day and then fly back overnight, from Kennedy to Heathrow. The Concord services both at Heathrow and New York, after landing, were speedy and hassle-free. Connie joined me on a couple of occasions on the Concord but was not as impressed.

Besides my routine weekly and monthly travels, there used to be occasional working trips to different continents and countries.

In 1996, I had joined the board of British Airways (BA) as an independent director. In 1997, I retired from Unilever and we returned to our own home in Bombay. The BA board meetings used to be held eleven times a year, mostly in London, except one outside the UK. To attend the BA board meetings, I flew to London almost once a month, and twice a year, Connie and I spent a few weeks in London, during spring and summer. The BA board meetings schedule also facilitated my attending the quarterly trustees' meetings of the Leverhulme Trust in London.

Travelling over the past several decades, in luxury and comfort, lulls one into feeling that it is what life is all about until . . . Connie's untimely passing away was my life's saddest setback, and the COVID lockdown brought about isolation at home for months. In a way, I am content to be homebound.

Casting my mind over the past, I wonder whether our generation was unusually fortunate. I mean changes such as airport security, and sipping cups, with the flight commander, in the flight cabin or being invited to the flight deck of the Concord to witness its take-off, are pleasurable memories. All things have their time and place. But life keeps moving, the Concord is now history, travelling itself has become somewhat of a hassle. Connie and I never took anything for granted. Before she passed away, we frequently reminisced of the happy life we had, and of which my memories linger!

Part V

Epilogue: My Better Half

My parents moulded me through my impressionable years, and even 'arranged' my marriage, in 1967. The rest of my professional and personal life blossomed over the next fifty-two and odd years, in ways which are the subject of this narrative.

Marriage makes couples anticipate and prepare for their journey together. This is true, both for what are 'love' as well as 'arranged' marriages.

Getting used to a life together takes different lengths of time. The majority of married couples spend a happy life together, some less so and a few not!

Connie and my arranged marriage settled down early, to decades of love and happiness. For two humans to blend as a couple requires understanding and adjustments. Although I was never conscious of the transition, as I cast my mind back to our early days, I know that changes took place, but subtly.

How It All Began

Connie's mother, Laxmi, and my mother happened to be second cousins. In 1961, Connie's father, Lt Col Bhattacharya, was posted at the Army Command Hospital in Santa Cruz, a suburb of Bombay. Their home was an idyllic bungalow, within a defence enclosure. Connie and her younger sister attended a suburban school, not far from their residence. My parents flat was in Worli, where I stayed, after returning from the US, in 1962. I had met Connie, briefly, during one of their social visits to Worli and ours, to their home. Shortly after my return from USA, I got a job with Hindustan Lever.

Arranged Marriage

In 1966, our parents arranged our betrothal and Connie and I were married in Kolkata in 1967. We returned to Mumbai and settled down, in my first office flat, on Pali Hill. My parents also lived with us at the time. After a few months, Connie had to return to Kolkata, to appear for her final BA (hons) history examination. By nature, Connie was a person of few words. Connie and I really did not know each other, even though we had met briefly, when her father was posted in Mumbai. After our wedding, we spent a few days in Darjeeling. She was by nature quiet and polite, but joined in if I started a conversation. The manager of our hotel in Darjeeling tried to entertain us in the evenings, spending time with us and playing a few Bengali records before dinner. Soon, we felt overwhelmed being served 'special' dishes at every meal. So we went out for leisurely walks after dinner. Walks, during Darjeeling summer, with snow-covered mountain peaks on the horizon, were spectacular.

Train Journey to Bombay

After returning to Kolkata, Connie, my parents and I embarked on a thirty-six-hour train journey to Mumbai, in air-conditioned comfort. I had booked separate suites on the train, for our travel, which provided privacy. My mother always carried, for herself, home-cooked meals on train journeys, while Baba, Connie and I had meals served from the restaurant car, catered by the well-known railway caterers Brandon or Spencer's. Those were the leisurely days of train travel. I was doing most of the talking. Connie told me later that she was amused by my endless stories, while breaking into laughter occasionally. After a good night's sleep, we were served morning tea. Then we washed up, and got ready for breakfast. I knocked on the connecting door, and went across to greet my parents; Baba was already having breakfast. The rest of the morning, until lunch, we spent time reading and occasionally chatting, especially when our train halted at a station. The taste of the railway chicken curry and rice has left lifelong memories, which no restaurant which claims to serve 'railway chicken curry' is able to match. It was only after we had been married for a short while that I understood that Connie was not only very gentle-natured, but she spoke sparingly. Most evenings in Mumbai, Connie and I went out for walks across what used to be a golf link in Pali Hill.

I chatted about the events of the day and other issues, and Connie joined in occasionally, as we got to know one another better and more closely.

Earthquake in Bombay

There was a major earthquake in December 1967, with its epicentre in Koyna. On the Richter scale, it was sufficiently strong for our beds and furniture to start shaking rather violently. Connie and I jumped out of bed, rushed out of our room, as did my parents from theirs. We all ran down the stairs, along with the other residents, to the open ground, in front of our building. The frequent aftershocks took a while to moderate, before we could return to our flat.

Final Exam

In June 1967, Connie had to go to Kolkata, to appear for her BA final university examination. I remember going to collect her from the examination centre. To surprise her, I wore a dhoti and kurta, which I normally only wore once a year, during Durga Puja. Connie seemed surprised, since she was not expecting me and even more, I imagine, by my outfit. She hurriedly left the group of friends she was walking with, and rushed to meet me, got into the car and we left quickly. I must have appeared silly in my outfit. She told me she was very happy that I had come to collect her, but did not tell me how ridiculous I must have appeared in my outfit. When I kept on, Connie admitted that she was slightly embarrassed.

The Unexpected

We celebrated our first wedding anniversary in 1968. My work as well as home life seemed well-settled, until, after some years, I discovered that Ma had been a source of tension at home while I was away at work and while Connie was preparing for her final exams, in 1967. I also learnt that Baba, who had retired, had dealt with these irritants and put a stop to them. All this took place when I was away at work, but Connie never mentioned even a word, during our daily evening walks. We were happy in each other's company. Connie loved listening to stories of my university days in Illinois, as well as my secondment in 1966, to Newaraelia in Sri Lanka, and Englewood Cliffs in New Jersey, to TJ Lipton. Sometime in late 1968, Dr Varadarajan, our research director, informed me about my likely posting overseas, to Unilever Research, but requested to keep the information to myself. Connie seemed pleased when I gave her the news that evening. A couple of weeks later, I was officially informed that Connie and I were to go to Holland, for a year, and then for six months, to London, in 1970, on secondment.

To prepare for the trip, we had to vacate our company apartment in Pali Hill, and the packers put our household stuff into storage. Ma and Baba moved back to their home in Worli.

Holland on New Year's Day 1969

Connie and I flew on New Year's Eve, by Air India to Frankfurt, and took a connecting KLM flight to Amsterdam. After takeoff, the crew laid on a New Year's Eve party, and each passenger was also presented a New Year gift. Connie's was a French perfume. Because of inclement weather, arrival in Frankfurt was delayed and we missed our connection and had to wait at Frankfurt for four hours for the next KLM flight. From Amsterdam, we were driven by road to Rotterdam and then to Hotel Central, where we were to stay initially. We were jet-lagged, and slept soundly for the next twelve hours. Europe was in the grip of its usual severe winter, with frequent and heavy snowfall.

Hotel Central took very good care of our stay. During the day, when I was away at work, Connie mostly remained in the room, trying to follow Dutch TV or reading books, which she had brought along with her. For breakfast and lunch, Connie went down to the dining room.

One evening, after I returned from work, the very hospitable and polite hotel manager asked me if I could spare a moment and then informed me that earlier that afternoon, while Connie was in the lobby, a massive and noisy procession of demonstrators had marched by. Connie had enquired with the manager what the festivity was about. The manager explained to me that he could, of course, not shock the lady by telling her that it was a gay parade, and was very apologetic. Holland was, at the time, in the forefront of social changes, legal smoking of mood-enhancing drugs, same-sex partners living together and not long after, legal euthanasia. When I explained to Connie about the manager's hesitation earlier in the day, we laughed because we had heard about major cultural shifts in post-war Europe. In the winter, it got dark very early. We usually went out for a walk in the nearby, brightly lit downtown pedestrian area of Rotterdam, and frequently had Dutch or Indonesian meals in one of the mall restaurants. One weekend, we discovered a Surinamese eatery, which served excellent chicken curry and hot chapatti. Surinam used to be a former colony of the Netherlands.

The Dutch had transported indentured labour, mainly from Bihar and neighbouring areas, to work on the sugar plantations in the West Indies, during the eighteenth and early nineteenth century. After Independence, a large number of Surinamese had migrated to Holland and there was a sizeable community in Rotterdam, and strangely, a Maithili twenty-four-hour radio station. During our walk, we also discovered the popular Dutch croquettes (minced meat and boiled potato roll, coated in breadcrumbs and deep-fried). We became addicted to croquettes during our stay.

Move to Schiedam

After the first couple of weeks, we shifted to a well-furnished Unilever apartment at 664 Gravelandse Weg (pronounced Shravalandsay Weg), in the nearby town of Schiedam. We were happy to move. Everything, to the smallest detail, had been taken care of by Mr Kooij (pronounced Kooy) from the Unilever administrative department, who ensured that all the amenities and domestic accoutrements were to Connie's satisfaction. (Incidentally, Mr Kooij, once again, in 1990, furnished my office and apartment, in Rotterdam, with the same dedication to detail, care and comfort.)

Our flat was on the fourth floor of a modern apartment building. All Dutch homes have a full glass front, as did our apartment, looking out on the main thoroughfare. The front curtain in Dutch homes is never drawn until bedtime, when the lights are switched off. Later, our Dutch friends told us that the Dutch families are house-proud, and an open-fronted home is also a welcome gesture. Connie and I were very happy to move into our new flat. During the day, when I was away at work, Connie used to go down to the large departmental store on the ground floor of our apartment building, to buy whatever provisions she needed—she enjoyed cooking our evening Indian meals at home. For lunch, the Dutch normally had sandwiches with one of the wide variety of cheese and cold cuts, usually with a glass of Karenmilch (buttermilk), followed by a shot of Dow Egbert Espresso. Most offices and all Dutch homes were usually equipped with the latest coffee machines. Connie loved the Dutch sandwiches, a wide choice of which were displayed in the supermarket, and usually a cafe latte, at home.

1969 in Holland

While we were still in Hotel Central, an Indian couple, Sudha and Bobby (Ramanujan) Iyengar, dropped by to introduce themselves and welcome us to Holland. Bobby turned out to be a fellow scientist at the Unilever Research, in Vlaardingen. We became and remained very good friends. After retiring, Sudha and Bobby returned and settled down happily in Bangalore. In Holland, they had a beautiful home in the suburb of Vlaardingen Holy, and we enjoyed frequent evenings at each other's home. With the advent of spring, and the blossoming of the tulip fields, we frequently drove together to different parts of Holland, as well as some neighbouring European countries and Scandinavia.

A Memorable Moment

On weekends, Connie and I sometimes took a train from Schiedam station to the next stop, the Rotterdam junction. We leisurely walked on the pedestrian paths, visiting some of the famous city museums, art galleries and the traffic-free zone in the centre of the city. Parts of the city, destroyed during the war, were still being rebuilt.

On the first Saturday after we moved to Schiedam, Connie and I had to go downtown, a couple of kilometres from our apartment, to register at the local police station. That January Saturday morning was bitterly cold and very windy, with a clear blue sky and bright sunshine. Connie, as usual, looked elegant in her sari, with a woollen scarf and her black winter overcoat. We gingerly stepped out of our apartment building and started to walk towards the town centre, carefully avoiding the ice patches. The temperature was well below zero. While Connie held on to my arm tightly as we faced a strong breeze, I remembered I had slipped on ice and took a mighty fall on the sidewalk across our apartment, on my way to work on the first day, after we had moved to Schiedam. Connie suddenly came to a stop and looked at me and said, in her measured tone, 'I am so glad, we came away. This will bond us as a couple.' I was left speechless. After this brief halt, when we started walking, I experienced a deep and intense sense of warmth and happiness. This event never came up, ever again, during the wonderful years of our life together. I frequently remember, even now, that bright and windy morning in Schiedam, when Connie shared with me the future of our life together. Starting with our arranged marriage, we had become a very happy and closely bonded couple.

Living Together

We soon, thereafter, reached the main town square and the Schiedam police station. As soon as we entered the premises, the tall, solitary policeman walked up to welcome us, by shaking Connie's and my hand. He then ushered us to the two chairs in front of his large desk, on which there was an old Remington typewriter and some sort of a form already in place. The policeman got to work, filling up details from our passports, and then looked up at me and asked to see our marriage documents. I tried to explain that we were married in a Hindu ceremony, presided over by a priest in the presence of our relatives and friends. The only document of proof we had were the photographs of the event. He heard me out without any expression on his face. He just asked, 'What should I write?' I promptly suggested, 'You could record it as living in sin!' The policeman did not think it was funny. Connie was embarrassed. The policeman recommenced typing, and told us he had entered 'Living together'. Our interview was over. He came over to the door to see us off, and wished us a pleasant stay in Holland. By the time we stepped out of the police station, the market was overladen with fresh fruits and vegetables, and customers. We decided to walk through the market. Almost everyone stopped to look at Connie, and greet us.

Social Life in Holland

We soon met socially and got to know some of the wives of my Dutch colleagues. The first time we were invited to one of my colleague's homes, I had asked what time we were expected; he had suggested between 6.30 and 7 p.m. would be fine. Connie and I assumed this was an invitation to dinner. We learnt later that families with young children dined daily at 5 p.m., while watching a popular TV serial *Mr Owl*. When they invite guests, the evening commences with coffee and cakes. Somewhat later, moving to alcoholic drinks, coffee and savoury snacks. The evenings usually pass quickly chatting and drinking, until quite late into the night. Connie and I, for the first time, learnt about this Dutch custom. We also started by inviting one or two couples, specifically for dinner at our apartment, on weekends. The Dutch loved Connie's kofta curry with rice, and Indian-style vegetable dishes. After dinner, like the Dutch, we served coffee and cake, and in a while, settled down to drinks and savoury sides. Our Dutch friends loved these evenings at our flat, and the word soon got around, and we invited quite a few of our friends home during our stay. Connie and I also introduced our friends to the card game of rummy, after dinner, in which a player may win or lose small change. These rummy games sometimes went on until quite late.

An elderly and internationally well-known scientist, Professor VanDorp, one morning stopped me in our Vlaardingen laboratory corridor, to tell me that he had heard that Connie served excellent Indian dinners at our home. I had a nodding but good acquaintance with him. Out of politeness, I asked if he would like to come on a mutually convenient evening, to our home. Prof. VanDorp immediately replied, if he and his wife could visit us on Saturday the same week.

Prof. and Mrs VanDorp seemed to enjoy Connie's Indian dinner enormously. We then settled down, as usual, for the evening. Our guest loved chilled beer—I had stocked enough to last several hours. In the course of that evening, Prof. VanDorp had asked Connie of her interests, and when he learnt that she had studied history, he wondered if she would like to use the famous history library, as well as the internationally recognized Sanskrit department at Leiden University. Not long after, Prof. VanDorp introduced Connie to Leiden—she started taking a train to Leiden two or three times a week, and very much enjoyed reading and browsing in the history library.

Settle in Holland

I had a great time working in the Dutch Unilever laboratory, a reasonably active social life and living in Holland. One morning, in the second half of 1969, to my utter surprise, I was offered a very

senior and permanent position in the Vlaardingen laboratory. I was
also informed that they would arrange Dutch citizenship for Connie
and me to settle down in their country. The offer came as a complete
surprise, and bewildered me. I returned to my office and phoned
Connie, told her what had just transpired. I further added that we
would discuss, as soon as I was back home, in the evening. By the
time I returned home, we had already had time to think. That while
the opportunity was exciting, we were not at all sure about settling
in Holland. Connie and I strongly felt that we wished to return to
India, after my secondment. Next morning, I met my boss, thanked
him for the generous offer, and conveyed our regret and said that we
wished to return to India. He was very surprised, but appreciated my
frankness, which he had got used to.

London, 1970

Our wonderful year in Holland seemed to have gone by very quickly.
On New Year's Eve, we reached London. The first couple of weeks,
we stayed in a hotel, before moving into a flat in Dolphin Square,
which is a well-known London address, as we were told later. The
flat belonged to Maurice Fitzmaurice, who worked in Unilever
and was moving to New York, on a six-month assignment. The
one-bedroom flat was neatly furnished and well-appointed and the
arrangement worked out well. His kitchen was, surprisingly, well
stocked with Patak's Indian spices and condiments. Maurice told
us that he was born in Nashik, where his father used to be the mint
master before India's independence. His fiancé invited Connie
and me to New Year's lunch at her mother's home. Our hosts
were very welcoming, and we had an enjoyable start of our stay in
London. Soon after we moved to Dolphin Square, we realized that
Connie was with our first child. A visit by a GP (general physician),
living in the same block of flats, confirmed the happy news, and
'advised' Connie to rest and relax and suggested that I should do
the domestic chores.

   My childhood friend from Bombay had settled in the UK.
He dropped by a couple of times, during most weeks, and used to

quickly cook a couple of Indian dishes, and the three of us would have dinner together. If the weather was reasonable, Connie and I went for a walk and had dinner in one of the number of restaurants around our place, before returning to our flat. Maurice's flat did not have a TV, but BBC radio programmes were very entertaining and informative. Occasionally, we went to watch a play in one of London's famous theatres. One weekend, we were thrilled to see the 'Swan Lake' ballet, performed by Dame Margot Fonteyn and Rudolph Nureyev, from Unilever's reserved box at the Royal Opera House, a thrilling experience for us. We were lucky to get tickets for the famous musical *Hair*. Sometimes we went to the cinema as well. The arrival of spring seemed to cheer up the city, after a grim winter and the long-drawn-out miners' strike.

Melded Life

During our time abroad, Connie and I had become very close to each other, and remained so during our lifetime. At the time, and even later, I was not conscious that I had also changed in many ways. Connie always possessed an inner strength, which was neither obvious nor overt, but had melded us as a couple.

Whatever I may have attained during my professional years or as a public personality, care of our daughters, their upbringing and their education, looking after my parents, her mother after her father passed away, were all, quietly and efficiently, managed by Connie, and was at the core of our life, together. Connie took care and managed everything at home so seamlessly, and although I was vaguely aware of, I later realized that I had been ignorant of all the vicissitudes. I was more than ten years older than Connie. I was keen in later years to take care of important matters for when I may no longer be around. Most unexpectedly and in a soul-destroying way, Connie passed away and left me totally bereft. Our life together seemed to have gone by in a flash, as our two lovely daughters grew up and completed their university education. Our elder daughter, Nivedita, married Christian, whom she had met at Oxford. Amrita lives down the road from our flat in Mumbai. She is a very successful professional.

When we celebrated the golden jubilee of our wonderful life together, with very close friends and family, I did not even remotely anticipate Connie would depart from the mortal world, leaving me alone and bereft, lamenting in self-pity and a life of sadness, and without meaning!

Solitude

How was Connie or I to even remotely contemplate that all the joy and happiness of our lifetime was to come to a crushing end, as it did! As the world shut down, in the COVID pandemic, my life plunged into an unknown darkness of solitude. Without Connie, my sole source of strength and hope, always by my side, I am engulfed in despair.

I now live in the eerie stillness of our home, which Connie built and adorned, leaving behind our daughters who are my only solace, besides the memories of our arranged marriage, which she told me was bonded in love, that winter morning, in Schiedam, when we were on our way to register our presence with the police, and Connie had suddenly held my arm tightly, as if against the fierce and chilly wind of the Dutch winter, to tell me, 'I am glad we came away.'

Part VI

Footnote

I had just returned from an unscheduled, one-day trip to London in November 1989, when I was told that I was to join the board of Unilever as an executive director, in April 1990. I returned to Mumbai, the same evening, by an overnight flight. Later that day, Connie and I drove down to my parents' home, to share with them the good news, and seek their blessings.

When I told Ma and Baba about my next job in London, my mother, as usual, was overjoyed. My father, who normally was not very expressive, suddenly seemed thoughtful and taciturn. Baba asked me why I had decided to go to England to work for an English company. His question was utterly strange and surprising. I reminded him that I had been working for the same multinational company for the past twenty-eight years. I was frankly bewildered by the unusual question from my wise and thoughtful Baba, and it worried me! Ma and Connie had gone very quiet. Later, while we were returning home, Connie said that she was unable to comprehend what Baba had in mind! I felt that the reason for what Baba had said may have been due to a feeling of insecurity at the prospect of not seeing us two to three times every week and having us a phone call away!

Baba's health and medical care was closely monitored by my colleagues and friends, Drs Jyoti and Ramnik Parekh. All the monthly administration, etc., was already being taken care of by Connie and my office. Our good friend Girija had helped already, engaging a live-in cook-cum-helper from Kolkata.

After moving to London in 1990, we remained in touch with my parents, through very frequent phone calls. Ma and Baba were happy to see us when we went to Mumbai, during the 1990 Christmas holidays. At the end of our holiday, in early 1991, we took an overnight British Airways flight to London. Bill Collier, who used to drive for us, was waiting to take us home. When we saw Bill, he told me that I had to call my office assistant, Barbara Lawton, right away. Barbara informed me that my father had passed away in the early hours of that morning, while we were still on our flight, and that she had booked me on the earliest available return flight, by Swiss Air, to Bombay via Zurich. I returned to Bombay, in the early hours, the following morning, and made arrangements for the funeral and religious ceremonies, later that morning. My mother seemed to have taken Baba's passing stoically, and we discussed with our family priest all that needed to be done for the eleventh day religious ceremonies, as per our custom. After a couple of weeks, once the religious ceremonies were completed, and ensuring all the arrangements were in place for Ma to live on her own, I returned to London. My parents had been married for fifty-six years. After Baba retired, they enjoyed frequent travels, visiting religious and other holiday destinations around India, and led a contented and restful life.

Over time, my father's reaction to the news of my moving to London had receded from my memory. That is, until the last few days, when I read a recently published book, entitled *Inglorious Empire*, about British colonial rule in India. The book begins with the East India Company being incorporated by the Royal Charter from Her Majesty Queen Elizabeth I, in 1600, to trade in silk, spices, etc., and which the company's representatives had presented at the Mughal court, in Delhi.

Our ancestral home was located in the village of Barti in the district of Barishal, in present-day Bangladesh. My grandfather moved to Benares, towards the end of the nineteenth century, where my father was born in 1905. Baba's father passed away when he was quite young. Baba went to Bombay in 1926, where one of his maternal uncles lived. Soon, Baba, at the age of twenty-one years, got a job in a British private limited company, named the Bombay Electricity Supply and Tramways, abbreviated as BEST.

Baba worked all though his career in BEST, except the last few years before retiring, when he had moved to Tata Electric.

After *Inglorius Empire*, I have been reading more about the colonial era, especially the final years of the Second World War. After the Japanese captured Singapore, and were marching on, the threat to India, Britain's critical bastion on the Eastern Front, seemed to have persuaded President Franklin D. Roosevelt, to push British prime minister Churchill to take steps for India's independence, and cooperation in the war effort. Churchill remained absolutely unmoved. Instead, with the support of the war cabinet and the viceroy of India, Sir Archibald Wavell, he had incarcerated and isolated Mahatma Gandhi and the individual members of the Congress Working Committee.

In 1943–44, Bengal and Assam were decimated by man-made shortages of foodgrains which led to unprecedented famine, and millions of Indians died of starvation. Wavell exacerbated the situation, using the traditional colonial device of fomenting communal divide.

During these final pre-Independence years, my father must have been deeply affected by the crude and cruel actions of India's colonial rulers, and the final devastation it had wrought, during the partition of the country.

I recall Baba used to routinely wear khadi clothes, in his private and social life. He completely abandoned khaddar on 15 August 1947, which may have been his way of protesting the partition of India, which led to the defilement and massacre of millions and permanently disfiguring the idea of India.

That evening, in 1989, when I had informed my parents about our move to London, and he had suddenly wondered why I was going to work for the British, he may have recalled memories of his youth and the final years of colonial rule! I have no way of knowing what he had in his mind at that moment.

Acknowledgements

The manuscript could not have reached its present format without the sustained advice, guidance and perseverance of R. Gopalakrishnan, a lifelong friend who happens to be a former and valued colleague.

The drafting and redrafting, which at times seemed unending, was patiently carried out by my longest-serving colleague, Mrs Amy Bharda. Three years back, Amy handed over the task to her equally dedicated successor, Mrs Dhanashree Purao. My heartfelt thanks to Amy and Dhanashree, for their perseverance and forbearance. My sincere thanks to Smt. and Shri Dinesh Verma, for their expertise and advice regarding the photographs.

The final copy of the manuscript was accomplished, with professional commitment, by Mrs Ketayun Bamji, who brought it to its present format. I am extremely grateful to her for the successful completion of this final task.